A PORTRAIT OF GEORGE MOORE
IN A STUDY OF HIS WORK

Mark Fisher, A.R.A., pinxit   W. E. Gray, photographer

A PORTRAIT OF GEORGE MOORE IN A STUDY OF HIS WORK

BY

JOHN FREEMAN

NEW YORK
D APPLETON AND COMPANY
1922

It were a kind of treason to remove the imperfections from me, which in me are ordinary and constant. . . . Do I not lively display my selfe? That sufficeth: I have my will: All the world may know me by my booke, and my booke by me.—*Montaigne*.

INTRODUCTION

FASCINATING as the art of portraiture may be, it is yet more difficult than fascinating when the medium is not the brush or the pencil, but the twenty-six letters of the alphabet. The difficulty does not arise from the poverty but from the richness of the medium, from its subtlety and confusions, hints and associations, from its uncertainty as well as from its simplicity, from its manifest variability as well as from its secret rigidity. The ideal craftsman—to disclaim a higher term—must needs subdue himself to his subject, and yet without the intensest realization of himself he cannot realize his subject; and hence the result of his labours, patient and faithful though they be, may appear as much a portrait of himself as of his sitter. And if he practise his hand upon several subjects his facility may show itself in nothing more plainly than in the involuntary portrayal of his native characteristics, and a mere generalizing tendency so far as his sitters are concerned. His only advantage is that he need not consult—as must the artist with the brush—the convenience or even ask the consent of the subject; but since that advantage does not affect the present occasion, I do not dwell upon it here.

But the fortunate artist with the brush may achieve at least an obvious likeness to the obvious features, and whatever greater success he aims at he will not inevitably forego this easier success; for the poorest of painters does not fail absolutely if he has skill enough to achieve a superficial similarity. There sits his victim in the flesh, or walks between fields, speaks, meditates—observable, amenable and at worst to be rendered as a piece of still life. Far different is the task of literary portraiture. It is not the face that has to be presented—nor, will the painter retort, is that the mere task for my brush. It is the character, the spirit, the inward history that must be expressed or suggested—and this, the painter cries again, this is the task of my brush also. But the literary craftsman will point out that the painter has one great advantage, the advantage of working upon visible physical characteristics, whereas for himself there are but the invisible and disputable mental characteristics. Intelligent readers of a certain writer will not agree upon the exact proportions of the individual and the common, the new and the old, the spontaneous and the mechanical parts of the subject's life and work; their perception of these parts is determined as much by predilections of their own as by invariable characteristics in the author. And another difficulty is to be noted. The painter with his brush has not to contend against masks and disguises and cunning defensive make-up; and unless his genius is splendidly wilful, he does not seek to show that the smile is false or the modest touch a trick, that frank eye shallow or that candid forehead cunning. But the literary craftsman, drawing his material from a few facts of external life and from a cloud of inferences touching the inner life, from a score of diverse books, from pages written lightly or gravely during a period of forty years, from works of imagination, of criticism, of reminiscence, has no guide but his own poor intelligence. His portrait may not be recognizable by his subject—that is indeed probable; but others also may find it wanting in verisimilitude. They may hold that all—or nothing—that the score of volumes tell of their author's personality is really true of him; they may believe that things said dramatically are historical, and things said historically merely dramatic. Thus it is that all that the literary craftsman may trust to (yet to what else should he dare to trust?) is his own critical imagination. Doubly difficult, then, is his attempt—and doubly desirable. And if the painter, seeking to end an argument with a flourish of his brush, cries, Confess, now, that the task is an illegitimate task, your craft, as you are pleased to call it, a bastard craft, neither portraiture nor criticism, neither biography nor commentary; the answer is silence and argument is over.

But assume that the painter forbears such a conclusion, the difficulty yet remains. Assume that the literary portrait is a possible aim, it is not equally possible between any subject and any craftsman. Pater may write of Marcus Aurelius and Watteau, Carlyle of Robespierre; but Pater would have failed with Rabelais and Carlyle with Donne. Antipathies, when they are precise, form the completest barrier to divination. Neither, however, will the craftsman more certainly succeed if he is completely subjugated by his sitter; for resistance is as necessary to light as to heat. But it is superfluous to pursue this notion, since the result alone can show whether imperfect sympathies needs must mar a literary portrait. Indeed, the only relevance which these first paragraphs may claim is their explanation of the method adopted in this study of George Moore, and also, perhaps, their assertion of the value of that method in abler hands than mine.

CHAPTER I

MAYO

I, who am king of the matter that I treat of, and am not to give accompt of it to any creature living, doe neverthelesse not altogether beleeve my selfe for it : I often hazard upon certaine outslips of minde for which I distrust my selfe ; and certaine verball wilie-beguiles, whereat I shake mine eares. . . . I present my selfe standing and lying, before and behinde, on the right and left side, and in all by naturall motions. . . . Loe here what my memory doth in grose, and yet very uncertainely present unto me of it.— *Montaigne.*

OF all confessed egoists among English writers, none has written more fully or more deceivingly concerning himself than George Moore. He writes, indeed, with seeming frankness, but that frankness must not mislead you into forgetting that he studies himself anxiously, adding here, brightening or diminishing there, and thus applying to autobiography the spider-like ingenuity of a novelist. Fact is to be distinguished from fiction, and yet fiction is not to be rejected; for in Moore's case it often serves him as images serve a poet. That is to say, it is false, and yet more illuminating than a narrow truth. But except for the purpose of apprehending the inward desire, the mental attitude, the fiction is not available for a portrait. To say, for instance, that in *Confessions of a Young Man* there is a display of shabby dissoluteness, of crude and plushy splendour, is to point out something which illuminates a certain aspect of Moore's early work, but which is obviously remote from the diligence and aristocracy of his mind. Yet it would be hard for the novelist himself, after more than thirty years' acquaintance with his own work, to affirm or deny the literary truth of a score of touches in that early book; and I shall not pretend to a greater skill than his own in looking either at *Confessions of a Young Man* or another book.

Happily, some things are certain; and of these the first is that George Moore was born in 1852 at Moore Hall, County Mayo, Ireland. It is claimed that the family has for illustrious ancestor Sir Thomas More, of whom certain portraits have remained among the family treasures. Curiously, George Moore does no more than allude to the lustre of this association, as a foil to the notion that Mr.

Yeats's belief in his lineal descent from the great Duke of Ormonde was part of his poetic equipment. All romantic poets, says Moore, have rightly sought illustrious ancestry; in Mr. Yeats's case the proof being, apparently, the existence in his family of spoons bearing the Butler crest. George Moore, however, has disdained emphasizing the place of that Mirrour of Vertue in Worldly Greatness, sometime Lord Chancellor of England, in the history of his own family; and it is a fair conjecture that had Sir Thomas been executed for promoting the breach with Rome, and not in order (as has been suggested) to make that breach irreparable, some musing upon the Lord Chancellor's fate might have been found in *Hail and Farewell*. No better starting-point could have been used for his descendant's discussion of Roman Catholicism and its antipathy to literature; and would not the romantic opening of *Utopia* have attracted the perpetual story-teller of our own day, who is fain to romanticize whatever appeals to his eye or memory? And surely the strange contrast between Sir Thomas More's own intellectual freedom and his intolerance of religious freedom in others might have appealed to the speculative mind of our novelist. Heresy, says the Lord Chancellor's historian, was naturally hateful to More, and while his mind was too clear to permit him to deceive himself with Anglicanism—how he could I do not know—he attached himself with increasing determination to the cause of the Pope and the old faith. Attractive, then, is it to think of George Moore hanging like a dragonfly over the still, pure pool of his ancestor's mind, for between the two humanists there are curious resemblances and divergencies. George Moore, like the great Chancellor, is touched with intolerance and indulgence; he would burn a contemporary for his stories, but not Verlaine for his morals; and if the torture of heretics at Chelsea is a charge against Sir Thomas, the dissection of Gill and Plunkett in the neighbouring study of Ebury Street is no more pitiful. Conscience, in the one as in the other, has urged the executioner; only, in the latter case, conscience is working through that more fluid and unstable medium, the æsthetic temperament, in which antipathies have more than the strength of principles, and integrity is at the mercy of a beard, an accent, a stutter, a smile, a hand-shake, an idle reminiscence or speculation. . . . It is possible to think of a wholly Protestant Sir Thomas More, but since no man may escape the influences of his time even while he moulds it, we cannot easily think of him as indifferent to religion and utterly disengaged from the great question that agitated the England of Henry VIII. But the question of Catholic or Protestant is not an inevit-able preoccupation for our novelist, and indeed it springs from a purely intellectual or æsthetic concern, namely, concern for the development of imaginative literature, which he finds with the suddenness of Revelation to be incompatible with Catholicism. Pity it is, to repeat the lament, that he has not pondered Sir Thomas More's seemingly easy reconciliation of intellectual liberty with religious subordination; for here he would not be able to resort, as he has done in later instances, to a charge of dis-honesty. Rather would he find a singularly clear case of the persistence of parallel loyalties—loyalty to the intel-lectual spirit and loyalty to external authority; loyalties persisting throughout exaltation and disgrace, and shining with equal brightness on the scaffold which the true friend of Erasmus regarded with a jest. He died as serenely as any of those he had persecuted, as serenely as any—states-man or artist—will die for the idea or the image which is more than his own life. 'After he had subdued them,' writes the author of *Utopia*, 'he made a law that every man might be of what religion he pleased, and might endeavour to draw others to it by the force of argument, and by amicable and modest ways, but without bitterness against those of other opinions.'

If, however, it is a fair conjecture that the religious difference prevented George Moore from hovering over the Lord Chancellor's character, it is fair also to remark that Colonel Maurice Moore has not the same reason for abstention; and it is to him that we owe (*An Irish Gentleman, George Henry Moore*, by Colonel Maurice Moore, C.B.) a more explicit reference. It is related, he writes, that a descendant of Sir Thomas More settled in Mayo and acquired lands near Ballina, and it is known that in the time of William of Orange, George Moore of Ballina held the title of Vice-Admiral of Connaught; his son and grandson were living in Ashbrook, near Straid Abbey, in 1717.

In Colonel Moore's book we find other admirable accounts of the Moores. It seems that the fortunes of the family were established by a George Moore, great-grandfather of the novelist, who ventured into Spain and there became the head of a prosperous Irish colony. He made a great fortune, two hundred and fifty thousand pounds, says our novelist, and married an Irish Spanish woman, one of the refugees from the penal laws. In those days there was great trading with Spain, and galleons had once come floating up the bay, their sails filled with sunset. Not only in certain buildings, it is said, but in flesh and blood also are traces of Spain to be found in Galway. 'It amused me,' you read in *Vale*, 'to think of the ships laden with seaweed coming round the Bay of Biscay from the Arran Islands to my great-grandfather in Alicante, and the burnt kelp filling the iron chest (still at Moore Hall), and quickly, with ducats, and my great-grandfather returning to Ireland, a sort of mercantile pirate of the Spanish Main.' Looking for a site whereon to build a fine Georgian house, 'he would have built it at Ashbrook if there had been a prospect, but there being none, he bought Muckloon, a pleasant green hill overlooking Lough Carra; and the Colonel mentioned that

our great-grandfather used to sit on the steps of Moore
Hall, his eyes fixed on the lake.' The house was built in
1780. 'I have travelled far,' he is reported to have said,
'but have seen nothing as beautiful as Lough Carra.' . . .
An elderly gentleman in a wig and a scarlet coat—'it is
thus that he is apparelled in the portrait that hangs in the
dining-room, painted when and by whom there is no
record. In it he is a man of thirty, and when he was
thirty he was in Alicante. It is pleasant to have a portrait of one's ancestor in a wig, and in a vermilion coat
with gold lace and buttons, white lace at the collar and
cuffs—probably a Spanish coat of the period. The face
is long, sheep-like, and distinguished—the true Moore
face as it has come down to us.'

Who has ever heard, George Moore adds, of a more
horrible discovery than to go blind in one's sleep? So
it was that his prosperity ended. 'On awakening one
morning he asked his valet why he had not opened the
shutters. The servant answered that he had opened
them. "But the room is dark." "No, sir, the room is
quite light." "Then I am blind!"' The rest of his life
was lived between priest and doctor, in terror of death.
Our novelist finds a significance in the circumstance of his
great-grandfather's burial, for the blind man had desired
that he should be buried with his ancestors in the
Protestant cemetery near Straid Abbey, but he was buried
in the Catholic chapel at Ashbrook. 'The Irish Spaniard,
Catholic back, belly and sides, would not have hesitated
to ignore her husband's instructions.' She wished, in
short, to conceal the fact that she had married a man
of such doubtful Catholicity that he had chosen to be
buried in a Protestant cemetery.

John, the eldest son, was concerned in the rising of
1798 and joined the French expedition which landed at
Killala. After a delusive victory he was elected first
President of the Connaught Republic, and when his small

army was overthrown he was only saved by influential friends from a court-martial. Escape was planned, but defeated by his own generosity towards a follower; and he died before his trial began.

Upon George, then, the honours and cares of the family fell; and his life also has been illustrated by Colonel Moore and our novelist. He was, it appears, a member of the Holland House circle, a philosopher and historian of the English Revolution and the French Revolution. He married a grand-daughter of the Earl of Altamont, a capable woman to whom he serenely left the conduct of affairs while he pursued a student's life in his library—an agnostic like his master Gibbon, we are told in *Vale*. He had married his wife in spite of the fact that it was her relation, Denis Browne, who secured the conviction of his brother John. It was on the completion of his sixty-fourth year that he wrote the ' Preface to my Historical Memoirs of the French Revolution, to be Published after my Death.' He left five hundred pounds to defray the expenses of issuing the History, but it was never published. ' Having written a history of the French Revolution, impregnated with all the feelings and sentiments of an Englishman, and written in a style, I hope, purely and thoroughly English, I am ambitious it should be read after me. I have had no celebrity in my life. But a prospect of this posthumous fame pleases me at this moment . . . We are so made that while we are living we think with pleasure that we shall not be forgotten in our deaths.' Is it only in the lineaments of a portrait which may have been painted by Wilkie that the Moore features may be traced; or is it not equally in the cadence of such sentences as these, in the serene simplicity that intimates and conceals depth, that a likeness between the two George Moores may be noted?

Of his three sons the eldest, George Henry, was born at Moore Hall in 1810, and it is his life that Colonel Moore, as I have already said, relates in *An Irish Gentleman*. At seventeen he writes from Oscott College telling his mother of his interest in painting and verse; he had written a poem of many hundred lines, *The Legend of Lough Carra*, which he intended offering to Murray or Colborne: and already he had completed *Irene* in five hundred lines, an Eastern Byronish poem. 'If I could get one hundred pounds from one of the booksellers for the child of my imagination, how happy I should feel in buying you a pair of handsome horses.' *Irene* was published, but there is no record of the hundred pounds or the horses, nor of the fate of *The Legend of Lough Carra*, which at any rate had the prime virtue of dealing with what the author best knew and loved; for Moore Hall stands just above the edge of the lake, a square Georgian house with a great flight of steps and big pillars supporting a balcony. The house and the lake dominated the young George Henry Moore, as they dominate his son, for whom indeed they have become not merely a memory but a symbol, a figure of recovered or recoverable Eden. Time has not diminished the beauty, for the green slopes, the light and shade holding planetary sway over the miles of water, the bridge, the horses and the men, have emerged as clear as dawn, as soft as noon, as quiet as evening, amid the stealthy, slow deposits of sixty years of reflection. That passage in *Vale* is famous in which the author recalls his journey to the old home, a journey he was loth to undertake, for he could see the wide long water, and all the slow curves of the bay along Kiltoome and Connor Island, with the mind's eye more clearly than with the bodily eye. Ballinafad, his mother's home, was near by, but it was become a monastery; why should he see it again? True the old house had not yet been pulled down that cells might be built instead; in fact, the only change would be a peasant in frock and sandals for a peasant in frieze. Well, the drive from Manulla to Moore Hall would show him the familiar woods of Ballinafad; and so driving he reanimates the scene. Joe Blake off to Castlebar with his arm round a servant's waist; the girls at Clogher—Helena, Lizzie, Livy and May—gathering cherries . . . he could see the dead girls quite plainly. The trees at Clogher seemed not to have grown a foot in forty years. Disagreeable hazels still hedged Carnacum Lake, and he recalled how once the trees were not wasted as now, for they used to be sold to the coopers at Derrinrush to make barrelhoops. Endless the stone walls; country and people were still savage; and why were there no windmills? He recalls, too, childish rambles with his governess through the unpathed woods, between silver firs and rowans: once the hillside was dark with adventure and mystery; and for a while he is a child again, only awakening into the denser air of maturity at the sight of the new gateway which his brother had removed from Newbrook, a handsomer affair even than he had expected to see. Looking for a tall laburnum, whose slim slippery body had defied his legs as a boy, he could not find it, but it still lived in his memory of Moore Hall; so, again, did the lost hawthorns and lilac bush, among which he had played at Red Indians. There, where the lilac bush was once large and leafy, he had thrown himself down, and discovered, it seemed, how to be happy; but the next day—he remembered it all now— he had asked Joseph Appely why he no longer wanted to crack his whip, hide in the lilac bush or roll in the hay? What Joseph Appely replied can only be imagined. Tree after tree was gone now, lilac and laburnum. But the house? the steps alone were to his taste, for he liked brick, and houses that had grown generation after generation. Nor did he like plate glass, and he thought that if ever he should live in Moore Hall he must have the windows refurnished with the old hand-made glass with rings in every pane.

It was a much experiencing and much remembering man that made the visit described in *Vale*, and when he

reached the house the old fondness for it seized him; the
whole passage showing how gravely and clearly the instinctive, profound past beats bell-like and soft upon the
rounded consciousness which is George Moore's present.
Going over the house with his brother, meditating upon
changes accomplished and dreamed of, upon the Adam
ceiling, the open yard, the bathroom that had once been
his father's dressing-room (the sight of which at once
recalls George Henry Moore to him and to us as vividly as
any passage in *An Irish Gentleman*), he confesses that he
would not have had the courage to make those changes,
so real is the memory of his father sitting in the room, or
standing shaving while the small George talked and
watched. It was on such an occasion that his father
asked him to read aloud from Burke, from an edition
printed with long *s's* : and when the boy stumbled over
these, as indeed he would do even now, his father,
stricken like one who found his son suddenly blind or
dumb, appealed to the child's mother and governess :—
Was there ever another child of seven who could not read
Burke without faltering over the long *s's* ? He averred
(and sincerely believed), his face still lathered, that he
had been accustomed to reading the *Times* aloud to his
mother at breakfast at the age of three.   For days there-
after child and governess were banished to the schoolroom
to read Lingard, listening apprehensively when Apply
brushed the master's hat, and breathing lightly only when
the hall-door told that he had gone to the stables.   And
now he could feel not his father's ghost alone, but his
grandfather's also animating the rooms : was it not for
that reason that Moore Hall had always seemed strange
and 'preoccupied' ?   No new influence had touched the
house since 1870, and he would never be able to live in
it; for he would always feel his grandfather sitting by
him and wondering that his grandson should practise a
prose style so familiar, so unlike Gibbon's.

'My father was too near the Georgian period to appreciate the house,' he murmured to his brother. *An Irish Gentleman* tells of that father, and if it says little of the literary powers which he transmitted to his eldest son, the latter is yet sensible of them; wondering how it was that his father could so indifferently destroy the letters in which his travels in the East were related. Maria Edgeworth advised the publication of these records of travel, saying that the man who could write such letters could write anything he pleased and become famous. Fame teased him not, and he remained, in his eldest son's opinion, singularly unconscious of the literary power that lay half kindled within him. He did not love literature for its own sake, and George Moore's sense of this lack caused separation between father and son. Why not make a book out of these? asked his wife; but he threw the letters into the fire, packet by packet, for he never wanted to look at them again. There were drawings, too, in his diaries, drawings of women, and camels with long, shaggy, bird-like necks, tufted and callous hides, 'bored ruminants, the Nonconformists of the four-footed world.' In these precise outlines there is a delicacy, a beauty which betrays the skill of a wise hand. Letters, diaries and sketches alike had their roots in romance. He was but twenty-two when his mother became aware of a secret love which he could not conceal nor she approve; she adjured him to leave England, and in 1832, declaring that he would never marry—never! he removed for five months to Brussels. Not long after his return to England he resolved to travel in the East, and it is the prefacer who tells us in *An Irish Gentleman* that it was for love of a lady that his father turned to travel, and for love of him that she followed with her husband. For two years his diary was forgotten, and it speaks again only to bewail the loss of the lady. He wandered in Russia, through the Caucasus, into Persia, Egypt, Syria and Greece; showing in the surviving pages of his diary the instinctive power of phrasing which he drew from his father and passed on to his son. He speaks of sweet and solemn reveries, of burning dreams, of immortal hours, in passages that are noticeably echoing, their music magnified or diminished, in the last pages of *Memoirs of My Dead Life*.

When he returned to England he was still but twenty-seven and disposed to fashion his life on the model of his father's; and when the historian died, in 1840, George Henry Moore devoted himself wholly to hunting and riding. Not until 1846, his brother Augustus having been killed in a racing accident and famine smiting the country, did he halt and throw himself with the same impetuosity into relief work, the building of a monastery and so on to the bewildering, rootless and fruitless life of party politics. He had already won a seat in Parliament when he married Mary Blake, in 1851, but after political disappointments which need not be mentioned here, he resumed the activities of a country gentleman. Colonel Moore tells of many of the incidents from which his brother has spun shining webs of imagination and fancy; and to him is due the precise sketch of Joseph Applely, prototype of the mysterious, pathetic Mr. Leopold of *Esther Waters*, already secretive and abstruse, presented by nature as a finished model to her artist. It was once our author's luck (he writes in *Vale*) to be thrown three times before breakfast, the falls irritating his father, who declared to Applely that no horse could unseat him; but next morning the boast was avenged, for he too fell and broke his collar-bone.

Of his father our novelist speaks with detachment touched with affection. He writes of his death in 1870 as he might tell of the death of an extraordinarily well realised character in a book, saying that he died of a broken heart, and that he would like to believe that it was by suicide, in the Roman fashion; an inclination which Colonel Moore has refused to support. 'This tragic death,' he adds, 'seems the legitimate end of a brave life; and in my brother's book he appears as wonderful as any character invented by Turgenev.' The phrase is written some forty years after the event, but is it not characteristic that the death of his father affects him imaginatively, and precisely as the death of Grandet or Bazarov might affect him?

It is in *Vale* that the simplest and frankest account of the death and the days following the death of George Henry Moore is found. His eldest son describes the journey and his own sensations, speaking aloud the thoughts which most of us rebuke into snake-like stillness; adding, 'We never grieve for anybody as we should like to grieve, and are always shocked at our own absent-mindedness.'

> 'I remember nothing till somebody came into the summer-room to tell my mother that if she wished to see him again she must come at once, for they were about to put him into his coffin, and catching me by the hand, she said, "We must say a prayer together."
> 'The dead man lay on the very bed in which I was born, his face covered with a handkerchief, and as my mother was about to lift it from his face the person who had brought us thither warned her from the other side of the white dimity curtains not to do so.
> '"He is changed."
> '"I don't care," she cried, and snatched away the handkerchief, revealing to me the face all changed. And it is this changed face that lives unchanged in my memory.'—

'The one pure image in my mind, the one true affection,' he exclaims of his father, in the heightened prose of the *Confessions*.

Pride of family is the commonest and pleasantest of frailties. George Moore, who has become so acutely sensible of the difference between himself and his contemporaries, and loves to assert a no less marked distinction between himself and his brother, is not without the common pride. Men are seldom reluctant to recall, to exalt, to illustrate the casual eminence of their ancestry; conspicuous beauty, wealth, courage and intelligence—these, and in this order, are the chief gratifications of a reverie over recent generations. It is sometimes with an envious, sometimes with a humorous sigh that they recount old splendour and excellence; even if, for instance, it is a sigh over the wealth that enriched not me but the British and Foreign Bible Society. And Moore is intimately aware of his father's and grandfather's part in him. The instinct for letters that distinguished the grandfather, the restless passion for experience that marked the father, are in him intensified and enlarged. The quiet instinct becomes energetic, the restless passion is new-winged with imagination and becomes vicariously active. He calls himself pagan, but that is, at least in part, an intellectual delusion; and he is at times so sharply concerned with religion, with religion in its personal aspect only less than in its social and æsthetic issues, that it is hard to forget that he comes, as he loves to repeat, of a merely shallow-rooted Catholicism.

And like another father and mother is the Mayo land-scape—the lonely face of field and lake, the soft, green-breasted country, the trees of the woods and the reflected water-trees, the landscape of which, reading in almost any of the later books, you will say—a Corot! a Moore! so finely has it impressed itself in those admired paintings and in this prose. The movement of the prose, the undu-lations never wandering past control, the unheightened and unlapsing phrasing, the colour and the quietness, the simplicity, the depth, the brightness—all these, the mere names of qualities, as trees are mere names of mysteries, are the artist's rendering in his proper medium of that which his youth has breathed, and which was in his veins before consciousness awoke. Supremely interested in himself, he is therefore interested in his progenitors,

although without the egoism of regarding them as his
precursors; and the tendency to reverie over childhood,
which his later books reveal, is directed almost as much
towards his father and grandfather as towards the infant
George. The mind of a pure artist is not to be tethered
nor its flight foretold; and if it be said that this reverting
of the eyes to youth was not to be expected from the
creator of *Esther Waters* and the author of *Evelyn Innes*, I
can but answer that it is none the less natural and uncon-
trollable. And who so well as Moore could become an
English Aksakoff, or to what finer devotion might his
powers be yielded? Aksakoff has clothed with new life
his father and grandfather, and called out of the mist his
own early years; and might not George Moore, who has
so often touched the personalities of two generations, and
himself admires so justly the portrait of *A Russian Gentleman*, enrich our literature with its first complete history of
a family, and include such an account of his own childhood
and youth as made Aksakoff's *Years of Childhood* precious?
Strange it is that this kind of imaginative chronicle, a form
in which the English genius might find unique liberty,
should have been so long neglected in England. The
literality of Defoe has passed away without stimulating a
higher faculty in his successors; and few indeed are the
attempts in a higher direction. Ruskin's *Praeterita*, and
Mr. Gosse's insufficiently appreciated *Father and Son*, are
isolated instances of what may be achieved; and for the
rest?—Even the narrowest form of autobiography is
shunned, except by those anecdotal writers who have
nothing significant to reveal. I think of Tolstoi and
Gorki, of Rousseau and Goethe, and I wish in vain for an
emulous zeal in England. All that another may tell is as
nothing compared with what an imaginative artist may
tell of himself. St. Augustine has quickened our minds
with those touches which reveal what most we need to
know—those episodes, of thought or action, which make

him a man of like passions to our own, and thus he too is
among the imaginative company of those that have revealed
themselves; but wanting that revelation, what could his
personality count for in our own day? It is by his own
story of his life that that life has been prolonged.

George Moore has made free with the character of
others—you may charge it equally as a fault and a virtue,
according as your attitude is individual or social, æsthetic
or moral—and no less candid concerning himself; and he
seems to me superbly gifted for such a creative task as
others in English letters have ignored or too briefly
attempted. 'Myself,' he says, 'was the goal I was making
for instinctively, in those early Paris days;' and that
preoccupation with personality is among the chief
essentials of imaginative autobiography. He has not
yet essayed the full desirable task, and his neglect
makes it necessary that something of his early life shall
be sketched or gathered here, however imperfectly and
inadequately. The need is greater since so much that
he now writes is called out of the dark backward and
abysm of sixty or fifty years ago.

'When I was a small child,' he says, 'I used to go with
my mother and governess to Carra Castle for goat's milk,
and we picnicked in the great banqueting-hall overgrown
with ivy.' The memory of those early excursions recalls
those he used to see; Mulhair recognized by his stubbly
chin, Pat Plunkett by his voice and Carabine by his eyes,
with Appely moving about in his unstarched collar and
too-large frock coat. Clothed with mystery are the earliest
scenes in a child's life; and the wonder has hardly
decreased as he thinks of the days when he longed to
explore the wilderness of rocks at the end of Kingstown
Pier, the great clefts frightening and sending him back,
ashamed of his cowardice, to where his uncles and cousins
sat listening to the band, as Dublin used to do in the

C

'sixties. One day he was bolder, and after descending
into that wilderness returned to tell how he had met the
King of the Fairies fishing at the mouth of the cave. But
his relations were not interested and thought him a little
daft; and one girl (with wide ugly mouth and loud voice,
as he sees her now) laughed harshly, saying, with a touch
of prescience, that George could not be taken anywhere,
not even to Kingstown Pier, without something wonderful
happening. The phrase marks him out for us. Such
gibes filled him with shame and he resolved to shun
adventures; but notwithstanding that resolve and subsequent vows, he has failed to see and hear as the heathen
do, and has gone on meeting adventures everywhere.
That phrase, again, its truth and its sting, marks him out
for us. Characteristic is it that he follows this story with
an incident showing how, when walking by the shore
with Mr. Yeats and Mr. Edward Martyn, and looking at
the sea moving against the land's side like a soft feline
animal, he and he alone saw three girls advancing into the
water, lifting their skirts high and laughing invitingly;
the boldest showing thighs whiter and rounder than any.

A shy boy, he calls himself elsewhere, and says it is
difficult for him to believe any good of himself. And
is that lack of belief a gift from nature, or was he trained
into it by his parents? It seems that he can trace his
inveterate distrust of himself to the years when his
parents used to say that he would certainly marry old
Honor King, a beggar woman; and he came to dread her
appearance and even her name, understanding that the
joke rested on the assumption that nobody else would
marry such an ugly little boy. Happily we need not call
for the assistance of the newest psychology in determining
the root of this shyness, nor yet to disgust us with an
explanation of another incident. It was at the beginning
of his childhood that he stole away one morning to St.
Stephen's Green, inspired by an unaccountable desire to

break the monotony of infancy by stripping himself of his clothes, tossing them out of reach, and running naked in front of his nurse or governess, screaming the while with delight. Had he not moralized the incident the temptation to do so would be irresistible now :—was the visit to Ireland, which was to produce *Hail and Farewell*, anything more than a desire to break the monotony of his life by stripping himself again and running, a naked Gael, screaming *Brian Boru*? There is nobody, he adds again, that amuses one as much as oneself. The incident illustrates my theme, and the comment increases the impatience of the cry, Why does not Mr. Moore write his autobiography? He had, even as a child, a curious and probing mind. He and his brother once built a children's house high up in a beech tree. A quarrel arose concerning the building, and to get his own way George pretended not to believe that his brother loved him, and so caused Maurice to burst into tears; whereupon, the elder's curiosity being provoked, he tried to think of what could make his brother cry again; but alas, the gibe was blunted upon his brother's indifference. Looking back upon the trifle after fifty years, the author of *Salve* cries, As detestable in the beginning as in the end! And thinking how (unlike the Colonel) he partook of a boy's cruelty and hunted the laundry cats with dogs, no one corrected him, he muses, no one reproved him; and so he grew up a wilding.

Perhaps we shall do well not to regard this statement too narrowly, but there was a happy wilding time when his father's *Croagh Patrick*, a famous brown horse, won the Stewards' Cup. George Henry Moore and his wife went with the horse to Goodwood, while the small eldest son, who had watched the horse in his last gallops at Cliffs before the race, stayed behind among the stable-boys to enjoy liberty and become familiar with that world which was to contribute so much to the excellence of *Esther Waters*. Truly Irish carelessness, says Colonel Moore in speaking of the surrender of his brother to the stables; but we shall not regret it. Nobody looked after this 'little kid of nine,' riding as he pleased about the country, until one day his liberty was ended. It was through the success of a horse named *Master George* that Master George was snatched from the horses and sent to school; such, the Colonel remarks, are the ways of Providence, calling them nevertheless devious. It is the wittiest phrase in his story of *An Irish Gentleman*. Other winners came out of the stables, and one racing historian, recounting them, hazards the remark that George Henry Moore would probably have disinherited his son had he foreseen the writing of such a book as *Esther Waters*. Providence, it seems, failed to prompt the novelist's father; but, indeed, *Esther Waters* might have been written by a disinherited son, and was actually written by an impoverished son.

The merest tantalizing crumbs of memories of horses and hunting are given in *Hail and Farewell*, shedding brightness on the story of the days that were ended with school. There was, for example, a race-meeting at Castlebar or some neighbouring town, with old men in knee-breeches and tall hats, young men in trousers, cattle-dealers in great overcoats reaching to their heels, wearing broad-brimmed hats, everybody with a wide Irish grin on his face, and everybody with his blackthorn. Especially was there a crowd watching a bucking chestnut, a sixteen-hands horse with a small boy in pink on his back. Now the horse, says Moore, looking on again with the eyes of a child, hunches himself up till he seems like a hillock; his head is down between his legs, his hind legs are in the air, but he doesn't rid himself of his burden. He plunges forward, he rises up, coming down again, his head between his legs; and the boy, still

unstirred, recalls the ancient dream of the Centaur.—
Bedad, the greatest rider in Ireland.

But while the fight between horse and jockey yet
waged, George Henry Moore rode up threatening the
crowd; if the course was not cleared he would ride in
among them on a great bay stallion. Master George
himself felt the pangs of fear as he looked on, for even
then a peasant's life was counted valuable. And it
seemed that his father was very cruel to the poor boy
whose horse would not keep quiet. . . . An equally vivid
character is cousin Dan—Dan, in his long yellow
mackintosh, and tall silk hat covering the long white
skull ribboned by a single lock of black hair; the same
long skull that George Moore has inherited, a long pale
face, and long, delicate woman's hands. Craft and
innocency were mingled strangely in Dan's face—by
heaven! a Moore face truly previsioned, you might cry,
looking from that to this. Dan has his secure place in
Hail and Farewell, and is indeed the occasion of a justification which our author usually disdains to give. To the
question, If you respect your family so much, why do you
unscarf Dan's frailties? he replies: 'If I did not do so, I
should not think of Dan at all;' and what we dread most
is to be forgotten. . . . Dan's love of his Bridget was what
was best in him and what was most like him. Our
interest in Dan is not lessened by knowing that the
writing of *A Mummer's Wife* was associated with him,
with Galway, and a riding horse which Dan lent Moore
—a great, black, shoulderless beast.

But Oscott interrupted the early familiarities. That a
boy should remember the first sight of his school is not
surprising, but it is faintly surprising that he should note
now the seeming heartlessness with which he met his father
and mother when they bade him good-bye. They were
shocked, but he could only think of the boys who wanted
to make his acquaintance; a phrase which betrays an early

sense of importance in a child of nine. Before the end of his first meal he had become a school character, and thought it a fine thing to offer to match himself against the smallest boy present in the play-room. George was beaten. . . . Is it not a familiar story he tells, of a child of nine rising at half-past six and getting beaten if he was late for Mass? Looking back, he perceives in others not the faintest recognition of the fact that he was but a baby, and he does not pretend now, as men so often pretend in later years, that the hard life was good for him. 'The injustice, the beastliness of that place—is it possible to forget it?' When his parents visited him they found the high-spirited child changed into a frightened little coward, blubbering for home; but he remained at Oscott until his health yielded to cold and hunger and floggings. Two years at Moore Hall followed, the best part of his childhood, with long days on the lake and bird-nesting in the woods, and the unconscious laying-up of treasures for discovery later on. He could learn nothing from tutors, and often asked his mother, Am I really stupid? without getting a clear answer; and all that an old governess could remember was that he was the most amiable of children.

It was about this time that he first read Shelley, during a ride of some sixteen miles in a C-springed coach; rocking about and discovering *The Sensitive Plant* in a little fat volume with the usual portrait which yielded nothing at all in the world. The name attracted him, as Byron's did also, and he started to read the English poets whose names most pleased him. Readers of *Avowals* will remember that Kirk White was an early choice. The desired parcel arrived, and he could scarce find patience to open it; but a line or two was enough, and he read no more that day nor any other. Shelley became the god of his idolatry. He was able to take the book to Oscott, reading it in secret while others were at lessons—they at heaven knows

what, George Moore at *Queen Mab*. No wonder he learned
nothing at Oscott; no wonder that his father was angered
at his backwardness; no wonder that Shelley has remained
the chief of his few poets. *Salve* tells us that the edition
of Shelley which he took to Oscott explained that *The
Revolt of Islam* was but a revised version of *Laon and
Cythna;* and that one day, coming from the refectory, he
said to the prefect that he had brought Shelley with him
and, reading it constantly, had begun to wonder if it was
wrong; for Shelley denied the existence of God. The
book was taken from him—a sacrifice designed to purchase
the blessing of expulsion, but a vain sacrifice. It was another
matter that played a chief part in his leaving, the in-
nocentest of innocent affairs with a little housemaid, the
only thing he could think of to break the monotony of the
Oscott day. A scruple of conscience harassed him and he
wrote to his father freely, saying that if the girl was sent
away he would have no peace and would be obliged to
marry her. Promptly did his father gallop off to Clare-
morris to catch a train, and then descending, unexpected,
upon the school, drew with his gentle manner and em-
barrassingly clear eyes all the queer little story, and the
threat which was not meant seriously. The young novelist,
you surmise, had been dramatizing a personal incident and
his own character, as children and their elders almost
equally love to do, and slyly exploiting it. He sees
himself even in those times just as he has ever been, very
provident about his own life, and determined to make the
most of it. The girl was not to be dismissed and this
prefatory *Memoir of My Dead Life* remained a mere
sketch, a hint, a dramatic titillation; ah, but there was
something far more serious, and his father's eyes lost their
kindness as he asked: 'George, is it true that you have
refused to go to confession?' It was true: he had found
nothing to confess, even after the excellent stimulus of
a flogging. His father agreed with the priest that there

were always sins to confess for him who chooses to seek, and the subtle boy was pressed into tiny admissions. . . . Was ever anything funnier? George Moore being brought to confess willy-nilly—George Moore, whose whole life has been an explicit, unchecked confession, and who may indeed be thought to have exceeded the demand of the most exigent confessional in the world!

The boy's resources were yet deeper: how could he confess when he doubted confession? And was that doubt a fault in him? And dare he communicate when in doubt? Why, the priest himself was not always a believer. After a while, father and son drove to Birmingham and talked of—Shelley. His father had but a moderate admiration for Shelley—'Why do you waste your time learning bad verses?'—but liked the opening of *Queen Mab*. A religious discussion followed and the boy's admiration of his father's intelligence declined from that moment, even while his sense of kindness increased. . . . George returned to Oscott for the rest of the term, but was forbidden to speak to his school-fellows. He enjoyed this outlawry, but the pleasantest moment of all was when he asked permission to say good-bye; and so he left in flying colours, or at least flying the colours he wished to fly. More than forty years after he recalls this affair, saying that he 'discovered' himself to be a Protestant and proclaimed his religious conviction (or shall we say the absence of a religious conviction?) to his parents: and while they did not oppose his claim to share the faith of his ancestors, they did not help him to attain it. And he will add to this now by saying simply: I couldn't breathe in Catholicism.

So ended Oscott. He had learned nothing there; and never was he able to learn anything he did not want to learn; such things remain dead to him—as now. He was to suffer for many years from the helplessness of an overgrown ignorance, and from the sharp perception of that most distressing affliction, literary clumsiness. One

living intellectual interest was noticeable in the recalci-
trant, and it is recalled in *Ave* as he thinks of the priest
of Carnacun, tall, gaunt, large-nosed with tufted nostrils;
and of that day in the 'sixties when the priest came to
Moore Hall in ragged cassock and battered biretta with
McHale's Irish Homer, saying that the Archbishop had
caught the Homeric ring. But was the Irish better than
the Greek? Reluctantly the priest answered no, and
read some eight or ten lines of the Greek. The discussion
gave the priest an interest in the boy, and it was soon
arranged that Father James should teach him Latin. The
name Propertius attracted him: might he read Propertius?
For aid he studied Cæsar diligently for a month:—in six
months could he get enough Latin to read Propertius?
It would take many years. But one day the priest said
that the time would come when George Moore would give
up hunting and everything for the classics. His mother,
hearing her elated son repeating this prophecy, burst out
laughing; and George surprisingly adopted her casual
attitude without question, emulation was slain by a look,
and the young scholar hardly ever saw Father James
again, except at Mass. . . . No, it is not surprising if you
remember his simple and sincere avowal of a great disbelief
in himself.

When he left Oscott he found Moore Hall a stable, for
his father was training racehorses; and as he has so often
done since, George Moore adopted the first ideal to hand,
as he calls it in his early prose; a phrase which he found
strangely endurable nearly twenty years later. He rode
and hunted and aspired to fame as a steeplechase rider.
What saved him but his father's political aspiration, and
its fruition in a return to Parliament in 1868? The home
was broken up and George perforce gave up racing in
Ireland for idleness and art in London.

It was from meeting Jim Browne, 'a great blonde man,'

who painted and talked about luxurious women, and from
that florid painter's opinion of the boy's sketches, that
George Moore received both impulse and discouragement
in art. Humbled but aspiring he would follow his father
through the National Gallery, and attend evening classes
at South Kensington, vexed that his subaltern brother
should accompany him. His father must have been
ashamed of his queer, erratic son, he surmises, for we all
want our children to be respectable though we may not
wish to be respectable ourselves. . . . He does not
proceed to the reason, namely, that we do not credit
our children with the courage which dictates and supports
our small unconventionalities, and instinctively want to
shelter them in the uniform of the world.

Hence it was, presumably, that his father concluded
that George must be got into the army if the army would
receive him; and it was settled that as Jurles was eminent
above all men in getting impossible boys through rudimentary examinations, Jurles should exert his thaumaturgy
upon George Moore. At that time, we learn, anything—
even Mrs. Jurles—was capable of awaking an erotic
suggestion; but no stimulus to military study was strong
enough to touch him. So self-conscious a youth was not
likely to be even half in love with easeful anonymous death
on a battlefield; and never has the mind of our author
been reducible to a formula. It seemed to him that
himself was his country, but wanting an alternative, for
all professions were repugnant, he was fain to accept the
army. But he realized that he could not be put into
the army without passing examinations, and the *Sportsman*
helped him to avoid passing. His sporting predilections
brought him into touch with betting and racing men and
their sumptuous mistresses; for we are speaking of fifty
years ago. But what would happen to George, thus
neglectful and uncontrolled? The sudden death of his
father in the spring of 1870 suspended the answer.

His mother would have liked to linger by his father's grave, but he gave her no peace, urging a return to London: 'We cannot spend our lives here going to Kiltoome with flowers.' An atrocious boy with engaging manners, is his note upon himself, and he adds that his mother died believing him to have been the best of sons, although he never sacrificed his convenience to hers. I cannot determine precisely the value of phrases like these, but even an atrocious boy may be humanized by regrets. Regrets, however, do not seem to have pleaded urgently for utterance.

The return to London was made memorable by his forsaking Jurles for the drawing-class of one Barthe, to which Whistler was a considerable attraction. The glimpse of Whistler does not please, and clearly is not meant to please; and Moore preferred to ally himself with a smaller celebrity, Oliver Madox Brown. . . . The story flows or eddies on with incidents of riding and shooting and the application of a nickname, *Mr. Perpetual*, due to his admission, or claim, of being always in love. ' To be ridiculous has always been *mon petit luxe*,' but I am sure he has never seemed ridiculous to himself, and he knows that only the pompous are truly ridiculous. Hence, I suppose, even a party of officers and ladies—a-stench with Victorianism—ending in an affray with sword and poker, is not really ridiculous; nor the notion of wearing for painting-robe the tea-gown of one of those ladies until Jim Browne ordered him to discard it. At Jim Browne's heels the future author of *Héloïse and Abélard* would swing along Piccadilly, Jim laughing at the lad's assertion that his hair was yellower than his friend's; and strange, and indeed thrice strange, is it to think of George Moore modelling himself upon Jim Browne, in both inward and outward aspects, learning his tastes in food and the looks of women and lap-dog loves (the story is a trifle tiresome even in *Vale*), and obsequious to his dictation in art. So humble was his obedience that for years and years he followed Jim's fondness for tall women with abundant bosoms, although in reality he liked hardly any, a gentle swelling being enough for his youthful austerity.

But Jim Browne's influence was suspected by George Moore's guardian, and Jim was driven to moralizing, and urged his friend to shoot in Africa or Abyssinia or seek the source of the Nile. The appeal found no response, and the source of the Nile slumbered on in unvexed obscurity. It was for art that he thirsted, and at last Jim said, ' If you want to learn painting you must go to France.' The call to France is variously related in the *Confessions* and in *Vale,* for the later book dispenses with the supernatural agency which, in the earlier account, was needed to dispatch him to Paris. He experienced, he says in *Confessions of a Young Man,* the phenomenon of echo-augury, words spoken in an unlooked-for quarter; and without appeal to reason they impelled belief. The echoing of one word, France, convinced him that he must go to France and become French. A more conspicuous and valuable instance of the Pauline phenomenon is recalled in *Hail and Farewell,* and may be noted later.

For a while he still hung back, disobedient to the heavenly echo. He was heir to a considerable property, and divined all that money meant. Lake, mountains, and woods uttered but one word—Self, the Self upon whose creation his mind was resolved; truly a poignant psychological moment. Self was to be created, expressed and nourished by art; and he was eighteen, with life and France to come. Art dominated all. Shelley had made him an atheist, and he is amusing in his account of a declaration to his mother that he declined to believe in God. He had expected to paralyse the household, but his mother shocked him with the indifference of her tone —'I am sorry, George, it is so.' It is odd to read in *Confessions of a Young Man* that the author hungered after great truths, the reading of *Middlemarch* and *The History of Civilization* being among his remembered spiritual moments. He preserves a different touch of the Victorian, again, when he writes that while he waited for his coach to take a party of 'tarts' and 'mashers' to the Derby, he would read a chapter of Kant's *Critique of Pure Reason*. He loved the abnormal, it seems, the self-conscious artist in him already fingering the tangled threads of personality. He boasted of fictitious dissipations, and his mother expected ruin; but ruin passed harmless beneath George Moore's windows as, standing there in the morning twilight, he watched the moon and repeated Shelley and dreamed of Paris.

CHAPTER II

A SENSITIVE PLANT

I can never mutinie so much against France but I must needes looke on Paris with a favourable eye : It hath my hart from infancy, whereof it hath befalne me as of excellent things. . . . So long as she shall continue, so long shall I never want a home or retreat to retire and shrowd my selfe at all times : a thing able to make me forget the regret of all other retreates.—*Montaigne.*

AN Irishman must fly from Ireland if he would be himself, Moore writes in 1911, when he begins to think of the soul he had lost in Paris and London, wondering if it is indeed true that whoever casts off tradition is like a tree transplanted into uncongenial soil. But in 1888 such questioning was impossible, for the ten years spent in France were still intoxicatingly remembered; and he notes that the most impressionable time of his life, from twenty to thirty, when mind and senses are awake, he, the most impressionable of beings, passed in France. Nor was it as an alien or an indifferent spectator, for he strove to identify himself with his environment and, shaking himself free from race and language, sought deliberately to recreate himself in the womb of a new nationality. Time slowly—yes, quite slowly—revealed the failure, but George Moore himself was half deceived into thinking it a success. *Confessions of a Young Man* gives the measure of that failure in its most immediate light, as well as the frank story of the desperate attempt. To his mother he had avowed that it was for education that he meant to go to Paris, rather than Oxford or Cambridge; he thought he could educate himself better in a café than in a university.

It was in art that his immersion was complete and his re-birth accomplished; and the tale of that long-proceeding change is luckily available. With trunks of clothes, books, pictures and an English valet, he started for Paris; the valet, Mullowny, becoming very soon the one superfluity of all these. Had Moore been an artist already he would not have suppressed the valet, but used him for delicious Chorus in the Comedy of Paris; but it is only the mature artist that sees the material nearest to his hand. The valet might have been at least as much to his master as is Alec to his auditor in *A Story-Teller's Holiday*. The chance slipped away unperceived, and *George Moore by his Valet* remains an imaginary fragment of biography. Mullowny, sick for home, wife, beer and conversation, counselled his master to return to England, and when the advice was refused, left him at the end of eight months; and Moore was glad to lose him. A valet meant conformity to conventions, but the young man who sets out on the great adventure of art must separate himself from all conventions; and he realized that Mullowny stood between George Moore and the artist. Above all he was twenty-one and wished to be himself, and he felt that to be himself he must live the physical as well as the intellectual life of the Quarter. So adroitly is a confession insinuated into the story of *Vale*.

His first business, then, was the discovery of a café where the evenings could be passed. Was it instinct or chance—was it another echo-augury—that brought him news of the café in which Manet spent his evenings? The Nouvelle Athènes sounded in his ears as though invented to lure him; I can see it now, he cries, the white nose of a block of buildings, stretching up the hillside into the Place Pigalle opposite the fountain. His retrospective glance in 1921 is as fond as it was in 1904, when he first revised the *Confessions*, or in 1888, when the book was first issued. He mixed, he says, with many men at the Nouvelle Athènes, with Manet, Degas, Pisarro, Renoir and Sisley, and once or twice talked to Monet there. . . . 'I have not the least idea why they endured me. One thing I learned, and that was from Monet, who taught me to be ashamed of nothing except being ashamed; yet who knows?' he will add (and again it is the note of 1921), 'perhaps that was not learned, but lay in me all the time.'

The writers among the group into which he was so suddenly and so deeply plunged were doubtful of their own art, and envied the art of the painter; and homage was paid to the painters as they trooped or sidled in. He recalls his longing to be admitted to their intimacy, and especially his shy regard for Manet, whom he had begun to recognize as the great new force in painting. Evening after evening he sat silent until at last Manet, observing him correcting proofs or pretending to correct proofs, asked if the café talk did not distract his attention: receiving then for answer, 'Not at all, I was thinking of your painting.' Friendship followed, and in the studio in the rue d'Amsterdam he came to understand the real, the Parisian Manet within the blonde, amusing face and clear eyes—face, beard and nose almost satyr-like, but with an intellectual expression. Bad art, he muses, reveals no personality, and is bad because it is anonymous; the work of the great artist is himself, and Manet was one of the greatest artists. Manet was a rich man, in dress and appearance an aristocrat; and for the sake of his genius he was obliged to forsake his own class and spend his evenings in the café of the Nouvelle Athènes among artists.

Of Manet's art, and of his almost alone, Moore speaks with unrestrained praise and fondness; and was it not partly because Manet urged revolt against the old that this younger rebel declared and maintained such a loyalty of admiration? because 'Adam standing in Eden looking at the sunset was not more naked and unashamed than Manet'? A pathetic hint falls across the tribute when he speaks of Renoir and Manet. He suspects Renoir's art of a certain vulgarity, yet Manet's last pictures were influenced by Renoir. Less pathetic, and not less significant, is the fact that Manet never sold a picture during the years that Moore knew him; the price, he adds, that one pays for shamelessness, for truth, sincerity, personality, is public neglect.

But I am wrong to dart thus at Manet, instead of remarking first that Moore approached the Nouvelle Athènes circle with no other pretension than the slender one assumed by any disciple in Julien's studio. And I must remark, also, that the tribute to Manet, like the tribute to others whose names brighten Moore's reminiscence, is not to be found in the *Confessions*, which immediately reveals the author's sensations and ideas, but in *Hail and Farewell;* and the slow emergence of these recognitions is a thing to be pondered over in any account of Moore's mental progress.

A typical meridional Julien, as Moore found him, with a large stomach, dark, crafty eyes, seductively mendacious manner and sensual mind. Julien consciously made use of his pupil, and the pupil unconsciously made use of Julien. Remember that Moore was twenty and talkative, eager and diffident, that his knowledge of French had been picked up in three months, and you will have a glimpse of the comedy of the situation. The studio exhaled a subtle mental pleasure—the sense of sex; but although that sense was very dear to him, he is explicit in affirming that he did not fall in love, and yet more definite in affirming, with the detachment which has grown in him and helped to make him an artist, that he was willing to stray a little from his path, but never further than a single step, which he could retrace when he pleased.

Of Julien a fuller and more amusing story is given in *Impressions and Opinions,* and it is necessary to refer to it in order to understand into what strange scholarship the new disciple was inducted. Julien, as Moore came to see him, was the most notorious and powerful personage in the art world of Paris, a dizzy position for a man who was

once a shepherd of extraordinary physical strength, and
free to choose between fame as a wrestler and fame as a
painter.—No, he did not toss for the decision; the village
settled his future by sending him to Paris, where he
pretended just sufficient talent to obscure the truth.
Failure as an artist diverted him into the life of a show-
man, and at the end of a season's wrestling-matches
Julien, as successful as Barnum, had accumulated a small
fortune, and as quickly lost it again. Why not, then,
open a studio? He opened a studio, and strove against
envious Fate with small luck until he bethought himself
of the power of medals. Since my countrymen love
medals, he cried, I will give medals—a medal every
month for the best drawing or painting; a medal and
a hundred francs. It is not hard to believe that in
three months the Salon Julien burst its doors and en-
gulfed all Paris; in three years M. Julien was a limited
company, and the late wrestler the managing director
at a large fee. The medal had triumphed. That the
triumph was not eternal matters nothing; which among
human institutions is eternal? The modern Tamerlane
had his day. When Moore wrote his account of the
rise and fall of the Julien despotism he had escaped
from the influence of the salon; he could even urge
upon young English painters the wisdom of staying at
home, avowing himself anxious to save them from the
commercialism of Julien's studio, and declaring it to be
unnecessary for them to learn in Paris. His own ten
years were over; he had escaped as by a miracle, and
he could not help reviling the prison of French art. He
even pleads for insularity, saying that only by being
parochial in the first instance may any man's art become
ultramontane in the end. It was not the course of his
own mind, and the acerbity of his reflections upon Julien
is in the main due to his tardy perception that those
ten years were wasted. But I think it was also due to

the fact that he could not forgive Julien for thrusting Marshall upon him, as he could not forgive himself for submitting to Marshall. In a moment we shall be considering his ten-years adventure in relation to his calling as a writer, but when he made his attack on the commercialism of French art he had scarcely written a line except in a cosmopolitan prose.

Henry Marshall (in the revised edition of *Confessions of a Young Man* he becomes Lewis Ponsonby Marshall) is the bore of the earliest account of Paris days. Would not most readers of the sketch be surprised to know that the name concealed a real person who died some years ago and therefore must have lived? Maybe Lewis Ponsonby Marshall sat for the portrait of Lewis Seymour, of whose shabbiness his own is a faithful forecast. . . . Perhaps memory, and certainly art, matures with years, and the slightly amplified account of the first meetings between Moore and Marshall is witness to the immense development from the poor skill of *Confessions* to the mastery of reminiscence which fills *Hail and Farewell.* Indeed, this is the sole interest by which the unfortunate Marshall survives. He had come from Brussels to Paris with a beautiful prostitute, Alice Howard, who could not refrain from exclaiming as she watched her lover, 'What a toff he is!' Not less surely did his manner, his looks, his shallow brightness of talent, captivate the novice who strove to copy his speech and bearing, yet knowing that his own was the rarer nature. But it was no unconscious subordination, for Moore was watching life with the patience of a cat before a mousehole, picking a single phrase out of hours of vain chatter; he used Marshall as he used all those with whom he was brought into close contact. The avowal was made in 1888, but how much more completely true it is now, every reader will know. Moore's art has always been

concrete rather than aery in its essentials. Yet it is
with no contradiction but in absolute candour that he
avers that he did not form relationships with designs;
never has he given a thought to the advantage that
might accrue from friendship. He read books and
friends with an equally disinterested passion, discarding
each when he had eaten his hunger away.

Moore says these things of himself in the revised
Confessions, but in the first edition they were said
dramatically in the name of Edwin (once Edward)
Dayne, a fact which need not deceive us into ignoring
their verisimilitude. . . . He lived at this time in an
old-fashioned hotel kept by an enterprising Belgian,
and he is at pains to describe his first Parisian friend, a
little fat neckless man—Duval in *Confessions,* Lopez in
Vale; the author of a hundred and sixty plays, not one
of which had been produced for twenty years. He had
written plays in collaboration with everybody, even
with Dumas père and Gautier, and the mysteries ot
collaboration thickened halo-wise around his head as
the young stranger questioned him in bad French, out of
a rapture of admiration and respect. The significance ot
this acquaintance appears when you find later on that
these radiant mysteries allured George Moore with the
question, Why not write a comedy? No matter that his
writing had been a few ill-spelt letters. With Marshall
for hero and Alice for heroine, with three weeks'
fermentation and the growth of a plot, there remained but
one enormous difficulty—how to achieve a prose dialogue?
At last he discovered Leigh Hunt's edition of Congreve
and other Restoration dramatists, and the fruit of study
was a comedy in three acts with the abstract title,
Worldliness. A bad play it was, but he thinks not nearly
as bad as might be imagined; and in that, let us assume,
lies the reason that his precipitate return to London to
get it produced was fruitless. As fruitless was his attempt

with another play, and with a closer view of the embarrassments of the dramatic writer he returned to Paris. The bibliography will show how often the desire of the theatre has irked him, and I must speak of other plays later on; here we need but record the attempt and the failure, and the unregretted absence of the early texts.

From *Vale* you are permitted to gather that the return to England arose from a pining for London and English food and speech, and his mother's house, where Millais used to visit. Edward Martyn also, he remembers, knew him during the eighteen months of his stay; and Edward, he declares, is right in saying of him then that he developed from a mere sponge to the vertebræ and upwards, for in those days he worked and grew unconsciously. But all the while Lewis, in Paris, was still shaping him in London, and when he returned to Paris he was so closely fashioned in his friend's likeness that Julien, catching sight of him on the boulevard, thought it was Lewis himself. Lewis he found *plus amoreux que jamais*, a young god wallowing in finest linen and in moral depths into which we need not very carefully peer; we need but note that Moore began to despise him, but nevertheless passed months in his company pursuing art and dissipation. It was to Lewis Marshall or Alice Howard that he owed his acquaintance with *la belle Hollandaise*, who passed from him with an enigmatic, I don't know what's going to happen to me! 'She passed out of my life for ever, and if I relate the incident of our meeting it is because I would pay tribute to her who revealed sensuality to me '— a phrase which prompts a question whether our author might not have become a self-sacrificing scientist instead of a self-sacrificing artist. The young men prided themselves on the versatility with which they used the language of the fence's parlour and the language of the literary salon, and appeared as much at home in the one as in the other. For the true artist, like the false, is a chameleon.

In a terrible slang they shouted benediction upon a plan to break into a crib, and then fancied there was something very thrilling in returning home to dress for a reception among the *élite*. The story is not entrancing. Art and Marshall's poverty wrought a change. The amorous friend, who always lapsed into extremes, retired to Belleville and settled down as a workman in a china factory; and Moore went to see him and related the story to Julien. What followed is not recounted in the 1888 *Confessions*, but is inserted in the revised edition and enlarged in *Vale*. The interpolation indicates how candidly the author looks back upon himself, since it explains that it was no unprompted generosity that led to his offer to make himself responsible for Marshall. Julien, it seems, urged him to save Marshall from living as a workman, and either make him an allowance or share rooms with him; a suggestion that rather shocked one who was concerned with his own genius more than with fostering another's. But he yielded, dismissed his valet, and welcomed Marshall. It was unpleasant, he reflects, to have a window opening only to an unclean prospect of roofs, to rise at seven, to work ten hours a day, to forego all pleasures—for the sake of a friend with whom he had entered upon an artistic duel. It was a year of great passion and great despair, defeat falling upon our author by inches, like the pendulum in the pit; and how could such a mind help suffering, so intensely alive (as he sees it later) to all impulses, so unsupported by any moral conviction? His own facility was unequal to his rival's, although in character and feeling his work was more individual and refined; but Marshall showed himself singularly capable of education, while we have Moore's repeated word for it, and the slow development of his own excellence, that the truer artist was not.

For nine months the struggle continued—vainly; and the burden of unachieved desire became intolerable. All that he wanted was art, and art was taken from him. At last, 'I laid down my charcoal and said, I will never draw or paint again. That vow I have kept.' And the rest? To the question, What should he do? there was no prompt answer. He strove to read, but it was impossible to sit at home, within earshot of the studio, and all the memories of defeat still ringing. Marshall flaunted success in his face; his good looks, his talents, his popularity, showing no pity or comprehension. It was not his vanity that distressed Moore, for that is rarely displeasing to him and sometimes is attractive; it was an insistence and aggressiveness which made the defeated feel only his serviceableness to the other's talent. Ten years hence, whispered the subtle Julien at a feast commemorating Marshall's success, a feast for which Moore himself paid, Lewis will be painting pictures at thirty thousand francs apiece; but man, adds our author, is such a selfish animal that it began to seem that he would prefer a great failure for Lewis to a great success. Yet if Marshall failed he would never get rid of him; and so he was as unhappy in the Galerie Feydeau as he had been at Oscott College. For relief he sought another circle, and was introduced to John O'Leary and others who interested him on his father's account. But the problem remained, and indeed grew acuter when Lewis broke into that other circle. No longer able to endure the frightful neighbourhood, he told Lewis that he was going to Boulogne, mentioning a Madame Ratazzi with whom he had acted in *La Dame aux Camélias*. Of his adventures as an actor I know nothing. . . . The story of the rupture is given in *Confessions*, but the author of *Vale*, admitting that his own was at once a shameful and a natural act, wonders if he has told sufficiently of his surprise at Marshall's indecency in staying at the *appartement* when he himself had gone. In fact, his return from Boulogne three months later found the old difficulty as embarrassing as ever, for Marshall ignored him and refused to leave, playing on his friend's weakness and almost forcing him to plead for forgiveness.

A new start was needed and the two went to live in the Rue de la Tour des Dames, Marshall to paint and Moore to read and write poetry. Marshall furnished the rooms with the imagination of a high-bought courtesan and a fifth-rate artist, the valuables including incense, a Persian cat, a python and a crush of gardenias. For as yet, it seems, impressionism was an ineffectual influence, and France as vulgar as England; and Moore had not discovered the satisfaction of the eighteenth century. The commonplace, he says, in speaking of de Musset, is constitutionally abhorrent to him; but clearly it was not always so, and he suffered the perfection of the commonplace —the common itself—to flush his sky.

But Lewis Ponsonby Marshall seemed to be sinking, and had given up hope of painting anything that would sell, resorting instead to writing ridiculous sonnets. Unguardedly Moore introduced him to the Nouvelle Athènes, and almost died of shame when a foolish question to Degas showed Lewis as guilty of the unpardonable sin—lack of comprehension. It was this and this only, if the memory of the author of *Vale* may be trusted (and he would prefer an æsthetic reason to any other), that compelled Moore to beg him to go at once. In a few days he went. Months, perhaps years after, he met Marshall at Barbizon, engaged in painting a picture of an old graveyard. Friends gave him kindly or unkindly hints, and nothing remained for Lewis but to paint the picture. But since a picture exists not in the composition or the drawing but in the touch, it would have remained 'tinny' had it not been for the advice of that true painter, Stott of Oldham, who showed Lewis how to draw the brush from right to left until the paint began to look less like linoleum; and Lewis thought he understood. The result was a successful picture which was sold for ten thousand francs. Lewis's conduct, says his friend, looking back on the success, was not very dignified; he could not restrain himself—the talent of *un détraqué;* with which remark we may dismiss Lewis Ponsonby Marshall from our tale. Vivid enough are these memories to George Moore, after so many years, and it is characteristic that if he speaks of them now (as, for example, the incident of Stott redeeming the badness of Marshall's technique), it is almost precisely in the same words, without addition or omission, as those used in *Confessions* or in *Vale;* so deeply have past things entered into his mind, and so consistent has been his view of them.

For himself, Moore says, both drama and art were abandoned for poetry. He talked of poems to Lopez, who gave him the innocent advice that he should choose subjects which might astonish the British public by their originality. Hence it was to Lopez that the first copy of *Flowers of Passion* was presented, and it was with Lopez that he so wonderfully discussed the possibility of an English and a French author collaborating in a play for Henry Irving on the subject of Martin Luther, even deciding that it should be written in a spirit of ardent Protestantism. Alas that nothing of these surprising, delicious discussions has been reported!

Proudly does Moore repeat Manet's words, ' There is no Frenchman in England who occupies the position you do in Paris.' A reserved young man would have been backward, but Moore was eager, maybe importunate, and he proved irresistible. It was to Lopez, again, that he owed an introduction to Villiers de L'Isle Adam, wild-eyed and dishevelled, with white feminine hand and long-falling hair. His reminiscence plays fondly with the names of artists who flamed in the forehead of his morning sky. Shelley had continued to be his joy, but that joy was swallowed up for a while on reading *Mademoiselle de Maupin.*

Gautier's exaltation of the body above the soul, the plain
scorn of a world of lacerated saints and crucified Redeemer,
conquered him. He had always cherished mystery and
dreams; but now so great was the change that the more
brutally his old ideal was outraged, the rarer his delight.
Never will he read Gautier again, but though he lived a
thousand years Gautier's power over his soul would remain
unbroken. That Gautier has nevertheless disappeared
from the subsequent autobiography of George Moore need
not surprise us, nor will it evoke a very profound regret
when we read *The Brook Kerith.*

After Gautier, Baudelaire. Mad and morbid, is his
phrase for the literature created by the enthusiasm of
1830. He was never quite subjugated by Baudelaire, and
now grudges him the honours of current criticism; declaring, for instance, that famous sonnets show plain faults in
every line, even faults of syntax as well as obscurities of
meaning, and prepared to prove that every sonnet has
such faults. Baudelaire, however, he admits, is saved from
neglect by English readers by their common ignorance of
the refinements of the French tongue; and Moore himself
escaped that ignorance only at the cost of ten years in
France.

Reading again his earlier and later musings upon French
literature, you require but a very faint effort to remember
that Moore's ten years in France were ten years of an
immature mind—the mind of twenty to thirty, without
traditions or other anchorage, and with ardour alone for
guide. He acknowledges the mere instinctiveness of his
tastes and his attraction to the sound and appearance of
names; and it is perhaps remarkable how clearly he sees
the French writers with his own eyes—Catulle Mendès,
for example, one of the muse's minions; a perfect realization of his name, with pale hair, fragile face and depraved
idealism. ' His words are caresses, his fervour is delightful,
and to hear him is as sweet as drinking a smooth perfumed

yellow wine. All he says is false.' No one's conversation was more fruitful, he admits; but a touch of the later sharpness is added in, 'Every country has its Catulle Mendès. Robert Buchanan is ours, only in the adaptation Scotch gruel has been substituted for perfumed yellow wine.' We need not ask whether Mendès is already so easily forgotten as Robert Buchanan.

For contrast, Mallarmé and Verlaine. Symbolism did not attract him—how should it attract one whose sole art is expressed in clarification and effusion; one for whom the obscure only is horrible, and the rainy morning light the sweetest in the world? No writer is less capable of mysticism, and fluid as his mind was, it flowed in its own bed and could not be confined to the ambiguous depths and iridescent shallows of the symbolist's world. Proof against Mallarmé's influence, he nevertheless admired and has continued to admire the poet, 'one of the saints of literature,' whom to know was an honour and a distinction such as fell upon the Apostles. The dedication of a new edition of *Memoirs of My Dead Life* to Mr. Edmund Gosse (exquisite the phrase concerning the book that 'so amiably solicits the protection of your name!') affords the opportunity of recording a recent visit to the neighbourhood which knew Mallarmé, and a testimony to the rare concurrence of acquaintance and admiration in the mind of our author. To Verlaine the response was more prompt, ample and prophetic, as readers of *Impressions and Opinions* will remember. Verlaine is sharply discriminated as a spiritual perversity—hate as commonplace as love to him, unfaith as vulgar as faith; yet poetry springing lily-like in whiteness and smell from the obscenity with which his mind was dunged. That is a vivid account of Moore's visit to Verlaine.—The poet had promised a sonnet on Parsifal for publication in a review, and Moore reluctantly accompanied a friend in search of the sonnet and the poet; and an amusing story of the exploration of a dim, eccentric region

of Paris introduces you to a dark corner, a door, and the
bald prominent forehead, cavernous eyes and macabre
expression of burnt-out lust, which were the outward
Verlaine. The head was covered by a filthy nightcap:—

> ' A nightshirt full of the grease of the bed covered
> his shoulders; a stained and discoloured pair of trousers
> were hitched up somehow about his waist. He was
> drinking wine at sixteen sous the litre. He told us
> that he had just come out of the hospital: that his
> leg was better, but it still gave him a great deal of
> pain. He pointed to it. We looked away.
> ' He said he was writing the sonnet, and promised
> that we should have it on the morrow. Then, in the
> grossest language, he told us of the abominations he
> had included in the sonnet; and seeing that our visit
> would prove neither pleasant nor profitable, we took
> our leave as soon as we could. But I remember one
> thing that seems characteristic. Speaking of a career
> for his son, whom he had not seen for twenty years,
> he said he regretted he had not brought him up as a
> *garçon de café*, avowing his belief that he could
> imagine no trade more advantageous than that of a
> *garçon de café*.'

Verlaine, he adds, believes, but there is no more than
belief, practice is wholly wanting; and he suggests that
the poet never quite realizes how he lives or how he
writes, for after giving an abominable description of the
sonnet he was pondering, he sent the depressed editor a
'most divinely beautiful sonnet.' Verlaine and Villon,
there is something of kinship between them beyond the
crude suggestion of alliteration. The whole man, in
Moore's view, is contained in an all-embracing sense of his
own unworthiness. ' He spoke of his miserable condition,
but without adjective or emphasis—just as the old woman
in the ballade might have done; he deplored the discom-
fort that the lack of the very smallest sums of money
involved, but without even suggesting that after all it was

a man of genius who suffered.' The picture is supremely sad: he was alive when Moore wrote of him—the prey of strange passions and constant sickness, dragging a pitiful body from hospital to hospital and sheltering among herds of workmen. It is a proof of Moore's sympathy and swift apprehension of a remoter genius than his own, that the tribute from which I have quoted was written when Verlaine was almost unknown; and our author himself is to be thanked if his tribute is no longer singular.

Yet another instance of the favourite echo-augury is asserted in Moore's discovery of Zola and naturalism. Hardly able to believe his eyes as they scanned a casual article by Zola, he read that one should write (surely no hard task!) with as little imagination as possible, that plot was illiterate and puerile, and so on; and he rose up a little dizzy, as though he had had a violent knock on the head. For a third time he experienced the pain and joy of sudden light—the 'new art' called naturalism; and at once vaguely understood that his Roses of Midnight were dead flowers, sterile eccentricities and what not. The *Confessions* abounds with the utterance of this mental excitement, and with the difficulties that rained upon the newest disciple when he meditated applying naturalism to poetry. It seemed that time was waiting for the poet who would sing fearlessly of the rude industry of dustmen, and Moore did not foresee that time would quite serenely wait until *vers libre* should lyricize the dustman's craft.

It was, he says, the idea of the new æstheticism that seduced him—the new art corresponding to modern life as ancient art corresponded to ancient life; for as yet, I surmise, he could not perceive the opportunity of art unentangled by current and local conditions. He could not perceive that what caught him so powerfully was transitory and not permanent, delusive and not solid, a formula and not a native mode. Reading Zola he had been impressed by a pyramidal size and strength, and a fugal treatment of various scenes; he did not know then, as he came to know later (how gradually his own books have shown), that it is only the artist that changes, art being eternal. No writer has changed more slowly, or more completely, than George Moore; no writer has become more devotedly an artist; but he had not yet found what he was, and for a while was subdued by Zola's immense energy and the simplicity of his prescription. Subtilize as he will, the creative mind of an artist craves simplicity, and what is more welcome than a new and energetic formula when the mind is perplexed and wearied with twilight subtleties?

Disguised as a Parisian workman, for the occasion was a fancy-dress ball in honour of *L'Assommoir*, and accompanied by the impressive Manet, he thrust through a Montmartre crowd and found himself speaking to a thickly-built, massive person—Zola himself—who chilled him with a bow and passed on. Not until he sought out naturalism in a temporary fastness did he really talk and listen to Zola, who was not yet the kindly and gracious host, but a bear cursing the universe—no, a Buddha with fat legs lying on a sofa. Buddha, however, finding he had not to entertain a fool, was ready to talk on Protestantism in art to the author of *Martin Luther*. 'I have made a friend,' repeated Moore again and again as he returned from his first conversation with Buddha; but the significance of the friendship was exaggerated. Years after, when *Confessions of a Young Man* was appearing in a magazine and Zola was under a promise to write a preface to a French translation of *A Mummer's Wife*, Moore called again and found that Zola would not write it. Why? Buddha, resuming whatever humanity he may be supposed to have discarded, pointed to offending passages in 'La Synthèse de la Nouvelle Athènes.' For there already Moore had discovered that Zola had no style, but sought immortality

E

in an exact description of a linen-draper's shop; and I
conceive Zola pointing out this enormity of recantation,
and others as huge, and disdaining his critic's pleading
hands. Vainly, and surely with no excess of dignity, did
the younger novelist urge that he was not giving his real
opinions—it was a synthesis of others' opinions—can't you
see? Not so, replied the re-humanized Buddha; you call
them Confessions, and when we use that word we mean
that at last we are going to tell the truth. Not that he
was angered: he merely found it impossible to write the
preface. Children will devour their fathers, he added,
mantling himself in an unapproachable reserve.

'There were tears in my eyes,' says our English
naturalist, as he recalls Zola's words and the simplicity
with which they were uttered; but the tears were
promptly followed with a more familiar sardonic smile, and
he goes on to say that at this time Zola was fat, and soon
after dieted himself into leanness; that Zola's house
revealed a large coarse mind, a coarse net through which
living things escape; that Zola once thought of giving a
ball, and so on. And equally characteristic is his return
to appreciation as he forgets the external man and considers the inward genius, until he cries—a most extraordinary imagination! Yet, alas, Zola was not naturally an
artist, and the quality of his writing does not seem to concern him any more than the quality of the things he buys;
and again, alas, Zola is a striking instance of the insanity of
common sense. All that Moore says of Zola is witness of
his own movement; revelation, recognition, discipleship for
the first steps, and again recognition, mocking and neglect
for the last. Paris showed him Zola, and the steady,
stealthy discarding of Parisian influences showed him Zola
anew—a gross imagination, the very enormity of common
sense. The illusion was violent, the disillusion complete.

There is scarcely a word of Zola in Moore's later
writings, and equally striking is the silence of our author

upon that other French master whose association with Zola was so honourably public. I refer to Anatole France. Moore's silence might be variously interpreted, but no interpretation is so sure as that the French ironist and the English imaginative artist are diversely endowed and that their superficial likeness—clear enough to one who regards but their humours—is delusive. I do not know how fondly Anatole France views the later writings of George Moore, and I can but hope that he does not look upon them with such a mortal indifference as George Moore opposes to the brilliance of his contemporary; for in his eyes Anatole France is but a small figure. He has praise neither for *La Vie Littéraire* nor for *Monsieur Bergeret.* True that the inherent cynicism does not repel him, but neither does the wit charm him. Moore and Anatole France were in Paris together, and met; but they were young, inconspicuous men, and I suppose previsionary glances prevented both intimacy and enmity.

A round-shouldered man in a suit of pepper and salt, with small eyes and sharp tongue—Degas—is a figure to be remembered by the side of his friend and rival, Manet, as you see him in *Confessions.* It was about 1876 that Moore became acquainted with Degas, wondering why he had been called harsh and intractable, an old curmudgeon. It was a mere legend, put protectingly forward by a very courteous and kind man whose sole objection was urged against journalists. Degas held that the artist must live apart, and his private life remain unknown; and you may judge of the strength of his hold upon our author's admiration when you read of his own breach in the privacy with which Degas surrounded himself. His doctrine was far other than the doctrine of George Moore, who called one morning at his studio, pulled the string at the foot of the stairs and ran up to question the painter about the very book which had so mortally chilled Zola.

Degas was reading the book and was pleased with it—so pleased, that the gratified author began to meditate an article upon his host, saying to himself that Degas' dislike of notoriety was purely imaginary. The article was written—you may read it in *Impressions and Opinions* —and attracted attention in France. Hence arose a dilemma; how could Degas consent to see Moore again, when it had been given out to the world that he would never speak to anyone who related his private life in an article? How could he speak to a friend—a dear friend even—who had flagrantly violated the rule? Degas preferred consistency, until he fell under the power of remembrance and sent word that he would see his old friend when he revisited Paris. But to renew an old friendship would be difficult, and they never met again. A breath of extreme sorrow is heard in the postscript to this story, when you read in a letter from a friend of the painter, 'Degas lives alone and almost blind, seeing nobody, without any kind of occupation,' and picture him hearing of the tardy homage paid to the achievements which his own eyes might never again behold.

Degas remains in his mind, no more alienated, type (if type he can be called) of the artists to whom George Moore's early devotion was freely given. Among those earlier contemporaries the painters alone remain undisturbed in eminence, for the writers have become rivals and his emulous ardency has not permitted them to prolong a casual brightness. Manet, Degas, Renoir and Monet—who began, Moore considers, by imitating Manet, while Manet ended by imitating Monet—these endure; for when our author discarded painting, he found his desires no longer rebuked by their accomplishment. We shall see later on that comparison has been a constant stimulus to his own work, as well as an amusement to his readers; and it is only in a kindred but remote art that disparagement has not followed quickly on the heels of familiarity. This at any rate Paris had achieved for him at the end of his ten-years effort to become a Frenchman.

But as a writer what did Paris do for him? He had failed to become a painter, and he lost a great deal of the fragmentary knowledge of the English language which he took to France. But he wavers when he asks himself what Paris did for him. At one time he wonders whether Edward Martyn was not right in saying that Moore had lost his soul in Paris and London; and when he reflects upon that expression of the soul which is called 'style,' or merely 'prose,' he counts himself lucky to have fled from France. Yet he hankered and has always hankered after French, and in his latest meditation upon himself he finds that those ten years were not wasted; Nature drove him forth from England, for in her strange wisdom she lamented the deeply-rutted road into which English fiction had fallen, and raised up a new Parsifal. To redeem mankind from too great admiration of certain writers—you are to presume contemporary English novelists—she sought out one who had resisted school education, one who had been a perplexity to his father and indulged himself in the pleasures of opéra bouffe until he was twenty-one, and sent him to Paris to forget English, and at the same time fail to become a French writer. A virgin mind, he notes, in this half-dazzled, swift, reverting glance. Shall we not echo his added tribute, that Nature's foresight and versatility are indeed remarkable? She put pebbles into his mouth, and they dropped out but slowly, one by one, with each of his laborious efforts to write English. We shall see them fall, we shall note the gradual clearing, the articulation becoming less laboured; modulations will be distinguished, civilities and humours will be heard, and when the last stone—a round French stone—has been ejected, we shall hear a voice speaking with unaccustomed ease and a fluency which is sometimes

near to monotony, yet never wanting the variableness of
the seasons of the year.

He wavers, I said, when he asks what Paris did for him,
at one time murmuring, 'So much,' and at another,
'Perhaps so little!' Even in 1921, in the prelude to the
new edition of *Memoirs of My Dead Life*, he has asserted,
'So much!' yet in the same year, answering the question,
How much? he murmurs, 'I don't know; perhaps, as
you say, the writer was in me all the time and Paris may
not have helped me much, even though you may be wrong
in thinking it hindered me. Who can say?'—And when
he is pressed with, After all, doesn't a writer, like any
other human being, simply become more and more intensely himself? And isn't his exercise partly a stripping
of the foolish accretions of his youth, and sloughing
numberless skins until his native brightness appears, his
Paris being but a thicker and tougher skin than all the
rest?—when he is pressed thus his eyes sink musingly
back into his head and he answers, 'Perhaps—who
knows?' and fails to remark, what I have only just
remembered, that in the preface to *The Coming of Gabrielle*
he himself has significantly pointed out the truth that we
grow into ourselves, if we grow at all.

It would be ill-manners to make George Moore a mere
warning to other writers, yet the significance of his mental
subjection to the French is not limited to himself. One
whose chief interest has for many years been animated by
English verse may be pardoned for thinking that a subordination to foreign influence is an evil thing to befall an
English writer. Imaginative literature is a fleet sailing
its eternal course over the seas of the world, and if the
newest commander of the frailest barque puts in at an
alien port and lingers on until hulk and shrouds alike are
decayed, he will find it a huge discouraging task to put to
sea again. Moore seems to have thought he could become
French merely by living ten years in France; but kindly

as his glance was, he perceived at last that he was not French and had but made his task as an English writer stiff with every possible difficulty. That certain English writers have been touched to fine issues by the study of another than their native language, proves nothing for the argument so far as our author is concerned; for he is an experimental writer, and how can you write from experience except in that language which is the chief gift of experience and of the deeper, unconscious experience called tradition? Ten years in France are not wasted if they yield an acquaintance with many and a familiarity with a few of the leaders of the impressionists, and at least—or at most—they may suffice to make an agreeably versatile writer upon English art; but in that other practice, the practice of prose, ten alien years may conceivably work an effect only less ignoble in prose than in verse. Denaturalization is an end beyond the reach of any truly imaginative writer, and usually beyond his aim also ; and the attempt is deplorable as well as vain, for the deflection of young vigours during a whole decade in a man's life—and in art how brief the longest life !—is a weakness which cannot pass unobserved, and which will persist long after the surrender has been annulled. I need not labour the argument, for has not Moore bewailed that surrender with eloquent and exact admissions? But even Moore himself has not apprehended all the consequences, and has often been complacent enough in his review of the past.

Yet a reservation must be made, for to generalize on such personal matters is neither interesting nor useful. The influence of France upon the creative mind may have been deadly enough in Moore's case, but upon the critical mind the same morbid influence cannot be asserted. Definitions of 'creative' and 'criticism' need not seduce our attention just now, for refinements of distinction are wasted where the facts are generous in their witness. As a creative writer George Moore had much to unlearn, much to forget when he left France for England, and even his excellences are marred by foreign airs and patches ; his clearest impressions being delayed until slow time and wandering change had released and renewed him. But as a critical writer it seems that in the years first following his return to England he owed much to France. It was his luck, as we have remarked, to be associated in varying degrees with many painters whose work has already become part of the nineteenth century's bequest to the twentieth. Of one of them, whose painting has the quality which George Moore's purest art itself manifests, I mean Corot, he speaks too little, but still with the admiration of an unavowed disciple. He approaches what he calls the mystery of Corot when he suggests that Corot's art has nothing in common with impressionist art ; for although Corot aimed at rendering his impression of a subject, his method of rendering it was contrary to the method of Monet and his school, Monet never having known how to organize and control his values. Usually, however, Moore's criticism is most acute when he has something to tell you of the painter himself or when he is challenging current tastes. He can strike sparks from the solid rocks of popular stupidity, as he sees it in the Royal Academy, but he contributes little to the foundation of principles which might purge the Royal Academy of stupidity in the future.

More frequently does he speak of Manet, Degas and the rest, and always with the admiration of a declared disciple. They could not teach him their art, but he could learn to look with their eyes and to weigh with their measure. Had he lived in the great period of English water-colour, his instinct would have led him into contact with English painters, and he would have shown the same discriminating zeal in proclaiming their virtues as he has shown in asserting the virtues of the impressionists ; it being plain enough that George Moore in his earlier writings is not an original critic but a very perfect and subtle echo. In those essays (as indeed in all his later work) he betrays no hint of speculation in his mind; his criticism is based not upon principles of æsthetics, but upon remembered sensations and personal influences. You will not look to *Modern Painting* or *Impressions and Opinions* for theories of criticism or theories of creation; and even now, although Croce may sweep all England with his new flame, Moore is shy of abstractions and remains unlit and unwarmed by any æsthetic speculation. Ivy-like he clings round his subject, his leaves gleaming brightly and precisely against the hard rind of created beauty and revealed truth; detached he falls. There is an exquisite responsiveness in his essays on art; the more closely he follows the intention of the subject the more happily you listen; and he is able to illustrate and support his opinions by a reminiscent familiarity which leads you to forget to ask for something fresh and independent in view. Thus in writing of Degas he says that Degas, with marvellous perception, follows every curve and characteristic irregularity, writing the very soul of his model upon the canvas; but you hardly stay to remark the vagueness of such phrasing because it is followed with :—

‘He will paint portraits only of those whom he knows intimately, for it is part of his method only to paint his sitter in that environment which is habitual to her or him. With stagey curtains, balustrades, and conventional poses, he will have nothing to do. He will watch the sitter until he learns all her or his tricks of expression and movement, and then will reproduce all of them, and with such exactitude and sympathetic insight that the very inner life of the man is laid bare. . . . And that Degas may render more fervidly all the characteristics that race, heredity, and mode of life have endowed his sitter with, he makes numerous drawings and paints from

them ; but he never paints direct from life. And as
he sought new subject-matter, he sought for new
means by which he might reproduce his subject in
an original and novel manner. At one time he
renounced oil-painting entirely, and would only work
in pastel or distemper. Then, again, it was water-
colour painting, and sometimes in the same picture
he would abandon one medium for another. There
are examples extant of pictures begun in water-colour,
continued in gouache, and afterwards completed in
oils ; and if the picture be examined carefully, it will
be found that the finishing hand has been given with
pen and ink. Degas has worked upon his lithographs,
introducing a number of new figures into the picture
by means of pastel. He has done beautiful sculpture,
but, not content with taking a ballet-girl for subject,
has declined to model the skirt, and had one made by
the nearest milliner.'

The lengthy citation may be paralleled by many others
upon other painters. It is not an illegitimate method, it
is a method that may teach much, but it is scarcely a
critical method. Rather is it an instance of Moore's
failure in detachment as a critic, and since painting is not
his own art, his criticism is useful not for understanding,
but for accepting a picture. The method would possess an
equal validity if applied to the praise of bad pictures, and
in fact when Moore writes of bad pictures he scarcely
shows you why they are bad, but simply how he hates
them. He does not rationalize his dislike, and is yet
farther from giving you the means of rationalizing your
own. To few men is it permitted to announce principles
of criticism, though many men evince an excellent, intuitive
judgment ; but criticism is something beyond the avowal
of intuitive likings and revulsions. Moore's conception of
pictures, attractive and stimulating as you find it, is one
to which the conscious mind has brought much less than
the unconscious ; while the great critic is he in whom

emotional is fused with intellectual apprehension. But the great critic is rare, and is seldom developed in the creative writer.

Nevertheless, I do not urge that George Moore's criticism is parasitic. The mendicant critic resorts to easy paraphrase, and with the facility of a fool will tell you what a picture is about—a trick perfectly legitimate in respect of inferior art, in which subject can be regarded apart from treatment, but sterile and impertinent in respect of original art. Moore has never yielded himself to such a folly. Instead of sinking to the description of a picture, he tells you of its effect upon him—a story of far more interest—or merely the effect of the painter's personality in sharp contact with his own. It is this, indeed, that lends half the interest that you find in his essay on Whistler. You will not fail to remember his personal dislike of Whistler on first seeing him, nor question whether that primary dislike was ever overcome. There is, for instance, a subtle disparagement in the phrase, Nature has dowered Whistler with only genius; if there is, also, a clumsiness which must have amused that acute stylist to tears. Whistler, Moore says, lacked physical power, but a painter needs the nerves of a bull; and then, oddly and innocently enough, he urges that if Whistler had been six inches taller, and 'his bulk proportionately increased'—I hope that the author of such a phrase will never chance on it now—his art would have been different. Innocent and odd are such sentences, but as you read on you find that they are introduced merely to give a living hue to Moore's dislike and a physical origin to the hysteria, febrility, anæmia and weakness which the critic affects to find in Whistler's work. Tributes to certain of the Nocturnes do not lessen the offence of a critical attitude which hazards such a twilight practice : and Moore even applies this practice to the details of painting, saying, Look at that ear ! in proof that the painter's nerves had given way once or twice. Unfortunate is it that these petulances of criticism should persist in the reader's mind even when the author proceeds to unrestrained praise.

It is pleasanter to observe that this critical mode does not touch Moore's affection for the French artists, to whom his submissiveness was almost as complete as prompt; though with these also the interest of what he says is mainly personal and reminiscent. . . . 'That marvellous hand, those thick fingers holding the brush so firmly, so heavily: he did with it what he liked, and my palette was the same to him as his own;'—it is of Manet that he speaks. 'A wise and appreciative Jew, looking like Abraham, with white beard and bald head, always following in another's footsteps, a will-o'-the-wisp of painting;'—it is of Pisarro that he speaks. And of Cézanne—'I do not remember ever to have seen Cézanne at the Nouvelle Athènes; he was too rough, too savage a creature, who used to be met on the outskirts of Paris wandering about the hill-sides in jack-boots. As no one took the least interest in his pictures he left them in the fields; when his pictures began to be asked for, his son and daughter used to inquire them out in the cottages, and keep watch in the hedges and collect the sketches he had left behind.' . . . Anarchical work was Cézanne's, but there is life in his pictures.

Moore is as French in what he says of pictures in *Vale* as in his writings of twenty years earlier. He assimilated the best that was around him, surrendering himself so easily that the worst had no chance. Thus his Frenchification was a positive gain when he approached English art, and if an English painter may have ignored or contemned his criticism, that criticism was too intelligent, too clear a mirror, to fail in affecting those who buy pictures. Happily it is not an unavoidable part of my task to trace the influence of Moore's writing upon current standards of art and criticism; I need only remind the reader that our author claims an honourable position, for instance, as an apostle of Verlaine, and that his unfaltering assertion thirty years ago of the excellence of certain French artists has been confirmed by the recognition of a discriminating public in England. Not without reason he plumes himself now on reflecting that those who took his early advice and bought impressionist pictures have made money out of them; and if this book were written for dealers it might be amusing to pursue the subject.

The volume in which the story of his Parisian years is told was not written until some time after his return to England. He has twice annotated the book since then, once in 1904 and once in 1916, without attempting the impossible softening of crudities, without, in fact, trying to make a silk purse out of a sow's ear. He does not despise it, and indeed regards it as a sort of genesis, containing the seed of everything he has written. He is gratified when he looks back and finds that his tastes in the early eighties are his tastes in 1916—an unusual admission and an unusual source of pride. The interest of the book is not the interest of literature, but for our present purpose it has a value almost beyond that of any other of George Moore's writings.

CHAPTER III
NATURALIST OR REALIST

In truth good Authours deject me too-too much, and quaile my courage. I willingly imitate that Painter who, having bungler-like drawn and fondly represented some Cockes, forbad his boies to suffer any live Cocke to come into his shop. And to give my selfe some luster or grace have rather neede of some of Antinonydes the Musicians invention; who, when he was to play any musick, gave order that before or after him, some other bad musicians should cloy and surfet his auditory.—*Montaigne.*

HE had gone to Paris about the end of 1872, and left it ten years later. 'As was characteristic of me, I broke with Paris suddenly, without warning anyone. I knew in my heart of hearts that I should never return, but no word was spoken, and I continued a pleasant delusion with myself; I told my *concierge* that I would return in a month, and I left all to be sold, brutally sold by auction. . . . Not even to Marshall did I confide my foreboding that Paris would pass out of my life, that it would henceforth be with me a beautiful memory, but never more a practical delight.' Yes, it is characteristic, and characteristic too that his return from France should be made to appear— for his readers—not only sudden but unaccountable. How completely narrowed his personal horizon had become, may be guessed from the fact that not only his first resting-place, but his centre of interest after leaving France was London. His father had travelled, swept off his feet, in his son's story, by a great passion; strange lands too had called him, but George Moore did not hear the voices which called his father forth. Neither the strong passion nor the beckoning of strange lands touched him when he left France; his preoccupation was already sedentary, and camels and ships and peasants' huts and snowy heights remained beyond his care. Whether a certain poverty of interest does not result from narrowness of contact, and whether indeed an urban life is a wise choice for a sensitive artist, are questions which it is a little ungraceful to ask and unnecessary to answer; and yet the infinite, rosy-hued cloud of might-have-been holds certain hints of other developments of the powers that were hidden in George Moore when he stepped into the inobsequious Strand, dressed in exuberant necktie, tiny hat, large trousers and

F   65

a beard. A like extravagance of garb is admitted in *Parnell and His Island,* where he describes his own apparition in the person of another suddenly breaking in upon the familiar house, with long hair, Capoul-like beard, Parisian clothes—*un être de féerie.* . . . And not less an alien in mind than in dress, his first business was, he recollects, with an agent who explained that Moore owed him a few thousand pounds; that being the first and perhaps most violent impact of external upon mental things. You are, in fact, to understand that it was this business that called him from France, since the Moore Hall estate, under the influence of Parnell and the boycott, was producing debts and not revenue, and even the modest remittances upon which his Paris life depended were to be discontinued. But this of itself meant but a brief interruption; a few days might have seen him back in Paris; yet he stayed, obedient to some gesture, voice or air sweeping the barrenness of his heart. He knew that it was determined for him that he should stay, just as it was determined later that he should go to Ireland and then again leave it. . . . The difficulty of money could be put by, but how evade the difficulty of a reinstated intelligence at odds with its home? Every outward aspect was new and strange, every face now Brobdingnagian and now Lilliputian, but all alike foreign. Preoccupied as he was with this separation, he was yet able to conclude emphatically that the difference between English and French is found in the men, not in the women, Englishwomen and Frenchwomen being psychologically very similar. But the opposition between the men of the two nations seemed temperamental and absolute. Generalizations of this easy kind are not, however, common in our author. . . . Picture him debouching from Morley's Hotel, meditating upon the departure of his agent and then, wherever he turns and whomsoever he accosts, dismayed by a ridiculous awkwardness of speech; an intensely French-looking

Irishman, anxious to become English and an English writer,
yet no longer at home in his native language nor secure in
his foreign tongue. Gulliver's isolation was never com-
pleter. Moore had heard of writing and speaking two
languages equally well, but he found it impossible; so
impossible, that had he stayed but two years longer in
France he would never have been able to identify his
thoughts with the English language. He is able to
determine, with melancholy exactitude, that the real
damage was done during his last two years in France,
when he had begun to write verse and occasional articles;
and it was with surprise that he found himself thinking
more easily and swiftly in French than in English. He
could write French verse, in the strict form of sonnet or
ballade, but for all his ease he knew it was harder to
write prose than verse, whether in French or English.
And even when he was once more in England, and could
write 'acceptable' English verse, the ordinary newspaper
prose was beyond his reach. Verses quoted in *Confessions
of a Young Man* are meant to show the kind of poem
admired in France when it was written in French and
translated into English; for surely that, and not the
reverse, must have been the process.

> ' We are alone! Listen, a little while,
>   And hear the reason why your weary smile
>   And lute-toned speaking are so very sweet,
>   And how my love for you is more complete
>   Than any love of any lover. They
>   Have only been attracted by the gray
>   Delicious softness of your eyes, your slim
>   And delicate form, or some such other whim,
>   The simple pretexts of all lovers :—I
>   For other reason.'

It is, he cries :—

> ' Happiness to know that you are far
>   From any base desires as that fair star

Set in the evening magnitude of heaven.
Death takes but little, yea, your death has given
Me that deep peace, and that secure possession
Which man may never find in earthly passion.'

Pictorial verse, truly, verse of the studio, verse queerly sentimental, verse to which you listen with a sense of the intellectual abasement and depravity that follow the hearing of an English drawing-room song. *Flowers of Passion*, published in 1878, and *Pagan Poems*, published three years later, comprise nearly all his verse, and neither volume has a present value except in the eyes of men who collect scarce books and grow rich by selling them again. Swinburne speaks in the *Ode to a Dead Body* :—

'Is it a garden of eternal sleep
    Where dreams laugh not or weep ?
A place of quiet below the tides of life
    Afar from toil or strife ? '

and the most innocent Swinburne in the 'audacious' Moore who wrote :—

'Poor breasts ! whose nipples sins alone have fed. . . .
Poor lily hands steeped in the mire of shame.'

Sins, strange sins and fuliginous remorse form the subject of these poems, which are immature even for the immaturest writer ; and it is wonderful that he should have been so well pleased with the Baudelaire-Swinburne of the earlier book as to reprint some of its contents in *Pagan Poems*. The book was denounced by Edmund Yates (who appears to have usurped some authority in his own day) under the heading of 'A Bestial Bard,' a folly by no means discouraging to the young poet. It is a dreadful thought that George Moore might have persisted in his devotion to verse, and indeed have become a prominent member of the Fleshly School of Poetry ; for the flesh has the whole field in these small volumes, and despair only saved the author from becoming a prolific bad poet. How strong and how obscure was the vital instinct for prose may be judged from the curious fact that the verse which he discarded after 1881 was, *qua* verse, so much better than the prose, *qua* prose, which he hugged to his bosom and pored upon by day and by night, with the fidelity of a dog and the assurance of a swallow. . . . Time passes quickly with young writers, and three years before thirty may witness greater changes than ten after thirty ; but in 1881 Moore stood, as regards poetry and its spell, very much where I find him forty years later, for it was not poetry but prose that he was born to write ; and hard though he has found it to write simple prose, infinitely hard to write his later and better prose, it was lucky that he did not increase his difficulties by confusing them with the no less tyrannous and subtle difficulties of verse. An acute critical demon saved him from pursuing English poetry, and he is aware of that mercy, for he still sees that he cannot express himself in verse as he can in prose. He remains interested in English poetry, scarcely less than in French, yet I wonder in which his appreciation is more limited. Certainly in English poetry his idols are few, and they are what they have always been—Shelley and Swinburne. His loyalty to these first loves may appear remarkable if you forget that it results from the almost childlike simplicity of affection which is a part of his many-stranded character. It endures even while he admits to himself that he will never be a poet, as he once whispered that he would never be a painter. He may still write French verse, but he will no longer pipe for English ears that have listened to Meredith, Hardy and Doughty ; and if I surmise that, with the eternal exception of Shelley, he most admires the verse that has the best qualities of French form, rather than the ampler harmonies and varieties of our English muse, he will scarcely dissemble his agreement. Ten years in Paris, those early impressionable years, determined not only his judgment of pictures but his affection for poetry also ; it is only in prose that he has travelled.

Before he was thirty, then, he had realized quite suddenly that minor poetry would not be an occupation for a lifetime, and so precisely is this discovery remembered that he can even localize it, the very place at the corner of Wellington Street in the Strand ;—indeed, as Meredith says, a fitting spot to dig love's grave. Painting and poetry had failed him, and the heavenly vision still beckoning, prose only remained ; and you may read in *Confessions of a Young Man* how bitter was the pursuit— nay, you may read it in book after book, now admiring the courage and now marvelling at the failure.

What he has said there is but what he has said in many other places and on a dozen other occasions. He recalls, for instance, with a quite dispassionate humour, Wilde's remark that Moore had to write for seven years before he knew there was such a thing as grammar, shouting out then his amazing discovery ; and then he had to write another seven years before he found that a paragraph was architectural, and again could not conceal his astonishment. And he wonders even yet why learning has always been so hard for him, and can only sigh amusedly as he adds that he could always learn what he wanted to learn, without precisely showing what that was. Wilde was right, he agrees : 'I did not know—I simply did not know how to write, and even now, after more than forty years' diligence, I've almost as much trouble with grammar as with spelling ; it's incredible, the trouble I have to take, in order to produce even the passable sentences which other men write unthinkingly. And the strange thing was, I had given up painting because I couldn't express myself in paint, and poetry because I couldn't express

myself in verse, although in painting and in versing I
could do passably enough. My drawing was not common
like Marshall's, and I could do tolerably well if the model
happened upon an attitude which I could use. And my
verse was—what you see (for my pictures, you can't and
will never see them); at least correct, rather sensitive if
not very impulsive ; and I gave that up too for the same
reason. But if you ask why, when I found I couldn't
express myself in prose, I didn't give prose up as well,
there's but one answer. . . . What is it?—Well, it was
the *story* that held me in thrall, the story that was and is
my *Belle Dame Sans Merci*. I've always been able to
conceive, to invent a story, and though I couldn't write,
I found that I could learn because I wanted to learn.
Words I have always, and in abundance, and an ear for
rhythm ; my enduring foe is composition.'

His drawing, in fact, was ' common ' in prose. I do not
know of a finer example of the industrious apprentice than
George Moore offers to the faint yet pursuing writer; nor
a more candid admission of literary impotence than he
makes in speaking of his early work. The prose of *A
Mummer's Wife*, for instance, is bad, and he quite meekly
acknowledges it :—' The book isn't written at all ; you
can't call a collection of sentences, or half-sentences,
prose, any more than you can call the inhabitants of a
hospital an effective regiment. The halt, the maimed,
and the blind do not make prose, even if now and again
a phrase stands upright, or a sentence moves of its own
power, or a whole paragraph luckily disguises the general
tendency to *locomotor ataxia*. *Esther Waters* wasn't my
first novel, but if you have any doubt of the truth of
what I am saying, you need but compare the opening
chapter in the original edition with the same chapter in
the revised edition. It isn't prejudice, or perverted
modesty; I know when the writing is passable, and
that is why (answering a question) the passage you

quote concerning the flood of gold, the dear gold, rolling into the little town, was untouched in the revision. But that's an exception. Sometimes I stumbled upon a felicity, but most often stumbled a thousand miles from it.'

It is tempting but inopportune to ask by what miracle of patience the prose thus laboriously learned has come to wear so perfectly the appearance of nativeness; yet I must interpolate the remark that, wanting that miraculous patience, the pen still stumbles and the drawing is still common. Thus a letter in which he sought to answer certain criticisms in a weekly journal on *The Brook Kerith*, a long and acute letter, contains evidence enough that the closeness of the argument and the brevity of time have prevented the author's attending to his p's and q's. A mere 'would' for 'should' is venial, but the absence of all characteristic qualities is a graver matter, and serves to illustrate Moore's admission that only by a persistent wooing is the sullen irresponsiveness of prose overcome. True the grosser flaws are missing, but forty years have passed and even the wilful mind slowly acquires the habits of that in which it works; yet none the less haste is still the enemy of that leisured lightness, that supple willow-like waving of images, which in the later books persuades you into thinking how easy it must be to write well, since the writing is so unstrained in its natural delight.

Let us not, however, anticipate that perfection. The business of a writer being to write, and the absence of that primary power rendering worthless a thousand secondary powers, it is proper to note more exactly George Moore's early qualifications, if that term be not too misleading; and let us take the novel already referred to, *A Mummer's Wife*, by no means the least excellent of the earlier novels. Now if words be more than names of things and acts, a single sentence will be sufficient to show how poorly words are used in the decent, hardworking

prose of *A Mummer's Wife*. True that the defect can be
assigned, if you will, to a sedulous naturalism, to a desire
to be literal and, in common phrase, let the facts speak
for themselves; but at the present moment I am concerned to note the quality rather than excuse it.

Let me choose, therefore, a passage in which the author
may, if he wish, find a temptation to avoid this solid
literality, a passage of that reminiscent kind which has
become Moore's lucky medium :—

> 'Montgomery was as light to Kate, and soon he
> became almost as necessary to her spiritual happiness
> as her lover was to her material. He was so kind,
> so gentle, and he allowed her to talk to him as much
> as she liked of Dick. Indeed he seemed quite as
> much interested in the subject as she was. It was
> always Dick, Dick, Dick. He told her anecdotes
> concerning him—how he had acted certain parts;
> how he had stage-managed certain pieces; of supper-
> parties; of adventures they had been engaged in.
> These stories amused Kate, although the odour of
> woman in which they were bathed, as in an atmo-
> sphere, annoyed and troubled her. As if to repay him
> for his kindness, she, in her turn, became confidential,
> and one day she told him the story of her life.'

In *Modern Painting* he has been troubled to define his
use of the term 'values,' insisting upon the meaning of
proportion and relation in the use of light and colour, a
note of music, a colour in painting, acquiring beauty
according to its association; hence the necessity of the
musician or the painter knowing intimately what it is that
secures contrast and similitude. The recital may seem
primitive, but it indicates the fault of this prose The
phrases contribute no more than their lowest meaning,
for they are but a series of phrases, lacking co-ordination
and luminousness, giving nothing and owing nothing to
one another. 'Beginning at the beginning, she gave

rapidly an account of her childhood, accentuating the religious and severe manner in which she had been brought up, until the time when she and her mother made the acquaintance of the Edes.' Formal speech could not be colder, grammatical clauses might never spare less of light and warmth and movement, in a passage in which a young woman, thrilled with love, is recalling the most intimate of her early memories. Strange that the meticulous revision of the story in 1918 should have found the sentence passable : nothing could be less associative, nothing less imaginative. From the same page you may pick the same insentient phrases — affinities of sentiment, sweetest currents of emotion, moments of divine abandonment, inexpressibly dear, delightful sensations of enthusiasm. . . . This is not prose, it is not speech, it is not even reporting—it is merely print. The writing of Thomas Hardy, especially in the earlier novels, is at times conspicuously awkward ('What can be more pudding?' cries our sardonic author), betraying an imperfect mastery of speech; but even in the earlier novels, as so frequently in the later, there are pages of felicity and beauty. But with Moore the case is altered; seldom does he write awkwardly, and yet infelicitousness is constant in the earlier novels; partly, I think, because the literality at which he aims is in itself a harsh and delusive quality, and partly because, as yet, he cannot help himself whatever his aim. The details do not 'compose' anything at all, and while superfluous detail is usually avoided, significant detail is likewise wanting. And when, in the last chapter of *A Mummer's Wife*, the narrative cries for something to mollify the crudeness of the pain, you meet with sentences which merely vex and exasperate :—

> ' It was like a costume ball, where chastity grinned
> from behind a mask that vice was looking for, while
> vice hid his nakedness in some of the robes that

      chastity had let fall. Thus up and down, like dice
thrown by demon players, were rattled the two lives,
the double life that this weak woman had so
miserably lived through.'

Disharmony is doing its worst.—Later on I shall have to
speak of the same disharmony in the characterization of
the concluding chapters of the book, but at this point I
am concerned merely to observe the maladroit intrusion of
the wrong note into the writing itself, and its dissipation
of the proper and sombre horror which it is intended to
deepen.

    In *A Mummer's Wife* the difficulties of grammar, of
which our author so frankly confesses himself a victim,
have been overcome or disguised, and the writing is no
worse, perhaps, than that of a dozen novelists whom we
read for the frivolous story's sake ; but what is surprising
is that the author of such frigid and inexpressive prose
should ever have discovered, even slowly, in later books
the 'control of his values,' and not only avoided infelicities,
but achieved a mastery which in its kind is unique. Prose
being an art, it would be an unamusing paradox to say
that Moore's case suggests that a bad writer may become
a good writer merely by taking pains, but the present case
proves nothing but the difficulty of art. Infinite pains
would not have given us the style of *The Brook Kerith* if
he had not been a born writer, though born to an inheri-
tance, or an office, which for years he could not realize ;
and the fact that a candid reader will deny the faintest
signs of the later writing in any of the earlier books must
remain what it is—a singular, inexplicable truth. Theory
misled him, and the influence of alien models ; he knew
too much of French and too little of English writers ; and
for years he was struggling, first against his native powers
and tendencies, and then again to recover them. It was
only by struggling that the writer in him was saved, but
the writer was in him all the time—an emaciated,

impoverished spirit, kept faintly alive, full of hesitations and misgivings, but slowly gathering strength from the simple failure of the alien to extinguish the native.

To the writing of prose which was even less articulate than that of *A Mummer's Wife*, Moore's earliest years in London were devoted. Necessity dictated journalism and ragged rooms in a Strand lodging-house, of which, as of his fellow-lodgers and 'the awful servant, Emma,' his memory is vivid enough. That note of unsympathetic externalism, which can be fairly challenged in other books, begins to appear in his story of Emma; for he was curious to ask her all sorts of cruel questions, in order to plumb her depth of animalism. Sometimes his questions were too cruel, striking through what he terms the thick hide into the human, and Emma would wince; but his intelligence saw her as very nearly an animal—one of the facts of civilization. Perhaps there is nothing in all his wantonness of speech, in another kind, more distressing and deplorable than this, but it is half pardonable—like those other offences—because it is only half truthful; later passages showing that he was kinder than he chose to appear, and that what he perversely dissembled was not an inhuman indifference, but a human warmth. Few characters, indeed, present a less obscure enigma than the character of George Moore; his secrets are usually open secrets, and he most artfully disorders those qualities which it is most impossible to mistake.

Living on two pounds a week in a Strand lodging-house, with an unsuccessful actress for neighbour and poor Emma for specimen, our naturalist and realist began journalism, seeking to express ideas that were like unripe apples. He did more—he read his contemporaries as he reads them no longer, and for our amusement and astonishment he has left the most unreserved record of his opinions. Henry James in those days had not written *The Wings of the Dove, The Golden Bowl, The Two Magics,* or the dozen of short stories which have delighted our intelligence in the last twenty-five years; but he had written *The Portrait of a Lady,* and it is in speaking of this that Moore murmurs—'Empty and endless sentimentalities.' He tells in *Avowals* how he discussed this novel with James, and how an expression of envy passed over his friend's vast face when he described the subject of *A Modern Lover.* I imagine it was not with envy that Henry James read it. . . . Moore read also Mr. Hardy and Blackmore and is able to speak of them in one breath—of the former, indeed, with a disdain which in 1888 was merely ludicrous, and which in 1922 is something worse. I am reminded that in writing of the revelation which *Marius the Epicurean* brought to him, he talks of a sweet depravity of ear, meaning, I suppose, Pater's ear; but surely the phrase describes his own in 1888. It is not, however, my present purpose to discuss George Moore as a critic, but to note the thoughts that eddied in his mind when he started to write himself, and to point out the beginnings of that absolute unreserve of judgment which has always been characteristic of his attitude. Let me but add, that when the preface to a new edition (1904) of *Confessions of a Young Man* was written, our author—earless and un-abashed as Defoe—found but one thing to withdraw, a reference to George Eliot, whom he had over-praised—singular excess! Constant reviser as he is, ruthless with himself and as ruthless with others, he found nothing else to revise in this early deluding book.

It was because of such opinions as these, as well as because his English was as yet rotten with French idiom, that literary criticism was soon closed to him, at any rate as far as leading journals were concerned; but still he wrote and translated play and opera and short story. Some of the short stories were printed, and so it was that our author sank into the literary world or half-world of

London. He could not learn to see life paragraphically, yet the book in which his adventures are dustily shown for perusal suggests that no other view of life was possible for him. But he longed for fame and notoriety, and again and again avows his shamelessness and his pride in it, bringing for proof the duel which he tried to force upon a 'beautiful young lord.' . . . Let the phrase pass, and that still more egregious phrase—' he is now, if he will allow me to say so, a friend.' It was for this duel that his old friend, Marshall, rehabilitated by success, was called from Paris to London; for our author had grasped the advantage at once—a duel with a lord and all the Conservative press on the lord's side and all the Liberal press on the author's. Need it be said that the duel did not take place? Letters passed, and George Moore returned to his ragged rooms in the Strand, to resume the writing of his first novel with a far more genuine passion than he could apply to anything else in the world.

Almost as ludicrous is that other episode related by Whistler's biographers. Moore, we are told, had introduced Sir William Eden to Whistler in 1894, and a portrait of Lady Eden was the result. A dispute followed concerning the price to be paid, and legal proceedings were begun. The decision of the case, which was tried in France, was adverse to the painter, and a sharp controversy between Whistler and Moore led to Whistler, who was then in France, challenging Moore and sending to England as his seconds M. Octave Mirabeau and another. For all his slighting and foolish criticism of Whistler, I do not imagine that Moore wanted to murder him, or that Whistler was anxious to rob the future of a book which might surely rejoice his own delicate perceptions—*The Lake*. Happy it was, then, that the affair ended with the seconds.

An amazing young man, he calls the subject of *Confessions*, looking back over sixteen years. Audacious

Moore, was Walter Pater's term, which is recalled with pride and fondness; but it is scarcely the term we should employ now, although we should agree with 'the author of the most beautiful of all prose books,' *Imaginary Portraits*, that Audacious Moore was losing by his cynical and therefore exclusive way of looking at the world. It is only too true. The young man was losing heavily and all but irretrievably, and if I have touched too often upon the book in which the young man first attempted literature, it is by no means because I share Pater's assurance of its literary faculty, but because the book frankly and eagerly proclaims the personality of its author in the sharpest pangs of birth. The writing of *Confessions* occupied the summer of 1887, the wonderful Jubilee summer, spent at Southwick, upon which Moore looks back so often and so fondly. His visit had been intended to last but two or three days, and really lasted two or three years; and in a lodging overlooking the village green, in the most English of English counties, in that year of the expiring sputter of English parochialism, that year in which the spirit we now so perversely detest or despise looked for a while eternal, George Moore toiled at his exotic chapters. Pity that we cannot feel any more cordiality for them than for that Victorianism which he and we equally abhor! His exoticism has been discarded, for thirty years is a long span in an artist's life; and far more beautiful—and as clearly in the English tradition as the green and the downs—are the few pages of *Ave* describing his Southwick life, than any part of the earlier *Confessions*.

Enough has been said of the qualities of Moore's early prose to permit me now to look at the novels under other aspects. I do not propose to follow our author faithfully through time to eternity, and in turning to his first novel, *A Modern Lover*, written in such a smoky atmosphere as we have briefly whiffed, the excuse is, of course, that after years of neglect it was re-written and issued in 1917 under a new title—*Lewis Seymour and Some Women*—with a preface betraying an author's unhappy fondness for his first-born. *A Modern Lover*, he says, was the work of a young man who in a moment of inspiration hit upon an excellent anecdote and, being without skill, devised an uncouth text out of memories of Balzac, Zola and Goncourt; yet it was such a true and beautiful anecdote that it carried a badly written book into his collected works. The anecdote is simple enough—three women work for a young artist's welfare; the first is a work-girl, the second a rich woman, and the third 'a lady of high degree'; and the first alone retains all her faith, the second loses part of it and the third loses all. Let us freely admit the truth of the anecdote, in order that we may consider the more carefully its beauty. But its beauty can only consist in its treatment, a dogma which needs no buttress, yet which so much of Moore's work nevertheless supports; its beauty is an effect, an impression which may be communicated and noted. The effect will probably be found in the characters, as much as in the incident, and a review of *A Modern Lover* reminds me that only one of the chief characters has attractiveness, Lucy Bentham; she alone contributes to an impression of beauty, or at least to a pathetic aspect which may serve in the absence of beauty; and if, as Moore has said, the first business of a writer is to find a human instinct, it is found in this happy-unhappy woman. Lucy Bentham is a figure cast in the old mould, the maternal mistress, and the pathos of her situation is clear enough; and as clear is the pathos of that minor person in the story, Gwennie Lloyd, the first of the women who suffered so that Lewis Seymour might succeed. But the anecdote is without the light and shadow of beauty; what dominates it is not the sacrifice of the three women, but the vulgar egoism of their idol. They gave what they could, only to be displaced in giving; and the worthlessness of the idol is but a cynical commentary upon that giving. Moral the book assuredly is, and I am not sure that its too insistent morality does not support the cynicism in expelling beauty. . . . It is, let me repeat, a first novel, and need not be judged severely : it need hardly be judged at all, but for Moore's tenderness in re-writing it and re-presenting the 'truth and beauty' of the anecdote.

Is it unpleasant to dwell upon what one deplores? Criticism flourishes quite happily as an art of complaint, and there are good reasons why a hundred things may be shown in blame, for one that may be hinted in praise of a subject. I cannot find the single point for praise in *Lewis Seymour and Some Women*, except the ease of style which has grown, as we have seen, almost natural, and which has in this book become a little lax ; but there is an enormous complaint to be uttered. To put it briefly, the anecdote has been deliberately and grossly sensualized, and the further degradation of Lewis Seymour, with the degradation of his women, makes beauty more impossible than mere cynicism might. 'These words made it plain to Lewis that if he could persuade Lucy to condone his conduct and forget it, he would one day be admitted to her bedroom.' That sentence is a summary of the book. Reiterated lecheries, is Rabelais' term for the subject; a joyous composition, surely ! is Moore's phrase for the book in which he employs it. . . . I think it is the sole instance of his ruining a poor book by revision or re-writing; and he has ruined it because the revision was conceived in a perverse mood—was it merely for the sake of shocking his amanuensis?—while bathing and meditating upon the imperfection of his first novel. The reader too might crave for a bath when he had finished it.

I remember that there was lately in London a respect-able brick building occupied by an honest tradesman

G

One day it was seized upon by a contractor, who cut away the front, demolished the decent brick, thrust in steel joists beneath the unwalled floors, and then built up—on four columns of Portland stone—a new stucco front with an elaborate cornice, above which the old roof still rose steep. The stucco was finished to look like stone, but the stone refused to look like stucco, and the building remains now a sad and haunting image of uncostly sham.

He went back to Moore Hall to write the novel which helped him to realize his own powers, using for it many experiences acquired in London. In London he had undertaken an English libretto for *Les Cloches de Corneville*, for which the original of poor Dick Lennox had given him £30 ; and in London the Gaiety bar (in which he so innocently hoped to find another Nouvelle Athènes) yielded both directly and indirectly much of the matter for *A Mummer's Wife*. How much more serious a book that is than its unfortunate predecessor needs no telling now, and what has been said of the writing of it must not blind us to the excellence of one of the best of all English novels written to a formula. I have said that the prose-writer innate in George Moore was slow in assuming the freedom of nature, and it is equally true that the story-teller also was far from rejoicing in that freedom when *A Mummer's Wife* was conceived. Formulæ were to be shed and forgotten before his true work could be attempted, but *A Mummer's Wife* represents the transient and brilliant triumph of a formula ; and perhaps that triumph was necessary in order that our author's final manner might wear the aspect of reaction and another triumph. Within the limits of meticulous recording and careful analysis, of the kind to which Government blue-books have inured us, the novel is an almost unique success ; and almost unique, again, among its author's works is the invocation of moral horror to whet the sense of tragedy. It is the

most exactingly moral of all George Moore's writings,
but the particular moral is implicit and not expressed,
and, as I have just said, is subordinated to the tragic
purpose. The point is clearly seen in a single glance
at a single character, Dick Lennox. Kate's moral weakness, her swelling and ebbing wantonness, is heightened
by being shown against the quite unmoral and unreflecting
good-nature of the fat mummer. Wanting the power to
hold Dick for ever, Kate sinks below the capacity of her
nature; but Dick, grosser and more buoyant, floats easily
upon the waters that have gone over her head. Tested
by the standards of morality, he is a thought lower than
Kate, but in his mere grossness he is more human, being
as incapable of her best as of her worst. Good-nature as
a practical basis for human relations, good-nature just
conscious of itself and of the lack of all else— is this that
Dick reveals; revealing also at the same time how far this
serviceable quality will carry a man whose moral being has
never known pure light. There is nothing else to be
learned by a repeated reading of *A Mummer's Wife*, and if
it be thought that the gain of knowing that is little, then
I have failed in putting the case for its author. The
inconstancy of the human factor in different people—to
assume the style of the book—and the stability of animal
vigour when a finer activity has died, it is these simple,
forgotten truths that the novel clearly illustrates. To
see it as a sermon against drink or against unfaithfulness
in husbands is, I suppose, possible but far from profitable;
yet books are sometimes considered on their lowest terms,
and it is stimulating to think of George Moore preaching
on either subject.

But all that has been said does not denude, nor is it
meant to denude, the tragedy of its proper horror. Object
as you will to the farcical impossibility of Mrs. Forest,
who makes love to Dick while his wife is dying of drink—
and even yet poor Dick, sunken to that lady's property,

does not lose his hold upon our good-nature, for his own is so unfeigned—object as you must, the tragedy of Kate is still true, a genuine offering to the tragic Muse. Few English novels prolong more surely than *A Mummer's Wife* that undertone of human and moral at war which is heard, for example, in Tolstoi, in whom it is, indeed, never quite faint and at length rises into a storm of intolerable discord. The Moore that wrote this book has disappeared, intelligence or something less easily definable has preyed upon him, and now he is as careful to avoid the direct moral impression as then he was careless to deny it. Was it the method that helped him more than he knew, or was it the theme that possessed him, and dictated all but the words—pity the words were left to the author's industry!—and gave him a touch of insight beyond what was common to his years? I cannot say, but I know that the Moore that wrote this book has disappeared and another Moore has been busy over his remains, telling us things maybe that we cannot think for ourselves, and 'telling' all with a new ease of persuasive force. The face changes—a line, a quality, a simplicity perhaps, has gone; another line, another look, another quality has come, perhaps a better quality. But the quality of common tragedy has gone; the face has changed.

An interesting point is recorded in the 1918 (revised) edition of this novel, which was dedicated to Robert Ross. Ross, it seems, thought no other book of Moore's so likely to live as *A Mummer's Wife*, saying that although *Esther Waters* speaks out of a deeper appreciation of life, in *A Mummer's Wife* there is a youthful imagination and exuberance. The tribute sets Moore wondering—'If I had lived here before, Jupiter knows what I should have written, but it would not have been *Esther Waters*; more likely a book like *A Mummer's Wife*—a band of jugglers and acrobats travelling from town to town.' An antique story rises up in his mind, a recollection of one of his lost works or an instantaneous reading of Apuleius into *A Mummer's Wife*—which? But he dwells no longer upon the sombre morality of the primary conception.

The face has changed, I said; but it did not change suddenly. Change is seldom sudden, however violent or unforeseen its manifestation. Moore was a young man when he wrote this novel of one of the Five Towns—it is seductive to think of Mr. Arnold Bennett poring over it in his first youth, and murmuring, Hanley, Hanley, why not? —and only two years older when he followed it with a book so differently schemed and placed as *A Drama in Muslin;* and it is not until you look broadly at his whole work as a novelist that you recognize how earnestly he has sought the greatest extension of his powers. . . . Moral! The moral of George Moore's whole attitude to his calling is overwhelming, the moral of priest-like devotion to the creating of a sphere in which his characters, the most commonplace in the world, may live and move and have their being. His later graces—and graces truly is the term—may disguise this devotion, but a moment of reflection shows it as enduring. Even in the beginning it was a conscious aim, for what I have termed the sphere of each book—Hanley, a theatrical touring company in one, Dublin Castle in another—was a sphere visible to his eye when he wrote, and visible still when he looks back and records that the author of *A Drama in Muslin* seems to have meditated a sort of small *comédie humaine,* a meditation that proved fruitless and is not now regretted. It was, he thinks, life and not simply its envelope that interested him in planning the two books; he sought Alice Barton's heart as eagerly as Kate Ede's; and plunging a little deeper, he sees that far less accomplished author, somewhat surprisingly, as a soul-searcher with a headlong, uncertain style, and beneath the style a real interest in religious questions, and a hatred, as lively as Ibsen's, of the conventions that drive women into the marriage market.

Ibsen was much more conspicuous a theme for discussion in 1886 than he is to-day, and perhaps we hardly appreciate the significance of Moore's comparison of *A Drama in Muslin* with *A Doll's House*. He points out that the subject of the two books is the same, and thinks it a feather in his cap that a young man of thirty should have chosen it instinctively, reminding himself and us very plainly that not until he had written half his story did he hear the first translation of *A Doll's House*. Equally emphatic is his statement that his own art, however callow, was at least objective, while Ibsen had renounced all objectivity ; but he confesses that he could not understand *A Doll's House*, being too much absorbed in his own work, and in observing and remembering life, to be interested in moral ideas. The story is the thing, as we must constantly remind ourselves, without, however, restricting too narrowly the possibilities of the story. He had chosen to write of a 'puritan,' but not of a sexless puritan ; and his story of Alice Barton frankly yields him the same kind of pleasure as a good drawing.

And having said so much of the author of *A Drama in Muslin*, the young man of thirty or so with lank yellow hair (often standing on end), sloping shoulders, female hands, and an engaging vivacity of mind (for so the mirrors of Dublin Castle yield him up to the mature writer of 1915), he cannot but regret a little that young man's failure to make a *comédie humaine* out of the later history of Alice Barton and Violet Sculley ; and he broods upon Violet's future until a vague shaggy shape emerges and a typically Moorish situation is breathed fantastically upon the air. Polyandry has settled down with Christianity, and the practice of acquiring a mere share in a woman's life, rather than insisting on the whole of it, has taken firm root in our civilization; hence, with this notion firmly rooted in his own head at any rate, he is able to dream of the polyandrous Marchioness of Kilcarney, and picture husband and lover discoursing with perfect amity and æsthetic justice upon Violet's perfections. . . . A very ingenious story, he cries, urging against it, however, the grave improbability that three people ever lived contemporaneously who were wise enough to prefer, and prefer so consistently, happiness to convention.

I think this speculation worth pondering, for it marks so plainly one of the differences between George Moore in 1886 and George Moore in 1915. The former, we will agree, would have written such a sequel as is suggested with a fumbling hand, or would have shunned the subject altogether; the simple reason being that the subject, as the later writer contemplates it, is not an imaginative one, and is not imaginatively conceived, but is rather one for such a sardonic intellectual exercise as his own phrase suggests when he speaks of preferring happiness to convention. I cannot regret, then, that when *A Drama in Muslin* came to be revised and even its title reduced to *Muslin*, our author did not pursue his characters with a theory, but was content with a touch here, a pruning there, and that general stealthy amendment which gives to his first books something of the beauty of the later.

Considering, however, the 1886 volume as it stands, and especially as a step in the development of an artist, *A Drama in Muslin* has a very definite value. Its position between *A Mummer's Wife* on the one hand, and *Spring Days* and *Confessions of a Young Man* on the other, is witness to the zeal with which Moore tested his powers, and the bold deliberateness with which he pursued his aim of becoming an English novelist of the better sort. When he sat writing it in the Shelburne Hotel, Dublin, looked out on St. Stephen's Green, and dressed his reflection in the mirrors of Dublin Castle, I doubt whether he regarded it as the exposition of the personal conscience stirring against the communal (another of his comments upon Alice Barton's story), and I am sure it would have lost much of its excellence if he had. No, it was his intense curiosity, his thirst for a story growing as he passed and repassed the mirrors, that taught him the spell whereby Alice Barton and her mother and Lord Dungory and Violet and Kilcarney were called to the surface again, and held there in almost unwavering distinctness until their eager artist had finished with them. If now he is tempted to rationalize his imaginative glimpses, it is because he is older, and prone to look with a very imperfect sympathy upon a work which was schemed in a mood so different from the mood of the retrospective critic. It is remarkable that he should be so willing now to spoil the impression of an imaginative story with a thesis, and so ill-content to let the story preach whatever moral it will; for this is the self-consciousness not of the artist, but of the theorist with a notion which needs must lessen the proper influence of the novel as a piece of life.

But in 1886 the social theorist lay almost silent, and the life that swirled and broke around the Shelburne was his engrossing concern; and in particular Alice Barton and Violet and May and Olive, puppets of the social drama and living persons of Moore's book, scarcely secondary being Mrs. Barton and her attendants. Occasionally the artist sleeps and the theorist wakes, and acute extraneous pages are pressed violently into the narrative; an intrusion so simple and crude that it belongs to satire of a primitive kind, resulting from an artist's irritability rather than from the impatience of a sociologist. The author has become expansive, spending his strength vainly upon a voluptuous description of a Viceregal drawing-room, as though he would fain be Balzacian by mere excess; but the simplicity of his story is never lost, and it ends as quietly and primly as it begins. Less significant as a novel than *A Mummer's Wife,* its place in the Moore canon is secure, for it shows him for the first and almost the last time as the author of the domestic novel which so many hands have attempted, and which is usually as tedious as *The Newcomes* and as unlovely as that other masterpiece of the commonplace, *Vanity Fair.* Its title to a place in the canon is confirmed by the revised version, in which the proof of the value of pure literary instinct at work upon something substantial but faulty may readily be found. In 1886 George Moore could not refrain from a sharp piece of satirical realism in describing 'the moral ideas of Dublin in 1882.'—A land of echoes and shadows, he exclaims; the young and the old, running hither and thither, curse the Pope for not helping them in their affliction. The pages are not to be found in the 1915 version. In 1886, Cecilia, the unhappy celibate, assails Alice Barton with morbid lauds and laments concerning mystical religion, the depravity of the human heart and the nature of Jesus, which it was undesirable or unnecessary to repeat in 1915, and which in the earlier version are followed by physiological speculations no more necessary thirty years later. On the other hand, his immature reflections upon man's modern attitude towards women are reprinted by the older novelist; but there is a significant change in a concluding scene—I refer to that in which Alice Barton and her husband, touched to tears by the aspect of an eviction, restore the ragged outcasts by paying the due rent; but in 1915 Alice's mind has grown subtle—'she wished her departure to be associated with an act of kindness,' which is, she fears, another form of selfishness; and her husband, consoling her for not being able to pay the rent, adds, 'Nothing lasts in Ireland but the priests. And now let us forget Ireland, as many have done before us.' It is not simply Alice's mind that is subtilized, the author's too has changed; and there has come into it a hatred of the picturesque attitude which it needed small prescience to forecast as a piece of his natural development.

Controversy has played a far from insignificant part in the life of George Moore, and the publication of *A Modern Lover* gave him an admirable opening for his pugnacity. The beginnings of the campaign are recorded in *Literature at Nurse, or Circulating Morals,* a pamphlet issued in 1885, in which he asserts rather than explains the position of the artist. *A Modern Lover* had met, he says, with the approval of the entire press (pray reflect before you ejaculate; it was published in 1883), but Mudie's declined to circulate it, alleging that two ladies had written disapprovingly. Moore was irritated into deciding (against the entreaty of Mr. Mudie) to publish his next book at a humble six shillings; and no one will be surprised that *A Mummer's Wife* should have been yet more warmly and assuredly more wisely welcomed. But again the libraries objected, and Moore's pamphlet cites at length the harmless passage which gained the book's refusal as an immoral publication. Readers who possess the first edition of *A Mummer's Wife* may judge for themselves whether this most sombre of conventional sermons might have a seductive effect upon pliable spirits; the pages denounced being those in which Kate Ede is sent down to open the door to her lodger and is kissed by him. The charge was so foolish that it hardly deserved a pamphlet, but the injustice was rank and the possible injury serious. Moore's answer was characteristic and amusing. He took three novels which had not been refused by the libraries, summarized their plots, and quoted a questionable scene from each, crying, ' Look on this picture, and on this ! ' The method is elementary but effective, although the unhappy novels chosen for this essay in comparative damnation were unworthily obscure—*Nadine*, by Mrs. Campbell Praed,

Foxglove Manor, by Robert Buchanan, and *A Romance of the Nineteenth Century,* by Mr. W. H. Mallock.

Much more stimulating, however, is our novelist's announcement of his personal attitude, expressed with a touch of juvenile petulance which we can very well understand. 'To speak candidly, I hate you ; and I love and am proud of my hate of you. It is the best thing about me. I hate you because you dare question the sacred right of the artist to obey the impulses of his temperament . . . because you feel not the spirit of scientific inquiry that is bearing our age along.' It was to Mr. Mudie that this outburst was addressed, and if Mr. Mudie rubbed his eyes and asked whether *A Modern Lover* and *A Mummer's Wife* exemplify or promote the spirit of scientific inquiry, the question and its answer went unrecorded. Little enough has the later George Moore to do with scientific inquiry, and it is strange that the earlier writer should not have been content to rest his case solely upon the ample rights of the imaginative artist. In another passage he is still a little ambiguous and ill-content to stand upon that sole unanswerable contention :—' I would not have it supposed that I am of opinion that literature can be glorified in the temple of Venus. . . . The middle course is to write as grown-up men and women of life's passions and duties.' The middle course—yes, but it is too exact a definition of the naturalistic novel to please the novel reader in 1922; yet might not 1922 welcome a naturalistic novel even, to cleanse the foul bosom of much perilous stuff ?

Literature at Nurse is merely the earliest of those challenges to the stupid which George Moore has always rejoiced in uttering. Whatever dignity he presents to our view—and it is almost solely the dignity of an artist's achievement—he has never cared to assume that of suffering fools gladly ; perhaps because it is an attitude which the fool himself can so easily feign.

It is tempting to regard all the earlier novels as a preparation for *Esther Waters*, but that is a fallacy which I refuse to share. True that Moore's growing experience did not yield its full value until *Esther Waters* was written, but *A Mummer's Wife* and *A Drama in Muslin* stand quite easily by themselves, and I am not sure that *Spring Days* also is not an independent witness of our author's zealous invention. It is as clearly an experiment as any of the early novels, and indeed in that circumstance consists most of the attraction which it exerts; an attraction less than profound, yet not too vague to be noted. The preface to the original edition reminds the reader that a companion book to *A Drama in Muslin* had been promised, a book dealing with young men and blotting out young women, or rather using young women merely for a decorative background. That book was to be called *Don Juan*, and *Spring Days* is the prelude to it and all that we have of Moore's *Don Juan*. 'Of this idea of man, so complete and so full of subtle psychological interest, the dramatist, the librettist, and the poet have given us only a pretty boy with whom numerous women fall in love'— a Lewis Seymour, in fact. Shall we regret that Moore changed his mind? His strength is not in his 'Idea' but in his story, as we are so constantly remembering; his first essay in the incarnation of the idea of Don Juan was—what we have seen; and this prelude to the unattempted second essay does not tease us with any sweet dream-apples of delight.

Spring Days is born of that prolonged visit to Sussex of which Moore has spoken in *Hail and Farewell*; it is cast in the midst of the same scenery as you glance at in *Esther Waters*. But *Spring Days* is far too arid a book to give the reader any pleasant prospect of the downs; it is filled with an unkind, shadowless light and the harsh voices of sex-conscious girls. If Moore had felt constrained to display middle-class vulgarity and futility in a single complete reflection, so that vulgarity and futility might behold the reflection and perish, some such novel with a purpose might have resulted; but I cannot attribute that passion to him, and must concede that he makes this experiment because he was amused at the setting. It was originally published in the year of *Confessions of a Young Man*, and in the preface to the new edition the author records how he was induced to republish it after twenty-five years of oblivion. Certain friends had liked it, and on re-reading the forgotten pages he found a zest which helped to explain the tenacity with which the book had clung to existence.

Arid, I have called it, but something more should have been said. It is a book of confused purposes and impressions, and only one clear impression survives the confusion—an impression of twilight vanity. A doleful comedy, you may say, as you hurry to the last page with a sigh, finding whatever is sad a little ridiculous, and whatever is constant pathetic. Simplicity and tenderness unite in a single page or so which I must quote for its immense relief of the harshness of the whole, remarking also that it unstops a minor music not heard hitherto under the restless fingering of our artist :—

> 'I knew my passion was hopeless, but I couldn't resist it. Had I known her I might have won her, but there were no means; I never saw her but once off the stage, and that was but a moment. I often sent her presents, sometimes jewellery, sometimes fans or flowers, anything and everything I thought she would like. I sent her a beautiful locket; I paid fifty pounds for it.
>
> Did she accept your presents?
>
> I sent them anonymously.
>
> Why did not you try to make her acquaintance?
>
> I knew nobody in the theatrical world. I was not good at making acquaintances. You might have done it. I am a timid man.

Did you make no attempt? You might have written.

At last I did write.

What did you write?

I tried to tell her the exact truth. I told her that I had refrained from writing to her for three years. That I quite understood the folly and presumption of the effort; but I felt now, as drowning men that clutch at straws, that I must make my condition known to her. I told her I loved her truly and honourably, that my position and fortune would have entitled me to aspire to her hand if fate had been kind enough to allow me to know her. It was a difficult letter to write.'

When *Spring Days* was re-issued the sufficiency of this recital was admitted by the author, who left it untouched, but the succeeding paragraphs of the original edition were wisely changed. The earlier novelist had indulged in one of those undramatic asides of which Thackeray had given him innumerable and worthless examples; an aside ending: 'And then those letters—the one saving sign of soul in the man—that they should have perished, when the thousands of vain expenses and sterile records of ineffectual calculations stood bound and numbered in so many volumes.' It is omitted by the mature writer. Generally the novel has been only slightly revised, but a comparison of the fourteenth chapter in the two editions emphasizes for the millionth time the necessity of taking pains. Moore has never been a careless writer, but if you assume that he did his best with a poor subject in 1888— a subject yielding savour of poisonous brass and metal sick—you may reckon the leap of his ability when you turn to the revisions. True enough, as he says, there's no more moral in *Spring Days* than in *Daphnis and Chloe*, but that is a negative virtue. Most of the characters jerk and drop in a vacuum, and are seen in such a distinct, cold light that their motions seem unimpulsive and without significance; Willy alone is saved by his fidelity and failure, and remains to justify the title *Spring Days* if you remember that in spring an east wind will blow and shrivel many a flowering branch. It was an experiment, and the aridity so sedulously achieved was not to be repeated. Skill was gained, and *Esther Waters* was to show more clearly the advantage of subordinating parts to a whole; yet *Spring Days* is more than a mere precursor, if less to us than it seemed to its author on re-reading.

The preferences of authors are usually engaging enough when contrasted with one's own, and I confess that I cannot follow the fancies of George Moore's mind when he speaks of discarding *Vain Fortune,* or relegating it to his dusty apocrypha, while nevertheless retaining a favour for *Celibates.* The bibliography of our author is itself significant of the mental processes, and in particular the jealousy with which he regards his work; *Vain Fortune,* for example, having been twice revised by this victim of the disease of re-writing. In 1895 he did not disdain it, and regarded it as being far from his worst novel, but in 1921 he has rather inexplicably frowned upon it. Most properly might the revised text have been included in *Celibates* when that collection of stories was published in 1895.

It is a mere episode in treatment, a short story in essence, and, like *Spring Days,* communicates an impression of futility; enriching that impression, however, with a sense of tragedy far graver than any earlier book save *A Mummer's Wife* unfolds. A reminder of another novel, *A Drama in Muslin,* is conveyed by the imaginative apprehension of a young girl's mind, in its isolation and mania; and it is a reminder the more welcome inasmuch as it thrusts the commonness of *Lewis Seymour* and *Evelyn Innes* yet farther into the dark of the mind. It is difficult to imagine a purely pathological study being executed

with more tenderness than is used in the study of Emily
Watson; and it is no less difficult to believe that Evelyn
Innes and Emily Watson, or Lady Helen Granderville
and Emily Watson, are the work of the same hand.
Emily is the natural foil to the celibates of the book so
entitled; she told her love, jealousy was cruel as the
grave, and her story yields a glimpse into the deeps of
our poor human nature over which custom and shame
have drawn a flimsy shroud. Well might a suspicious
reader gasp in anticipation of offence in such a situation,
and there are many novelists who would not disappoint the
sorest anticipation; but the restraint of *Vain Fortune* is
the restraint of an artist who cares more for his art—that
is, for his story—than for the pleasure of shocking. It is
a restraint which I am bound in candour to emphasize, for
the lapses from it in other books are yet to be deplored.

I said it might have found a place in *Celibates,* meaning that it is the exact counterpart of stories in that
volume; for it has this in common with them—that it is
written in illustration of a theme, or selected as a type
in the true spirit of a new *comédie humaine.* There is no
reason why a good novel should not be written in this
way, but it is not a way which is littered with success.
Tess of the D'Urbervilles presents a pure woman, but if
you admire the book more than George Moore does, it is
not because it faithfully presents a pure woman, but because
it presents Tess; the novel, in fact, gaining nothing from
the faint suggestion that it presents a type. In the
scheme of *Celibates* the suggestion of presenting types
is more definite, but no more valuable. It is superfluous
to point out that the adoption of a type involves a purpose
beyond the purely creative purpose of the novelist. He
may, if he please, offer us a type of a sot, or a swindler, or
coward, politician, zany, boor, but he will scarcely interest
us if he gives us merely a type; and it is not wholly
absurd to insist on the simple truth that it is the task of

an imaginative artist to create imaginatively, not intellectu-ally, and to breathe into his characters an independent life as wanton and self-sufficient as his own.

It is the defect of *Celibates* that the stories in the book illustrate a theme; they are written upon the idea of celibacy, and every character is bitted and saddled alike. You cannot wholly escape the notion that the stories are intended to prove something, and even if you are willing to accept the proofs, you are apt—such is the natural wryness of the mind—to resent their interpolation in what should be an imaginative work. 'Mildred Lawson,' for instance, the first of these little novels, begins excellently and runs naturally until the first lover of this celibate dies; and there the story might have ended, perhaps a little subtly, but surely a sufficient ending. Instead, it begins over again and begins differently, as though to bring a fresh piece of evidence to the argument; and the delicacy of the earlier impression is ruined. . . . I know it is egregious to deprive a novelist of his right to his own story, but I cannot help feeling that Moore has robbed us of our rights in his characters; the rights, I mean, that a reader may properly assert in characters which he is invited to endenizen in some close corner of his brain. The dictation of a formula is felt even in the first chapter, where Mildred too artlessly unfolds her antecedents in a meditation of loneliness; you are given a summary of relevant facts as coldly and as formally as might be in the Probate, Divorce and Admiralty Division. Again, in tempting a second lover she becomes psychologically inconsistent with the Mildred of the first part, and is merely a ludicrous liar, the texture of the story being grossly coarsened for the sake of the argument. And again the reader demurs.

An escape from the domination of the theme is hardly achieved until the third story, 'Agnes Lahens,' is reached; for this is no simple illustration of an argument, but a

H

queer, painful episode of a genuine existence, an anticipation of Tchehov. The argument is subdued to the characters, and hence the interest is no longer extrinsic. It may be admitted that the vileness of the Lahens circle is as profound as need be, but it cannot be thought incredible; nor can the attitude of the child's father be thought incredible in its pitiful protest against the foulness of his wife's iridescence. ' One day I was told that as I paid for nothing I had no right to grumble. Your mother said, in reply to some question about me, that I was merely an expense. I believe the phrase was considered very clever, it went the round of society, and eventually was put into a play. And that is why I told you that money is everything, that it is difficult to be truthful, honourable, or respectable if you have no money; a little will do, but you must have a little, if you haven't you aren't respectable, you're nothing, you become a mere expense. . . . I've borne it for your sake, dearest.' You may read the whole of the few pages of this little novel without suspecting that an argument has ever entered the author's head, for Agnes and her father are not types but individual beings.

Between these two stories there stands ' John Norton,' a study in that religious sensualism which Moore himself has called elsewhere terrible. Condensation has made it easier to read but harder to appreciate, for in the earlier version ('A Mere Accident'), published eight years before, you were not asked to take so much for granted, and could test a little more accurately the weight of impulse and circumstance. But now—'the story will of course be no more than an experimental demonstration of the working of the brain into which we are looking.' Cumbrous phraseology, you will remark, and the experimental demonstration in itself hardly less cumbrous; the working of the brain being manifested not only to the eye but also to the ear in the creaking and clanking of the rudimentary machine, which in this story performs the office of the brain. . . . It loses another interest by the mutilation to which it has been subjected, since John Norton's early fondness for *Marius the Epicurean* and pictures by Monet, Degas and Renoir indicates the author's tendency to write autobiographically even in his immaturest work, as well as in his ripest. But mutilated as it is in *Celibates*, it yet holds a horror of its own. I do not know what could have possessed Moore to write this story, except the desire to illustrate his types of celibacy by a morbid invention. Consciousness of failure may be assumed, I fancy, from the abstention from another experiment of this kind, for which it is not wholly ungracious to offer a reader's thanks; although that consciousness does not prevent his pondering a third version of the story nearly thirty years later, and staring wistfully at the obstinate stone.

Between *Spring Days* and *Celibates* there was published a novel, *Mike Fletcher*, for which you must search the second-hand book-shops and which Moore himself disdains, including it with certain books to be reprinted only as the work of a disciple—Amico Moorino. He is not the only author who has mixed singularly good with singularly bad books; the curious may be referred to Thomas Hardy for another puzzling instance of the instability of genius or intelligence. Between *Tess of the D'Urbervilles* and *Jude the Obscure* you are confronted by so immemorable a novel as *The Well-Beloved*, and, more wonderful yet, between *Far from the Madding Crowd* and *The Return of the Native* you are perplexed by *The Hand of Ethelberta*. In Hardy's case this strange alternation seems to be due to a sluggish invention yielding slowly to habits of industry, but in Moore's case to an eager, fumbling uncertainty of his own mind and strength. He presses hither and thither, experimenting and failing, ardent and inconstant, yet maintaining with morose patience his resolve to become a man of letters. He falls

from *A Drama in Muslin* to *Confessions of a Young Man*,
rises a little to *Spring Days* and drops again like a bewildered bird down to the half-familiar depths of *Mike
Fletcher;* and once more he is miraculously ascendant
with *Esther Waters,* and once more falls with *Evelyn Innes.*
To follow the beating of his wings up and down the sky
yields the excitement of the incredible, for in a few brief
years extremes meet and inconsistency alone can be
counted upon. A splendid courage, truly, is it that
enables him to rise to *Esther Waters;* a pathetic fallacy,
surely, that weighs him down with *Mike Fletcher.*

The fallacy, or the lure, is the strange fondness for
the corrupt and wanton, for Lewis Seymour and Mike
Fletcher, for Mildred Lawson and Evelyn Innes; and
the strain of wantonness in Moore's intellectuality, expressed in so many of his characters and opinions, in
dramatic and undramatic utterances alike, responds only
too punctually to the stimulus of his subject. It is not
a mere simple fondness for shocking the easily shocked,
although that is a youthful proneness which he has never
wholly outgrown; the corrupt mind genuinely interests
him, as luxury interests him in *Evelyn Innes* and poverty
in *Esther Waters.* All these engross his intellectual
sympathies, and unless the reader, too, finds corruption
and luxury as interesting as hate and love, revenge and
despair—if abstractions may be seriously discussed—the
novelist's repeated choice of subject and character may
be deplored. There is no interest in Mike Fletcher's
attempted outrage upon the conventual Lily, because
there is none in Mike himself, and Lily is but a foil to
his coarseness; but when Richardson deals with the same
subject, and gives you the heart of Clarissa and the mind
of Lovelace, your own passionate interest is engaged
throughout the prodigious reiteration of his story. Moore
himself has taught us to be critical, and incident *qua*
incident does not delight, even though it be seduction,

nor monologue *qua* monologue, even though it be licentious. If character is wanting, then story is wanting and all else is vain.

But this is to anticipate much that ought to be said of *Evelyn Innes*, and meanwhile there is something else to remark, although that again is equally noticeable in *Parnell and His Island*. I refer to our author's penurious trick of using familiar material over and over again. Fletcher, for example, returning to Dublin and after prolonged absence calling on his father, finds him flute-playing: 'Oh, is that you, Mike?—sit down,' is the nonchalant salutation that greets him. The incident is treasured up and used again (of Marshall) in *Vale*. Again, Frank Escott reappears from *Spring Days*, no longer the careless youth but the editor of an impecunious review; and Lizzie Baker, shedding the virtue which dimly distinguished her in the earlier book, is at length become his mistress. And Harding, the eternal cynic, the literary effigy of *Vain Fortune* and *A Modern Lover* and I know not how many other books, here again seeks to display his damp squibs. Another small significant circumstance is Fletcher's meditation upon a trilogy on the life of Christ, a subject to be left for the maturer mind of our author himself. The influence of Balzac is still strong; not until long, long after *Mike Fletcher* did it yield to the influence of Turgenev, when, instead of Paris in London, you were confronted with microcosmic Russia in Ireland, and *A Sportsman's Sketches* begat *The Untilled Field*.

Perhaps I shall betray no very close secret in saying that in 1920 George Moore had retreated sufficiently far from the mood and manner of 1898 to decide that *Evelyn Innes* and *Sister Teresa* should be shut out of the canon of his works. His reasons for saying this will appear now and justify him amply. They are simple and amount to this —that both before and after writing *Evelyn Innes* he had written books so immeasurably superior, and again I say in mood and manner, that the shabby character of that unfortunate work is rebuked beyond revival. But the wisdom of the artist is often thwarted by the tenderness of the parent, and a few months after he passed judgment he appealed against it, saying, in the preface to the revised text of *The Lake,* that although he has very little admiration for *Evelyn Innes* and *Sister Teresa,* the writing of them has been useful to him, for had he not written them he could not have written *The Lake* or *The Brook Kerith.* Hence it seemed ungrateful to refuse two of his most successful books a place in the canon, merely because they did not correspond with his æstheticism. . . . On such points the author's word must be taken, and though it is hard to see that the writing of *Evelyn Innes* was an inevitable prelude to the writing of *The Brook Kerith,* I cannot question the assertion; all that can be said, speaking still æsthetically, is that the price was great. He follows the assertion with one of his many wise dicta—A writer's æstheticism is his all; he cannot surrender it, for his art is dependent upon it. Neither Moore nor any other artist has ever spoken more clearly a fundamental truth; and the interest of any study and portrayal of our subject lies in the determination of that æstheticism and the author's loyalty to it. My complaint is that the æstheticism out of which *Evelyn Innes* was shaped is obscure and shallow; luckily it was a mere disorderly quarterly tenant and not a freeholder, and when it was cast out (never was such an emaciated spectral being of ragged silks, coarse scent and arthritic gait!) a better spirit entered in and besomed the house. Moore himself cast it out, and I am only sorry that he inclines to tenderness in saying that his single concession to the wandering refugee is that if, when he is gone, an overwhelming demand for *Evelyn Innes* and *Sister Teresa* should arise, they must be reprinted from the original

editions but offered to the public merely as apocrypha.
I wish that his æstheticism had been a little less
imperious when he made this concession.

Between *Esther Waters* and *Evelyn Innes* there was an
external change which had a marked effect upon the
novelist. Remarking upon the good achieved by *Esther
Waters*, he adds that it did evil to him, the evil that
surrounded him when he lifted his eyes and saw a handsome flat, peopled by Manet and Monet and Berthe
Morisot with spiritual creatures. The flowered carpet,
the pretty furniture, the satisfactory cook—all represented
evil; for this 'thoroughly healthy' book had demoralized
its author. It is pleasant to think that the best of the
earlier books should have been the most successful also,
and we have no solid ground for assuming that if our
author had lived a long life of privation he would have
avoided the snare of *Evelyn Innes*. No! the demoralization
that leaps hugely before us is a purely æsthetic demoralization, symbolized almost perfectly in the contrast of the
dominant house in *Esther Waters*, the simple, busy home
of the Barfields on the Sussex Downs, with the dominant
house of *Evelyn Innes*, in Park Lane, with flashing horses
always waiting outside. The external impression of
Evelyn Innes is a strange one; few novels are so lavishly
furnished, so luxuriously upholstered. There is a story
in *Salve* which amusingly illustrates this:—

> 'Apologizing for spoiling the story, Sir Thornley
> told me I must take for granted the racy description
> of two workmen who had come to Upper Ely Place
> to mend the drains in front of my house. After
> having dug a hole, they took a seat at either end,
> and sat spitting into it from time to time in solemn
> silence, until at last one said to the other, "Do you
> know the fellow that lives in the house forninst us?
> You don't? Well, I'll tell you who he is: he's the
> fellow that wrote *Evelyn Innes*." "And who was
> she?" "She was a great opera-singer. And the story

is all about the ould hat. She was lying on a crimson sofa with mother-of-pearl legs when the baronet came into the room, his eyes jumping out of his head and he as hot as be damned. Without as much as a good-morrow, he jumped down on his knees alongside of her, and the next chapter is in Italy." '

Quotation readily shows the æsthetic disintegration so thinly concealed, and if the style appears incredible the task of proving it authentic may be left to Moore himself. Certainly his own word might be asked, in proof that this is indeed by the author of *The Lake*, written not long after; it is a passage describing the first meeting between an innocent and devout Catholic girl and Sir Owen Asher, Bart. :—

> ' Her intense consciousness of this tall, aristocratic man frightened her. She saw the embroidered waist-coat, the slight hips, the gold moustache, and the sparkling grey eyes asked her questions to which her whole nature violently responded, and although her feelings were inexplicable to herself, she was overcome with physical shame.'

The second meeting repeats the impression :—

> ' In a sort of dream, through a sort of mist, she saw the embroidered waistcoat and the gold moustache, and when the small, grey, smiling eyes were raised from her father's face and looked at her, a delicious sensation penetrated through the very tissues of her flesh, and she experienced the tremor of a decisive moment; and then there came again a gentle sense of delicious bewilderment and illusion.'

Throughout, the story is the same—their sense is with their senses all mixed in. Moore dedicated *Evelyn Innes* to Mr. Arthur Symons and Mr. W. B. Yeats, ' Two contemporary writers with whom I am in sympathy;' and I am amused to note the parallel currents of Moore's and Mr. Symons's works. For Moore is a prey to influences and streams of tendency. Moore and Mr. Symons have been fascinated by the French, one mainly by Manet and the rest, the other by Mallarmé and the rest. Each has been attracted by Baudelaire, and then by Verlaine, but Moore has revolted from Baudelaire instead of merely neglecting him. Each has been subjugated by Pater, each writes carefully, one better than Pater, the other worse. *Evelyn Innes* shows Moore wonderfully concerning himself with Saint Teresa and Crashaw; Mr. Symons's poems show an equally remarkable concern with Patmorean odes and St. John of the Cross.

Intellectual sympathies, however, are sometimes imperfect and sometimes transient. *Evelyn Innes* is a novel of the 'nineties rather than of a particular author, and, like much of the work of the 'nineties, it provides a submorality for the use of those who care to note it. There are pages in the book which form only too minatory a sermon upon the terrible monotony of wantonness, a monotony not broken even by Evelyn's hint to her confessor of unlimited lasciviousness beyond the moderate sexual life which she believed was maintained between husband and wife. Thankful enough are we to the discreet confessor who interrupted the luxury of this abasement with, 'You have said enough on that point;' although his interruption was only half effectual. Evelyn, in fact, is Moore's chief example of the wanton, the ivy woman whose body alone thinks; her weakness as a type is that she lives in his book not for herself and of herself, but to assist towards—what? The first English novel of passion!

It is by a sheer fatality, then, that for counterpart to Evelyn he falls back upon Sir Owen Asher, whose grave occupation was the seduction of his friends' wives and who is introduced to you with a remark with which he had embarrassed his reigning mistress—'Of course marriage is necessary; you can't have husbands without marriage, and if there were no husbands, who would look after our mistresses?' A sheer fatality is Owen in a novel of passion, for a virgin passion is wanted and Owen is impotent for the purpose. Moore's own view, again, is that a man with ten thousand a year is not a possible subject for art; and although I do not admit a purely arbitrary limitation, I cannot forget that Owen has twenty thousand a year; for the author never permits that to be forgotten. An accomplished seducer, when he obtains Evelyn he fears to lose her as he has lost others, dreading most of all the first intimations of reviving morality or religion; for had he not found that when a wanton begins to weary of her lover she preludes her sighs for another by obstinate questionings about morality or religion? He seeks, therefore, to seduce her intelligence in order to command her sense's loyalty, drenching her mind with Spencer, Darwin and Huxley; hence the book itself is soaked with an attempted philosophy of sensualism, a philosophy expressed partly by Owen and partly by his successor, Ulick Dean—Dean relying upon Blake instead of Spencer for his success. He taught her, for instance, on Blake's authority, that we must seek to exalt ourselves, to live in the idea; and though sexual passion was an inferior state, mean content was the true degradation. 'In the pauses of their love-making, they often wandered round the walls participating in the mystery of the Wanderers, and the sempiternal loveliness of figures who stood with raised arms by the streams of Paradise. It seemed a profanation to turn from these aspirations to the enjoyment of material love, and Evelyn looked at Ulick questioningly. But he said that life only became wrong when it ceased to aspire.' . . . Dean gives a varnish of mysticism to the hard surface of materialism prepared by his rival, and in this aspect the book is a modern Harlot's Progress. Just as Owen had swept her off to Paris and pleased her with the fripperies of expensive women's shops ('Owen's taste was for garters, and the choice of a pair filled them with a pleasurable embarrassment '), so Ulick sweeps her out of Owen's power and teases her with metaphysical fripperies not less delightful.

For Evelyn was truly ivy:—'Obedience is a divine sensualism; it is the sensualism of the saints; its lassitudes are animated with deep pauses and thrills of love and worship.' 'No sensuality,' says Moore, in another book, 'is so terrible as religious sensuality.' Her conversion is but an introverted sensualism, springing partly from the perplexities which naturally abound when an opera singer has committed herself to two lovers; and her own account of that conversion is amusing enough when she says in dismissing Owen: 'We have only a certain amount of force. A certain amount goes to support life, and the rest we may expend upon a lover, or upon our spiritual life.'—A longer passage is needed to illustrate the development of the wanton:—

'By a special dispensation from the Reverend Mother, her watch before the sacrament was increased from half an hour to an hour; she was therefore put on an equality with the choir nuns; and kneeling before the sacrament she thought of God as intimately as she dared, excluding all thought of the young Galilean prophet and seer, allowing herself to think only of the exquisite doctrine. She did not wish Him to take her in His arms until one day, starting suddenly from her prayers, she asked who it was who stood before her. She seemed to see Him among His disciples, sitting at a small table with a love-light upon His face. She scrutinized the face, fearing it might not be His. She seemed to have seen it. Presently she discovered Ulick; and tremblingly she remembered the night she found him among his disciples. So she did not dare to think of Christ any longer; and with regret and tenderness, and yet with a certain exaltation of spirit, she turned to the Father, to the original essence which had existed before the world needed a redeemer. She lost herself for a time in the vast spirit which hears the song of Nature through space and the ages. But very soon she turned to the young Galilean prophet again, and His exquisite doctrine seemed to her to be all that a man needs to bring to perfect fruition the original germ of immortality implanted in him.'

Evelyn Innes is not a novel of passion, but of intellectual sensualism. Culture and mammon do their best to be exalted, passionate, distraught; they remain at heart elegant and vulgar. Moore's interest in passion—and clearly he means passion as the French see it—is an intellectual interest; out of his critical contempt for the narrow range of the English novel he has projected a little world in which passion shall spin the plot, and the English novel at length burst the straight bonds of custom and prejudice. Once again Balzac beckons him with the enormous improvisations of his *comédie humaine,* but the energy of Balzac is wanting.

Dogmatism is easy and foolish, yet I cannot help saying that in attempting his novel of passion in English, for an English audience, Moore was heavily handicapped. The English genius is distinguished in this from the Latin genius, that its attempts in this kind have not achieved success but have wallowed obscurely in dim circles far below, shifting furtively between vulgarity and stupidity. It is an obvious gibe to say that the novel of passion needs passion for its success, and no one will want to gibe at Moore's attempt or deny that passion is absent from it; for appetite is not passion. When (in *Sister Teresa*) Evelyn turns from opera to prayer, it is not a revolt against sin but a simple revulsion of the tired mind and body; her sense and not her soul is sick, and she no more sways your sympathies as a convert than as a mere wanton. She foreshadows quite exactly the externality of Doris and the nameless lover of Doris in 'The Lovers of Orelay.' The merest echo of passion is that which you detect in the lavish and unflagging chapters of musical experiences and criticism; at the name of Palestrina Moore's eye brightens, at the name of Wagner his ears tingle and he bends all his powers upon the communication of his pleasure. His own enthusiasm for the Rhinegold, for instance, his vivid memory of that astonished first hearing, hinted at rather than described in *Hail and Farewell,* are the prompters of the prolonged musical disquisitions in *Evelyn Innes.* Not even his youthful excitement at the first reading of Shelley exceeded the intensity of his excitement on first hearing Wagner; and the chapters begotten of that fascination are at any rate written with a full heart. Sensuality exalted into something so high and fine as to have become almost spiritual-minded—that note of music's power is the note which he has surely touched in this novel; for it was first touched in himself; and he writes truly only that which he writes out of his own heart.

It is, again, the author that speaks in the attitude towards the Catholic Church. The sharp resentment of later writings is not traceable here, for music has softened the harshness of dogma accepted or dogma opposed, and the constraint of the religious life is never made ridiculous. I cannot imagine the thoughts of a Catholic upon the conversion of our operatic Magdalene, nor can I imagine his judgment upon her egoism when it wears the religious habit; but I can easily imagine Monsignor Mostyn pausing before he again cries to an errant beauty, *Get thee to a nunnery!* You are asked to believe that peace comes when Evelyn loses her voice, and perhaps a symbol is here of the spiritual gain from carnal loss; but did her egoism exist only in her marvellous voice? Alas, not so easily do mortals escape from the weakness of their being; and if our author should cast upon Evelyn such a musing regard as he gives to Violet Scully's future, he would find a teasing

problem for his fancy. Probably his later exasperation
with the Catholic Church, and in particular with the
priesthood, would tempt him anew into the rich per-
versities recorded in *Hail and Farewell,* and in the pages
dealing with his sudden discovery of an antagonism
between Catholicism and literature. But such an
epilogue would make the story even less a novel of
passion.

' I sat wondering,' says the author of *Ave* in speaking of
the joy which a reading of *Esther Waters* gave him some
years after its publication—' I sat wondering how it could
have happened to me to write the book that among all
books I should have cared most to write, and to have
written it so much better than I ever dreamed it could
be written.'

It is from *Esther Waters* that Moore has derived the
only pleasure which his books have given him, unless
his experience since *Hail and Farewell* should tempt him
to qualify that statement now; and he speaks frankly of
the unhappiness and anxieties that his writings always
cause him—an experience common to creative minds. A
harmless joy is his term for that pleasure, and he con-
gratulates himself somewhat surprisingly that this book,
though pure of all intention to alleviate suffering, has
perhaps done more good than any other novel written in
his generation; a concession to popular demands, surely,
which George Moore would ordinarily be loth to make,
especially since it may be freely admitted. The goodness
of *Esther Waters* is a subject which we may contemplate
now without reference to alien standards, and all that
need be added is the remark that the moral value of the
book was not originally undisputed. But the confusion
of art with morals is senseless, if almost inevitable, and
certainly has no use here except as an indication of the
commonplace to which the bright mind may sink.

' As characteristically English as *Don Quixote* is Spanish,'
cried the author on another occasion, referring to *Esther
Waters;* and at another time : the only English novel that
treated a servant-girl seriously, as chief person of the
drama.   And again, it was the Englishman in him that
wrote the book ; and yet again, was it likely that he who
had written the most English of all novels should be able
to describe Ireland ?   Could he write at all except about
England, and in leaving England and his inspiration wasn't
he leaving a literary career behind ?—More precisely, he
remembers that the book was written in the Temple, and
again the recollection pricks him with the notion that he
would have written better if he had stayed there ; for it
was in the Temple that his poor laundress used to tell him
every day of her troubles, and through her he became
acquainted with the life of poor people, and spontaneous
sympathy and kindness grew.   How mean we seem when
we look back !   He gave her five pounds when he left,
and with a candour that helps to redeem the coldness, he
confesses to having forgotten to answer the laundress's
son, who asked him to help her in old age. . . . She
did not inspire the subject of *Esther Waters*, it appears,
but she gave the atmosphere required for the book ; a
talk with her at breakfast being an excellent preparation
for the day's writing.

Esther Waters, then, was born in London, the fruit of an
unequal match.   It is hard to dispute that it is the most
English of all novels if a saving clause, since *Tom
Jones* and *David Copperfield,* be added.   A single sentence in a newspaper gave him the subject of *Esther
Waters*—' We're always complaining of the annoyance
that servants occasion us, but do we ever think of the
annoyance we occasion servants ? '   Pondering upon that
as he stepped out, he rejected the notion of a young lady
in love with her footman (a mere incident in the story as
we read it now), and imagined a girl, a kitchen-maid,

anxious to get a living. He thought that on fourteen pounds a year she could not rear her illegitimate child, but needed sixteen pounds. The life of a human being valued at two pounds a year was the subject, and before he had passed from the Temple to the Law Courts the story was decided upon. It is a story in which character and incident are balanced and interdependent; and if it has an excellence beyond our insular achievement it is the excellence of form. Pity that form should be regarded so often as negligible; but Moore at any rate has been admonished that creation demands form, and that in the medium of prose the presence of form is essential even if it be half concealed—like unwearing rocks, that shape the current of the tide—and showing only at moments of ebbing inspiration. The evil Victorian tradition of the formless, a tradition disastrously honoured in Tennyson's *In Memoriam* and Thackeray's *Vanity Fair* and Meredith's *Diana of the Crossways*, is a tradition which George Moore has been among the first to disturb. If the admonition came from France or Russia, if it came in fact from his admired Turgenev, it was an admonition to which his whole intelligence responded with the eagerness of a mirror to the light. His earlier novels had wanted this care, and although *A Mummer's Wife*, for example, had a beginning and an end (two parts of the obvious want), it lacked the continual evidences of a shaping spirit which are to be detected in the later masterpiece. And if it be acknowledged that the exact repetition, in the opening sentences of the conclusion, of the first lines of the first chapter, forms too rigid a pattern, it is the largest concession that need or shall be made. *Esther Waters* has a beginning and an end, and because all between is an easy, harmonious development, flowing like water to a stream or like branches to autumn and winter, the quiet end has the beauty of music and clouds. The story sinks in the west, clouds are lit and dimmed, and while a laggard blackbird still sings, Esther Waters, her son and her mistress stand clear and firm in the twilight, and the shadows of departed characters, William and Randall and Ketley and Sarah, step from obscurity and resume their places beside them. The close of the book is a luminous example of the formalizing effect of unity. . . . I have not attempted a definition of form in relation to a novel; it is suggested by the metaphors just used. It is the result of the co-operation of imagination with intelligence, of imagination working upon intelligence, at once sustained and strengthened by the sober counsels and curbings of the lower power. Put it more simply, and so far as it can be described as an effect rather than an influence, it is the result of the artist's complete possession by a definite idea, to which he is fain to give the shape, members and unity of a natural creation. It is not easily achieved, nor achieved at all by any who lacks the passion and discipline of art.

The trunk of the tree is Esther herself. That it was left to an Irishman to create this typical Englishwoman is not at all singular, for what was needed was neither Englishman nor Irishman but simply a man of genius who should be capable, as Moore candidly avows, of holding the mirror steadily up to a particular phase of 'nature.' This attractive, blunt-featured Cockney servant, with a religious severity imposed upon natural honesty, has the literal fidelity of a photograph and the warm animation of a painting. Could Manet have repaid Moore's constant lauds by a critical appraisal of his disciple's work, he would have found his sufficient occasion in this portrait. The triumph is the more delightful when the portrait is contrasted with the sketches in *Mike Fletcher* among the earlier and *Evelyn Innes* among later novels. The punctiliously but not quite perfectly revised text of 1920 (the book was first published in 1894 and Moore's growth as a writer of English prose is mainly

I

twentieth-century) gives a precise impression of the physical woman in the description with which the book opens: 'A girl of twenty, firmly built with short, strong arms and a plump neck that carried a well-turned head with dignity. Her well-formed nostrils redeemed her somewhat thick, fleshy nose, and it was a pleasure to see her grave, almost sullen, face light with sunny humour; for when she laughed a line of almond-shaped teeth showed between red lips.' And towards the close of the book, when the too-cunning or too-simple repetition of the first movement begins, the description is: 'A woman of seven or eight and thirty, stout and strongly built, short arms and hard-worked hands, dressed in dingy black skirt and a threadbare jacket too thin for the dampness of a November day. Her face was a blunt outline, and the grey eyes reflected all the natural prose of the Saxon.' But the truth of the book does not depend upon explicit but rather upon implicit things; and of these the chief is Esther's own regard of her early lapse. A girl of religious tradition and training, she is not appalled by her betrayal; she does not become a tragical creature, impressive and grotesque, or a type of woman's weakness; she is conscious of social disgrace without raging at that disgrace, and her native religiousness is untouched. The temptation to heroics is so steadily resisted that I wonder if Moore was tempted at all; rather is it likely that, possessed by his theme, not one of a million devils had power over him —not even that simian devil of sensuality who comes so quickly if Moore but whispers, had power to seduce the artist from his art. Happy are those whom an engrossing task secures against temptation!

One objection to *Esther Waters* has often been rehearsed —that for all its skill and verisimilitude, it fails in animation and heat, being written from without and not from within, coldly and not fondly. The charge is somewhat vague, and the vindication can be little less

vague, if more strenuous. I think it is the presence
of form in a rare degree that suggests coldness; the
uncommon quality being assumed to exclude a common
quality quite inevitably. But that exclusion is far from
inevitable; it is merely the slackness of the mind that
calls violence power, and restraint coldness. Argument
of this kind, however, is too abstract to be useful; turn
rather to the pages in which Esther watches her husband
die. It is conceivable that restraint may be mistaken for
coldness, but if it is my business to distinguish, I do not
find it hard to distinguish tenderness there.

Let it be granted, nevertheless, that passionate heights
and deeps are not touched in this novel; but let it also be
granted that they are not within its aim. The naturalistic
novel moves within definite limits, and it has not the
power of Ariel to fly or run at will. Of the French
naturalists it has been said that they found life unpleasant
and left it hideous; but the excesses of reaction are a
commonplace. The French naturalists reacted against
romance, and in turn the symbolists reacted against their
predecessors. Moore is the most eminent of those who
have sought to transplant or maintain the naturalistic
formula, but I have already called attention to his
apostasy from the ardours of Zola. In another book he
has said that a man may write twenty volumes of poetry,
history and philosophy, but a man will never be born who
will write more than two, at the most three, naturalistic
novels; the naturalistic novel being the essence of a phase
of life that the writer has lived in and assimilated. . . .
Esther Waters was clearly conceived in that tradition, and
it happened that the tradition, lightly observed and
sparingly infringed, offered the ideal opportunity for a
faithfully English novel. Written in another tradition,
it might have gained a romantic attraction and lost in
fidelity. Yet it differs utterly from *Celibates*, in that its
restrictions relate to form and not to idea. *Celibates*, I

have said, is spoiled by the domination of a theme; the theme of *Esther Waters* is enhanced by the observance of form.

Esther Waters has a special interest for its author, since it shared the fate of *A Modern Lover* and *A Mummer's Wife*—it was banned by the libraries whose circulation was still at the mercy of strange cerebral congestions. The insult and the injury have not yet been forgiven, and in *Avowals* you may see Moore's resentment bursting into new flame, and again that queer resolve to justify the book by the good it achieved; the new proof being that four years after *Esther Waters* was published a nurse was so impressed by it that she renounced the projected foundation of a convalescent home, and started a home for the infants of unmarried working mothers. I could understand his insistence 'upon the practical argument if he were still pleading with Mudie's, Smith's and the rest; I fail to understand that insistence when he is pleading the cause of art before the privileged few for whom privately printed books such as *Avowals* are issued. To one creative writer was it given to reconcile now and again the imaginative and the moral; by sheer pressure of genius Tolstoi was able to constrain the wine of a supreme imagination into the bottles of a dogmatic morality. I do not suggest that his art was the worse for this noble attempt, I do not see that it is better; but the attempt assuredly manifests the superb strength of the Russian realist. ' Always more of a moralist than an artist!' cries our author of Tolstoi, forgetting that in his inconstant fusion of the two Tolstoi becomes one of the great shaking forces of the modern world; and naturally repelled by his huge, dark, irregular genius as by a wild mountain storm.

It is scarcely a derogation to say that in neither imaginative nor moral power is George Moore the equal of Tolstoi. Faithfulness to his subject is Moore's excellence, not the imaginative intensification of the subject.

Turning from *Ivan Ilyitch* to *Esther Waters* you turn
without shame, although aware of a descent from clouded
heights to easy plain; but from *Ivan Ilyitch*—nay, from
Esther Waters itself to *Lewis Seymour* or *Mike Fletcher* you
cannot pass without shame, sorrow, nausea. . . . Moore's
master was first Balzac and then Turgenev; he turned
from force to beauty, from energy to order, and it is not
complainingly that his inevitable choice is noted here, if
choice it can be called that was so purely dictated by an
alert, unimpassioned nature.

It is characteristic of our author, as we shall have other
occasions of noting, that the theme of *Esther Waters*
haunted him like a remembered phrase of his admired
Wagner until (in 1911) he had turned his novel into a
play. A French actress wanted to take the part of
Esther, and so the first three acts (as good as the novel,
he thinks) were written and the last two stitched on
during rehearsals. He had never put his back into a
play, but now he made an attempt, and if I hazard the
crude opinion that the result was a novel in dramatic
form, I am driven to admit that this opinion was
apparently not shared by the Stage Society, which
produced *Esther Waters, a Play in Five Acts.* The division
into five acts is purely arbitrary, and made evident by
the resources of the printer rather than the art of the
author. Moore's dilemma may have been a concealed
one, but it was real enough. To adhere closely to the
story of the novel was impossible if a good play was to
be written; to depart from it was to provoke resentful
comparisons. *Let well alone!* is the appeal of the reader,
an appeal which becomes urgent as he turns the last
pages of the play. Compared with the art of drama, the
novelist's art is slow in development as a growing oak;
but the play moves with the swiftness of a building of
five floors. And is it not a pity to cut down a mature,

green-leaved tree for the purposes of a dramatic house?
I shall have occasion to note in a moment the strange itch
that touches Moore (as it has touched worse artists) when
he looks upon the easy-seeming success of the theatre.
It is as if he said in his secret mind—for even Moore has
a secret mind for his work, which all his frankness does
not betray—Look at this play and that play by such and
another worthless author; a play made out of a novel,
and running for a hundred nights. Isn't *Esther Waters*
a far better novel, and can't I make a no less superior
play?—Well, he has tried, but it is a play in which the
dramatic does not happen. There is not a half-note of
difference between the pitch of one act and another. A
different ending is provided, but the reader is pre-con-
vinced that a different ending will be a weak ending—as
it proves; and on the other hand such undramatic scenes
are faithfully retained as that of the dispute between the
servants over the *Silver Braid* sweepstakes. It is not
an isolated flatness. Moore's preface to the play ends
amusingly :—

'*Esther Waters* was produced by Mr. Clifford Brooke,
and from the first rehearsal he seemed to have the
entire play in his head, and to see it on the stage in
its every detail. So I never interfered; there was
no necessity. Once I did interfere. It seemed to
me preferable that the prayer should be recited in the
middle of the stage in front of the audience, and in
this it appears I was wrong; at all events, a well-
known actress, and one of great talent, complained of
this bit of stage management. Her suggestion was
that Esther should hide her face in a cushion; that
would give an idea of family prayers, and from the
point of view of the public and the artistic producer
I am sure she is right; but as I very seldom write
plays and shall never own a theatre, nobody need
be seriously annoyed because I think everything
outside of the text and the acting is mere vulgarity.'

The natural jealousy of the artist, upon which the whole craft of the stage so unerringly infringes, has seldom been more sharply expressed; for Moore's anxiety to write a play is after all a subordinate anxiety, and his insistence upon the supremacy of his own kingdom remains un-weakened. At any rate, failure as a dramatic writer has not weakened his conviction, and there has been no success to sap it. 'Everything outside of the text and the acting is mere vulgarity'—yes, he is at times con-temptuous of the theatre, even if that contempt wears the hue of envy; for he is not removed from the weakness of the wise and the failings of those who have succeeded.

Esther Waters, a Play in Five Acts, is not the only one of his books in which the preface atones for the disappoint-ment that follows it. It was while listening to an actress who took a minor part in the Stage Society's performance that the author murmured, 'There is no doubt that acting tells something that no other art can tell.' But if you ask what it is, Moore does not answer; it is an unguessed secret, and anxious as he is to guess it and achieve a victory over the alien medium, a secret it remains. His natural jealousy reappears in his allusion to another actress who did not think that Mrs. Rivers would speak of suckling her baby; to which his retort was that he did not propose to reopen with her the question of his choice of a profession; a retort which many might wish to make and few utter aloud, and fewer yet record as uttered. Moore smooths out the allusion with an added—'I've nothing but good to say of everybody; the little fault-finding being very little indeed.'

The sharp itch for the drama may not have been wholly responsible for that oddly-begotten play, *The Bending of the Bough,* but I cannot believe that Moore wrote it without trying to write as well as he could. *The Bending of the Bough* confesses the influence of Ibsen more plainly than *The Strike at Arlingford,* but it shares equally with the earlier play a harshness of subject and a dulness of tone surprising in our author. The harshness and dulness are happily redeemed by speeches which make agreeable additions to experimental philosophy, even while they diminish the dramatic interest for which you needs must look somewhat narrowly, if not quite in vain. Kirwan the mystic utters those truths which Mr. Yeats, distant pupil of aery philosophers, must often have dropped into the playwright's ear—'You were dissatisfied even with the earth under your feet ; the air was empty of supersensuous life. . . . There are only two chains, the material and the spiritual . . . there is but one way to attain the spiritual, and that is by sacrifice.' Assuredly Mr. Martyn was sardonically gratified if he read this version of his own despised play, and perhaps turned to the preface with a simpler pleasure to note how heartily Moore despised the theatre, from which—in writing, scenery and acting alike —intellect had been sullenly excluded. Art was produced in the youth of a nation. It had left England, but in its bewildered passage might it not rest for a space on that forlorn Atlantic island where the Irish Literary Theatre was lifting a wan head ? . . . The preface, save in antici-patory phrases, is hardly the work of the author who was about to draw from Ireland his rarest impulse ; but had it been tenfold brighter and lighter, it could not vivify a dull play. One beautiful prelusive passage might be noted—'In artistic England the pallor of centuries shines in the inactive autumn air. The thrush is silent, the nightingale has flown, and the robin sits on the coral hedge piping his little roundelay.'

A far better play is *The Coming of Gabrielle,* the re-written form of the comedy which originally bore the title *Elizabeth Cooper.* That it should have been neglected by those obscure Incomprehensibles, the theatrical managers, may appear astonishing. Something of the quality of Congreve's dialogue—and Moore is among the admirers of that alert elegance of action and speech which enchants

the reader of *Love for Love* and *The Way of the World*—
has been preserved in *The Coming of Gabrielle,* and tempts
one to indignation at delays exceeding the law's; for I
think it cannot often happen that a play that is so truly a
comedy is neither rejected nor produced. The changes
which have been wrought in the original composition are
valuable, but even in *Elizabeth Cooper* there is much of
the wit and lightness of the new version. Moore's attitude towards the theatre is once again freely expressed in
the preface, in which he condemns the realistic play even
while he yields a faint obeisance to it. He would revert
to, and start from, the old five-act comedy form, each act
with its several scenes changed before the eyes of the
spectator; for in such a form there would be room for
more story, variety, life. The story, once again, is the
thing.—Well, there is story, complexity, movement in
The Coming of Gabrielle, even without this reversion to an
earlier type; but if the author may be credited, not the
greatest of public success would induce him to write
another play, his thirst having been slaked in the writing
of this sole comedy that pleases him. It is as if he had
tried and tried again, and having at last succeeded and
convinced himself that he could write not only novel,
romance, reminiscence, and essay, but comedy as well, and
therefore was so much the more completely a man of
letters, he was content with this single, conclusive proof,
and, indeed, no longer envious but merely proud. Gabrielle herself I can conceive as a brilliant triumph on the
stage, granting the discovery of an actress superlatively
endowed with vivacity and intelligence, able to match
with hers the brightness of the later Congreve. That the
theme of the play is merely a deception which does not
deceive, concluding with a light revenge foregone, will
not blind the reader to the dramatic excitement of a performance, even if it be played only within his own brain
by the nimble and capricious puppets of imagination.

CHAPTER IV

NON DOLET!

The parts I most esteeme in my selfe, reape more honor by accusing then by commending my selfe. And that's the cause I more often fall into them againe and rest upon them. But when all the cardes be told, a man never speakes of himselfe without losse. A man's own condemnations are ever increased : praises ever decreased. —*Montaigne.*

THE year 1887 saw the publication of a curious, chaotic book, *Parnell and His Island*, a study in a forsaken mode of political-social interests, with the familiar Balzacian interventions and interludes. It is not the Moore we best know that writes—' And still dreaming of my Irish France, I listened to the monotonous story of a broken barrel-organ, and, looking at the poor devil of an Italian, I knew well that nobody here, except perhaps the distiller, is rich enough to throw him a penny.' The same forgotten disciple writes of Dublin—'Town of miserable vice and hideous decrepitude;' and of the Shelburne—'The pen of a Balzac would be necessary to describe it.' . . . The country exudes the damp, flaccid, evil smell of poverty, and never has he observed in the peasantry the slightest æsthetic intention; never was a pot of flowers seen in the cottage window of an Irish Celt.

The scenes of the book, he says, have been chosen because they seemed typical and picturesque aspects of a primitive country and barbarous people. Unconcerned with this or that interest, indifferent to this or that opinion, his desire was to produce a series of pictures to touch the fancy of the reader as a Japanese ivory or fan, combinations of hue and colour calculated to awake in him fictitious feelings of pity, curiosity and nostalgia of the unknown. But have these scenes been 'chosen' at all? I call the book chaotic, and a slight glance will show that it is made up in part of the material used in other books. Cut out of it certain considerable passages to be found in *A Drama in Muslin*, and you cut out much of the best of the book. There is the fashionable dress-maker, for instance, the ear for all confidences and intimacies in both books; there is an almost precise repetition of that oddly effective scene in the novel, in which the Barton tenants insist upon a reduction of their rents by twenty-five per cent.; but in *Parnell and His Island* the spectator is the poet who, intensely wearied, strives to amuse himself by recalling a sonnet of Mallarmé's. Another incident in this early essay is used with how much finer an art in the passage in *Vale* where our author relates his visit to the grave of that adventurous ancestor who established for a while the fortunes of the Moores. . . . These returns and renewals illustrate once again his frugal habit; for Moore's is not a royal and prodigal gift, and for all his supreme interest in the story and ease in telling a story, there is no careless largesse anywhere, but rather the anxious concentration which a growing accomplishment has taught him both to increase and to disguise.

It is related that Douglas Hyde, discussing with Moore the possibilities of the novelist's aid in the revival of the Irish language and literature, pointed to *Parnell and His Island* as an obstacle, saying that it would go against his aim, so far as the League was concerned. ' I should have thought,' Moore answered, ' that the League would have accepted those who are willing to help Ireland to recover her language, and not to bother about my past.' Enduring as well as he could the irritating little laugh of his friend, he listened as Hyde wonderfully proceeded—' The League might be reconciled to your book if you were to issue it with a sub-title—*Parnell and His Island, or Ireland without Her Language*'; for wasn't it perhaps Moore's best book ? —If indeed Douglas Hyde was guilty of such a notion, Moore's continual revenges throughout *Hail and Farewell* were not inexcusable. ' Mere gabble ! ' was his immediate answer, for he had reason to taste to the full that intimate shame which the true artist feels on a revisiting glance at work which he wishes had never been written or read.

Parnell and His Island is scarcely such a book, but although I cannot pretend to combat an Irishman's view, I can see clearly enough that its only interest now is for the craftsman who seeks to discover a small sign of the author in it, and determine what place it holds in his Pilgrim's Progress from a half-real to a wholly real world. He stands but precariously in a half-real world when he writes—'I am a close observer of life, and am, I think, as free from prejudice as any man, but this I am bound to admit—that it is impossible to over-estimate the patriotism of Irishmen. . . . Their love of Ireland is, as it were, a sort of constitutional vice that nothing can, that nothing will be able to uproot.'—And there is no godlike indifference to either sphere when he speaks of the terrible Irish incubus, wondering what measures Salisbury and Randolph Churchill will adopt to rid England of it, and finding himself obliged to admit the existence of a race-hatred. In two years from 1887 a free Parliament would be given to Ireland, Irish-Americans would flock back, and in a short, phantasmal seven years all traces of seven hundred years of Saxon conquest would disappear. What then?—when the inevitable war with Russia began, the Irish-Americans who would be governing in Dublin would declare independence. Unhappy is every prophet, exposed to stoning even when he is wrong as well as when he is right; and it is not without reason, for the prophet who prophesies falsely is only less maddening than is he who prophesies truly.

But to deplore the book—and it has been deplored—is to exaggerate the influence of literature upon affairs. *Parnell and His Island* is an essay in literature, and its real value is that of the marking on a wall by which a towering small child's height is taken on successive birthdays. As politics it need not be read, much less censured, and as literature it can be remembered for the simplest uses of history and portraiture.

Moore has acknowledged freely enough how quickly the Irishman in him evaporated at the contact with London and Paris; but when that disguised heavenly agent beckoned him from Paris back to London, and sent him, so curiously garbed, visiting Moore Hall again, the Irishman began slowly to re-solidify, and childish scenes, as I have said, reasserted their power while the novelist was seeking after his own. I am satisfied to note this in passing, and to say that in meditating or writing *A Mummer's Wife* and *A Drama in Muslin* in Ireland, he was unconsciously preparing for the more instinctive expression of *The Lake* and *Hail and Farewell;* and if one certain thing may be observed of this most fluid and changeful writer, it is again and again this—that his own earth was needed to renew and enhance his imaginative power, even for the sake of books of so foreign a setting as *The Brook Kerith* and *Héloïse and Abélard.*

Fondness for his native country—it needs no boldness to assert the eminence of that affection in almost every imaginative writer in the English tongue; a fondness sometimes restricted to the physical shape and character of the land, to its hills and rivers and magical dark woods, sometimes narrowly localized and enfolding a single aspect or a single county, and sometimes extended to the whole tradition and history of English life and character until it becomes metaphysically wide but still sensitive and passionate. The point is sharpened if half a dozen English writers of verse or prose are contrasted with half a dozen American, for the American writers betray no such fondness—nor, indeed, any other national characteristic, strongly marked as American characteristics appear in other transactions of the human spirit; for it seems that contact with their Western earth enfeebles the free intelligence, and that the excursion of Hawthorne and the exile of Henry James were equally in the spirit of Christian's flight. I cannot allow this dogmatism to be invalidated by the delightful instance of Mark Twain. On the subject of nationality in art, says Moore, one can talk for a long while.

Fondness for his native country may not appear to be a chief mark of the genius of George Moore, and *Parnell and His Island* may even seem the plainest contradiction of such a claim. Yet it is obvious that he has, at any rate, that primary affection which, as we have just observed, is restricted to the physical shape and character of the land, the local affection which is naturally stronger in poets than in other men. He would fain be esteemed a citizen of the world but, like the poet's, his heart lodges in a narrower field. Even this early book is redeemed by touches of that deft and tender drawing which twenty or thirty years of work were to bring to delicious mastery; for among the first of countless sketches of patrimonial scenes is—'The day dreams tenderly, and in the genial sunlight the pink dresses of the girls are sweet spots of colour, and the wide lake, with all its reeds and islands and shallowing shores, sparkles like a hand-mirror in the sun.' Other passages of the same affection occur, and if they have now mainly an historical or psychological interest, they serve also to give a pleasanter tone to an uneasy, complaining book.

The years that crept by after the publication of *Parnell and His Island* were years of imaginative divorce from Ireland; and it was long before he awoke and realized that the question of nationality was one which would not for ever leave him at peace. *Ave* opens with that question, and as he ponders he recollects his own half-unconscious truism that art must be parochial in the beginning to become cosmopolitan in the end.

'I began to think of the soul which Edward Martyn had told me I had lost in Paris and London, and if it were true that whoever casts off tradition

K

is like a tree transplanted into uncongenial soil.
Tourguénéff was of that opinion : " Russia can do
without any one of us, but none of us can do without
Russia "—one of his sentimental homilies grown
wearisome from constant repetition, true, perhaps,
of Russia, but utterly untrue of Ireland. Far more
true would it be to say that an Irishman must fly
from Ireland if he would be himself. Englishmen,
Scotchmen, Jews, do well in Ireland—Irishmen
never ; even the patriot has to leave Ireland to get
a hearing. We must leave Ireland ; and I did well
to listen in Montmartre.'

The talent he brought into the world might have produced rarer fruit if it had been cultivated less sedulously,
he muses ; Ballinrobe or the Nouvelle Athènes—which ?
But the question is not merely a personal one ; Ireland
itself—was it not strange that Ireland should have produced so little literature ? for there is a pathos in Ireland,
in its people, in its landscape, and in its ruins. Pondering
all this and putting it by and returning to it again in an
exquisite mood of reverie, he adds, ' I haven't thought of
Ireland for ten years, and to-night in an hour's space I
have dreamed Ireland from end to end. When shall I
think of her again ? In another ten years ; that will be
time enough to think of her again.'

It was less than ten years later that Ireland revisited
him in the persons of Edward Martyn and a stranger—
' Edward great in girth as an owl (he is nearly as neckless),
blinking behind his glasses, and Yeats lank as a rook,
a-dream in black silhouette on the flowered wall-paper.'
Their business, it appeared, since it was no doorstep
casualty, was to found a Literary Theatre in Dublin and
to get Moore's support. 'Ninety-nine, urged Martyn, is
the beginning of the Celtic Renaissance ; and Moore
quickly replied that the Celt needed a renaissance badly,
for he had been going down in the world for the last

two thousand years—a suggestion which his visitors may
very well have thought a little ungracious. Dublin, said
one of them, was the capital of the Celtic Renaissance;—
A new Florence? was the incredulous or scornful reply,
followed by the assertion that Ireland and Moore had
ever been strangers, without an idea in common. . . .
His scepticism yields to the subtle influences which steal
from Mr. Yeats's lips, until he becomes deliciously excited
at the thought of an Irish Literary Theatre and his own
participation in the Celtic Renaissance, and recalls the
first performance of the Independent Theatre, which he
had himself organized. With the story of that performance *The Strike at Arlingford* is involved, but it need not
detain us just now. *Ave* tells of the gradual entanglement
of our author in the snare of the Irish Literary Theatre;
of Moore and Martyn walking together to the rehearsals
of *The Heather Field,* 'Edward's bluff and dogmatic
shoulders contrasting with my own very agnostic sloping
shoulders;' of the rehearsals of a nondescript company
towards whom Moore soon assumed a surprisingly master-
ful position; and of the departure of the sifted and
re-sifted mummers for Dublin. 'Are you not coming with
us?' cried his oldest of friends from the moving train at
Euston, a question reinforced by a telegram of which the
words (you are invited to believe) as well as the sense ran,
'The sceptre of intelligence has passed from London to
Dublin.' Significant is it that, years after, Moore found
in that telegram the masculine persuasive force that bade
him from his study to Dublin.

'Again and again I read Edward's telegram. If it
be true, if art be winging her way westward? And a
vision rose up before me of argosies floating up the
Liffey, laden with merchandise from all the ports
of Phœnicia, and poets singing in all the bowers of
Merrion Square; and all in a new language that the
poets had learned, the English language having been

discovered by them, as it had been discovered by me, to be a declining language, a language that was losing its verbs.'

Rousseau-like, Moore acknowledges his disappointment at his unfriended entry into the new Florence; he expected, if not a deputation, at least some acquaintances to meet him, but notwithstanding his heralding telegram, there was nobody at the quay, nobody at the station, nobody at the Shelburne. He entered that hotel as any stranger from America might, unknown, unwelcomed; and it was with a sinking heart that he asked vainly if an invitation, a mere note even, had been left for him. Was it an anticipation of that later hint from Mr. Douglas Hyde that the newest of apostles might be more useful to the cause in England than in Ireland?

Happily he did not, he could not remain for long an embarrassed phantom; he was promptly immersed in the grotesque difficulty of producing such a play as *The Countess Cathleen* in the Antient Concert Rooms. His part in the adventure of the Irish Literary Theatre was admirable, and was freely acknowledged by Mr. Yeats in the first issue of the magazine published by the theatre —*Samhain* :—

'When Lady Gregory, Mr. Edward Martyn, and myself planned the Irish Literary Theatre, we decided that it should be carried on in the form we had projected for three years. We thought that three years would show whether the country desired to take up the project, and make it a part of the national life, and that we, at any rate, could return to our proper work, in which we did not include theatrical management, at the end of that time. A little later, Mr. George Moore joined us; and, looking back now upon our work, I doubt if it could have been done at all without his great knowledge of the stage; and certainly if the performances of the present year bring our adventure to a successful close, a chief part of the credit will be his.'

'I hope,' he says, in speaking of the future of the Celtic Renaissance, 'I hope to get our heroic age into verse, and to solve, for all Mr. Moore's unbelief, some problems of the speaking of verse to musical notes.' He did not want dramatic blank verse to be chanted, as people understand that word, but neither did he want actors to speak as prose what he had taken much trouble to write as verse. *Ave* reveals how complete was the difference between Moore's idea of production and the idea of Mr. Yeats; but nevertheless our author was not discouraged, and his confession of faith (in *Samhain*) will give you part of the reason. He was moved to join his friends because he had come to know the hopelessness of all artistic effort in England; he had discovered the English decadence before he discovered his own conscience, and saw nothing around him save intellectual decay and moral degradation. But the rest of the reason was still hidden from him when *The Countess Cathleen* provoked denunciation and uproar. Was it simply the sense of beauty? '*The Countess Cathleen*,' he says, 'awakened in all who saw it a sense of beauty, and a sense of beauty, once awakened, is immortal.' Moore's loyalty to that sense had been constant.

'There has been no more disinterested movement than the Gaelic League. It has worked for the sake of the language without hope of reward or praise; and if I were asked why I put my faith in the movement, I would answer that to believe that a movement distinguished by so much self-sacrifice could fail, would be like believing in the failure of goodness itself.

'Since we began our work plays have been written, some in Irish and some in English, and we shall be forgiven if we take a little credit for having helped to awaken intellectual life in Ireland. Many will think I am guilty of exaggeration when I say that the

Irish Literary Theatre has done more to awaken intellectual life in Ireland than Trinity College.'

One does not like to speak of a double self, he murmurs, as he looks within and without and reverts to his visit to Dublin, but he thinks it necessary to speak of his self-consciousness; for although that is a quality which he shares with every human being, no two human beings are alike in everything, and his self-consciousness may be different from another's. His, then, has always been a good friend to him, for as he walks through the streets scene after scene rises up in his mind, in which he takes all the parts and utters all the dialogue. 'In my novels I can only write tragedy, and in life play nothing but light comedy, and the one explanation that occurs to me of the dual personality is that I write according to my soul, and act according to my appearance.' His opinion of his own appearance, as that of a comic writer and comic actor, is itself amusing, for that noticeable, mood-matching countenance, which is so attractive to watch in its changes and responses, hardly shows 'the secret of a smiling face.' For these unwritten scenes almost any event is sufficient impulse or pretext.

'Never did Nature furnish me with so rich a theme as she did when Yeats and Edward came to see me in Victoria Street. The subject was apparent to me from the beginning, and the reason given for my having accepted to act with them in the matter of the Irish Literary Theatre (the temptation to have a finger in every literary pie) has to be supplemented. There was another, and a greater temptation—the desire to secure a good part in the comedy which I foresaw, and which had for the last three weeks unrolled itself, scene after scene, exceeding any imagination of mine. Who could have invented the extraordinary rehearsals, Miss Vernon and her psaltery? Or the incident of Yeats's annunciation

that Edward had consulted a theologian in London?
My anger was not assumed : Yeats told me he never
saw a man so angry; how could it be otherwise,
ready as I am always to shed the last drop of my
blood to defend art? Yet the spectacle of Edward
and the theologian heresy-hunting through the pages
of Yeats's play was behind my anger always, an
irresistible comicality that I should be able to enjoy
some day. And then the telegram saying that the
sceptre of intelligence had passed from London to
Dublin. Who could have invented it?'

Yes, art is outfaced in such an exquisite disarray of
possibilities as these incidents present, the whole forming
a kind of first act in which our Sterne-like author was
privileged to be both actor and audience. The second act
of *The Irish Literary Comedy* began to unfold itself in a
scene between Moore and Mr. Yeats, the theme being the
ecclesiastical opposition to *The Countess Cathleen*, developed
inconsequently in succeeding pages amid interruptions and
diversions, and charming irrelevancies such as a conversation with Gill, and Gill's scheme for a kind of Dublin
Nouvelle Athènes.

A further note on the call to Ireland is given in the
speech which Moore delivered at a dinner to the Irish
Literary Theatre ; for although he avows that he is the
only living Irishman who cannot speak for ten minutes, he
is able to read a speech and to smile at the event. It is
an amusing, reminiscent speech, ending with the phrase,
' Twenty years hence this week in Ireland will be looked
back upon with reverence.' Alas! and twenty years have
gone.

The story of Mr. Edward Martyn's play, *The Tale of a
Town*, as Moore relates it, forms the third act in *The Irish
Literary Comedy*. A shadow used to come into the play-
wright's face at the thought of his responsibility in writing

The Tale of a Town, for heresies frightened him; and
when Moore read the whole five acts and concluded it
was a worse play than *The Heather Field,* he conceived it
his duty to write to dear Edward, saying that not one of
the five acts could interest any possible audience, Irish or
English or Esquimaux. Beautiful is a durable friendship,
founded in boyhood and surviving the rude, imperious
shock of æsthetic candour; and no friendship is more
wonderful than this between George Moore and Mr.
Edward Martyn. . . . Discussion of the play was reserved
until the friends journeyed to Bayreuth, but discussion
anywhere is difficult when one party is silent and allows
but dim glimpses of his reproachful soul. The pity which
had been gathering in our novelist's breast melted away
at the thought that the dramatist was but an amateur
after all; and then again his natural kindness revived on
hearing that his criticism had really poisoned his friend's
recent tour with a party of archæologists. 'You're a very
good critic,' repeated Martyn again and again, as Moore
tapped and tapped his sharp points in; proving obstinate
when alterations were offered, because they were not his
own. 'The amateur always puts himself before his work
. . . whereas the artist is interested in the thing itself,
and will accept readily a suggestion from anyone, if he
thinks that it will be to the advantage of the work to do
so. *Je prends mon bien où je le trouve.* . . . Anybody who
can improve a sentence of mine by the omission of a
comma or by the placing of a comma is looked upon as
my dearest friend.'—Perfect and austere passion of the
artist! How imperfect is Mr. Martyn's judgment, and not
only in the matter of his play, is sharply discovered in a
story of his mistaking a window exactly six years old for a
thirteenth-century window, a story told not to display his
ignorance but his vagueness—'in order to show Edward
when the fog descends upon him. His comprehension is
never the same. . . . He is like Ireland, the country he

came from : sometimes a muddling fog, sometimes a delicious mist with a ray of light striking through.'

The third act develops but slowly, the subject emerging in the arrival of the friends at Bayreuth, when Moore asked dear Edward about the revision, and for reply received the manuscript with hardly a word in propitiation of doom. A *séance de collaboration* would have passed the morning nicely, but Mr. Martyn could not collaborate any more than the sheep with the butcher. His play needed revision, and revision was left to Moore, who not infrequently carried the manuscript away and forgot it in music, or in walks in the shady avenues of the town, or in the Zoological Gardens, where the finest of lions proved more beguiling. ' He seemed as lonely as myself,' says our author, ' and I often imagined us two together, side by side, *The Tale of a Town* in my left hand, reading it aloud, while with the right I combed his great mane for him. Which would he resent, the reading or the combing ? '—And so from Bayreuth home-ward, until the friends parted with the necessary alterations still unachieved, for at the mention of altera-tions Mr. Martyn's face clouded ; and when the discussion was perilously reopened at Tillyra, ' Leave me my play ! ' he cried, adding that he could not act otherwise, for Moore was giving the play a different colour. Moore thereupon altered it himself, and then the opinion of Mr. Yeats upon the changes was sought. Pity, or a resolve to be gentler than Mr. Yeats, tempted Moore to say that he could see no reason why the play should not be performed ; but conscience forbade the lie. Hence *The Tale of a Town* by Edward Martyn became *The Bending of the Bough* by George Moore, for the original author refused to have anything to do with the later version and would not allow his name to be used. There was nothing for it, then, says Moore, with meek remorse, but to sign a work that was not his own :—' I, too, am sacrificing to Cathleen ni Houlihan; one sacrifice brings many.' And with that smile the comedy of the Irish Literary Theatre, as Moore conceives it, may be said to end.

It seems that *The Bending of the Bough* was written or finished not in Ireland, after all, but in London, a fact which is made the occasion of one of many sudden transitions in the cunning retrospect of *Hail and Farewell*. Into the simple eddies of dramatic composition a great stone was cast. 'It seemed an exquisite joke to voice Ireland's woes, until one day I stopped in Ebury Street, abashed; for it was not a victory for our soldiers that I desired to read in the paper just bought from the boy who had rushed past me, yelling, News from the Front, but one for the Boers. The war was forgotten, and I walked on slowly, frightened lest this sudden and inexplicable movement of soul should be something more than a merely accidental vacillation. It may be no more, and it may be that I am changing.' When a great stone is cast into such a quiet and such a secret pool, the violence of the movement is almost startling to those looking on; and in truth this sudden shock of external upon internal, of the crude active upon the subtle quiescent, caused or disclosed a change in our author of which he was morbidly conscious, asking his friends if it had not touched his countenance. Was there indeed something in the external world which had for him the hitherto unapproached power of an æsthetic problem? 'The morning paper was picked up from the hearthrug, and the news of the capture of our troops read again and again, the same thrill of joy coming into my heart. The Englishman that was in me (he that wrote *Esther Waters*) had been overtaken and captured by the Irishman.'

Nothing more lucid has been said of George Moore than this that he has said of himself. Despair of art drove him to Ireland, Ireland taught him the value of freedom in South Africa, and South Africa in turn taught him how much he owed to Ireland. The dramatic faculty, and even the more simple and candid narrative gift, have their several seductions; and it is hard for such an inward-gazing writer as Moore to refrain from inventing experiences which will justify his literary expression of them. A glance at his incessant dramatizing habit suggests that since his own delight in a sometime passion for a free Boer State is so transparent, it may have been quickened only when it became necessary for his narrative. But such a doubt is unfair, and he is as near to the truth as any man can step in writing of himself, when he records that out of the wreck and rubble of his former self a new self had arisen; he had learned that ideas are as necessary to us as our skins. But sitting like one flayed, he wondered what new ideas would clothe him again, and into what new life he was being led. When he remembers his former self, he hates it as much as he hates England; but we know that although he is a good hater, the inward discord which is both hell and heaven has seldom fretted the deeps of his being. His casual hatred does not preclude enjoyment, for he took pleasure in the midst of his sorrow—a grim pleasure, truly, as he admits—in calling on his friends and watching their faces while he assured them that the recall of the English troops in South Africa would be the wisest thing that could be done. 'Love of cruelty is inveterate in the human being!' But human beings are complicated, and the invisible telegraphy of affections and ideas flies over many wires, or is broken, jangled and lost; for all that cruelty, nothing but the war interested him, the obsession becoming more terrible daily and the surrender of his sanity more imminent. A shameful materialism revolted him, the revolt being aggravated—and his eyes clear again in noting this—by memories of his former love of England; and musing upon England, with all that was once sweet turned sour, his thoughts lapse characteristically into a meditation upon the æsthetic ignobility of the English, until he wonders whether even Shelley, whose poetry he loves more than anything else in the world, was free from the taint of England. Unuttered but implicit in all his impeachment and complaint is the thought—Must he again leave England, and for longer than before, and seek in Ireland for redemption from moral degradation and æsthetic futility? Revisiting the familiar Sussex Downs he found no more than an uneasy anodyne, and after a while the discontent with England waxed sharp again, until even the face of the country wearied him as he looked along the hills, or at night saw shining garlands hung between the coast towns.—For there is no country in England, even the hills are enriched with lights. His thoughts turned to the neighbourhood of Moore Hall, the dim waste about Lough Carra, to other places and other times; for an idea had come into his life, without wishing and without warning, and, although repulsed, had taken possession of him and made him hate all that he had loved.

But it was something far more particular and definite that forced him back to Ireland, for the Irish Literary Theatre was taking three fresh plays to Dublin, including that sad monument of another's magnanimity, *The Bending of the Bough.*

His immediate task was the reading of a paper on the literary necessity of small languages, asserting opinions that are merely intellectual opinions, invented, he says smiling, to justify the existence of the Gaelic League. Candour again persuades him to write that some Gaelic Leaguers who heard him were cynical, for they had not forgotten or forgiven *Parnell and His Island;* nay, it was whispered that he had returned to Ireland to write about the country and its ideas, and would afterwards make fun of them if it suited him to do so. . . . Dangerous is it to suggest revenges to repulsed genius; and often must the cynics have deplored their prophecies. Some months later, when the cloud cast by this minor comedy over his belief in the Celtic Renaissance had dissolved, another theme was developed, presenting another occasion of escape from England—the proposal that Moore should write, in conjunction with Mr. Yeats, *Diarmuid and Grania*. The scene of this rare collaboration, this impossible conjunction, was fixed at Coole, already (if the phrase be not impertinent) a kind of twilight nursing home for the Irish Literary Theatre; for there had plays been brought forth in the ardour of the cause. ' In years to come Coole will be historic, later still, it will be legendary, a sort of Minstrelburg, the home of the Bell Branch Sing rs. . . . We shall all become folk-lore in time to come, F ns and Diarmuids and Usheens, every one of us.'

What collaboration was possible? I do not propose to insert here a character of Mr. Yeats, for a whole book would be wanted. Who doubts his genius, his yet more eminent skill in the craft of words, by which even faint thoughts and fading imaginations may be dressed in beauty? Extravagances have been uttered in his honour, but who does not excuse them by saying, He is a delightful artist? The most froward of critics would do no more than hint a fault and disguise an uncertain dislike; and very few would listen. Mr. Yeats has this in common with greater writers—that his genius is proven by its inconstancy. Talent is constant, and the mere craft of language may be unvarying; but Mr. Yeats's gift is uncertain and incalculable, sometimes abased to a mere decadence, as in the lyrics upon a certain lady who was dying :—

' Propped upon pillows, rouge on the pallor of her face.
She would not have us sad because she is lying there,
And when she meets our gaze her eyes are laughter lit,
Her speech a wicked tale that we may vie with her,

Matching our broken-hearted wit against her wit,
Thinking of Saints and of Petronius Arbiter——'

sometimes lifting upon stronger wings and sounding the
purer music of how many lyrics of his earlier and later
periods alike. Nor in verse alone has his genius shone
brightly, for there are certain essays and that too-brief
fragment of autobiography, *Reveries Over Childhood and
Youth*. His genius is truly individual and lonely in its
finest exercise, owing little or nothing to school or
influence; only his weaker writings may be assigned to
the influence of others. But I think that if we could not
have Mr. Yeats's work without having the Irish Literary
Theatre—the largest of concessions to the improbable—
the Irish Literary Theatre would yet have been justified
abundantly. Nor may we forget the influence which Mr.
Yeats in turn exercised on his friend, who now, for all his
asperities, freely admits his debt; for he never shrinks
from acknowledging what he owes to others who have
helped him to write a little better.—He was an excellent
schoolmaster for me, he will say of Mr. Yeats.

But the conjunction of genius with genius is perilous,
and what collaboration was possible between Moore and Mr.
Yeats? Collaboration?—'Feeling like a swordsman that
meets for the first time a redoubtable rival, I reminded
Yeats that in his last letter he had said we must decide in
what language the play should be written—not whether it
should be written in English or in Irish (neither of us
knew Irish), but in what style.' But Mr. Yeats also was a
swordsman and too wise to seek a bubble reputation. Of
what good will your dialogue be to me, he retorted, if it is
written in the language of *Esther Waters*? Words followed
upon the use of dialogue. Moore admits his own regret
that he should have suggested to his rival so hazardous an
experiment as a peasant Grania? We're writing an heroic
play, he cried, and dialogue would render heroes farcical,

for folk is always farce and it is not (he subtly muses, I presume, long after this reconstructed duel took place)—it is not until the language has been strained through many brilliant minds that tragedy can be written in it. Surely the play had better be written in the language of the Bible.

And once again, what collaboration was possible, since Moore argued that they would have to begin by writing a dictionary of the words that may not be used and the ideas that may not be introduced? Every writer has his own catalogue of inhibited words, his own rhythm, his own voice, his own ear; and working with another the most that can be looked for is an antiphonal concord. But the inhibitions proposed for joint observance were not limited to ideas and words, for Moore protests against the poet's wish that he should not waste time by writing descriptions of Nature.—Is it not amusing, for who more winningly than Moore can write descriptions of Nature? and to forfeit that exercise was a hardy request. Primitive man, Mr. Yeats had said, did not look at trees for beauty but for use, but Moore contends that it is safer to assume that primitive man thought and felt much as we do; and again the argument turned upon the virtues of dialect. 'But, Yeats, a play cannot be written in dialect, nor do I think it can be written by turning common phrases which rise up into the mind into uncommon phrases;' and he adds a sigh, for it seemed he had come to Coole upon a fruitless errand—that he would never be able to write *Diarmuid and Grania* in collaboration with Mr. Yeats.

Many pleasant hours, nevertheless, passed in quarrelling as to how the play should be written, Lady Gregory, Moore remembers, coming to their help with a suggestion that one should write the play and the other go over it; while they were together they should confine themselves

to the construction of the play. To this important aspect
Mr. Yeats contributed his theories, saying that the first
act of every good play is horizontal, the second perpendicular, while the third is circular, being a return to the first
theme. There, he exclaimed, as he recounted the story of
the first act—there we have the horizontal; you see how it
extends from right to left. But Moore, who is a man of
letters rather than an æsthetician, wondered if it did not
extend from left to right; and when the second act was
likewise explained and termed perpendicular, it became
necessary for Lady Gregory to beseech him to be calm.
No comedy conceived by the novelist alone or by the poet
alone might be half so perfect as the comedy issuing from
their fond and vain co-operation; Sterne himself hardly
created a situation more humorous. A desperate suggestion
that Moore should write the play in French was seized on
by the others, resulting in a midnight proposal that his
French text should be translated into the English of Lady
Gregory, the English translated into Irish, and the Irish
re-translated into English—for Mr. Yeats to put style upon
it. Strange are the innocencies of genius, stranger is the
fact that Moore should have left England to do his part
by writing the French text. *Hail and Farewell* contains a
piece of his French dialogue, and his own comment that
a writer can think, but not think profoundly, in a foreign
language. Only by printing a specimen of this dialogue
could he hope to convince anybody that two such literary
lunatics as Mr. Yeats and himself existed contemporaneously
in Ireland. What was all this nonsense that kept on
drumming in his head about the Irish language and Anglo-
Irish? Vexed and humiliated, he suddenly left France
and returned to England. As for Mr. Yeats, he announced
Diarmuid and Grania as a prose play in three acts by
Moore and himself, founded on that most famous of all
Irish stories, the story of the lovers whose beds were the
cromlechs. He believed there was nothing in it to offend

anybody, but made no promises. 'We thought our plays inoffensive last year and the year before, but we were accused the one year of sedition, and the other of heresy. We await the next accusation with a cheerful curiosity.' When the Irish Literary Theatre wound up its three years of experience with the production of this strangely begotten play, he recorded the large audiences which it drew, but acknowledged that it was a good deal blamed by those who knew only the modern text of the legend; the version used in *Diarmuid and Grania* being fully justified by Irish and Scottish folk-lore and certain early Irish texts. . . . Extravagant as the whole episode appears, I wonder if it might not have been yet more amusing had Mr. Yeats followed this relation with his own.

Moore's unpremeditated return to London (as we are to presume it to have been) was really a return like that of a wanderer to the fold; for at once the noise of the South African War reached him again, and his thoughts were resolved into a prayer for the humiliation of the oppressors of that distant southern Eire—a prayer not very likely to be answered, and yet answered. Far off now is the struggle of De Wet. It seems that while it was drawing near to an end, Moore received letters telling him that quarter would not be given if a token of surrender were raised. Too horrible! he cried, and tried to publish the plot; but London newspapers refused. Only in Ireland, then, was there any sense of right, and so he hastened to Dublin, dictated the story to the editor of the *Freeman's Journal*, and at length drew from the military authorities a repudiation of the 'plot.'

One virtue of Moore's great romantic autobiography is that it displays the surface as well as discovers the depths of his mind; and he has not scrupled to attribute to himself a pettiness which makes his righteousness appear merely self-righteousness. He believed himself, he says,

L

to be God's instrument for saving an honest Protestant people from the bad designs of a Jew and a nail-maker. The dramatic instinct, you will say, had not decayed; Ireland's apostle had become the Boer's saviour, and he saw himself as protagonist in a spiritual war. Hence his mind was prepared like St. Paul's on that journey which was so strongly to impress the author of *The Brook Kerith*. As he walked towards Chelsea it seemed that a presence followed him; a thin sensation at first, but deepening every moment until he dared not look behind lest he should see something which was not of this world. In a devout collectedness he heard an external voice behind him saying distinctly, *Go to Ireland!* but when he looked there was no one near. And again the voice sounded as he walked on. It is the third instance of the echo-augury in his reconstructed life, but the first in which the call was moral and not æsthetic. Was it for that reason that he questioned the voice? Hard it seemed to abandon his project of going to live in what he thought was his own country, France; but the command was now repeated, *Go to Ireland! Go to Ireland!* the voice speaking within five or six inches of his ear, and so distinctly that his hand was stretched out to the speaker. A few weeks later, being still disobedient to the heavenly charge, the 'presence' seemed to fill his room and overpower him; as he strove to resist, it forced him to his knees and he could not help praying. Doubt was no longer possible, he had been summoned to Ireland.

Under Providence, then, De Wet and Kitchener and Chamberlain had conspired for the sake not of South Africa but of Ireland; their strife, blind and uninformed, had resulted in the appointment of a Celtic Messiah; they were the prime authors—if in this dark, mysterious world any can be called prime authors—of *Hail and Farewell*, a book not to be written until years had elapsed, for the art of writing it was not yet discovered. The stars in their courses never poured stranger influence upon the wandering heaps that flow between the shores of men, than at the beginning of the twentieth century, when the conquest of a people was needed to send a writer to Ireland to beget a masterpiece of imaginative art. Nor have they often been kinder to letters than when they permitted that echo-augury to be repeated, so providing a full and perfect close to the first volume of this autobiography.

His tardy response to the bidding was complete and uncalculating—he himself tells of the difficulties he became involved in before he was able to disappear from London and emerge like a new-washed orb from the Irish Sea; and the Irish difficulties seemed as great as the English, for he had almost as much trouble in finding a new habitation as in leaving the old one. The search is made the occasion of a study of A. E., that kindly, whimsical, Moorish creation, about whom our author loves to group his fancies, speaking of him now as a child speaks of his father, now as a father of a loved child, and always with that affection which we bestow upon slightly diminutive and precious things. To A. E. he confides his enthusiasms and disappointments:—Nobody wanted him —why had he come to Dublin? He had hoped for a welcome, without bonfires and banners, but not without some appreciation of his sacrifice ; and once again his hope was vain.

What was that sacrifice? He tells the story of Whistler saying to him, years before—I suppose nothing matters to you but your writing. 'His words went to the bottom of my soul, frightening me ; and I have asked myself, again and again, if I were capable of sacrificing brother, sister, mother, fortune, friend, for a work of art. . . . One is near madness when nothing really matters but one's work.' It was a lucid madness, and a lucid madness it has remained; and if we accept that term madness, we must always emphasize the qualification. He thought the Boer War disproved Whistler's charge, but *Hail and Farewell* shows the height and the depth, the length and the breadth of his renunciation, and how secure the love of letters remained.—Why had he come to Ireland? The lack of welcome disturbed his faith, for if England was hateful, Ireland was somewhat repugnant.

Again and again he turns to A. E., to the A. E. of his quick invention, often to share his joys, often to banish his doubts, but most often to answer his arguments. 'When he left me, a certain mental sweetness seemed to have gone out of the air.' A. E. tempted him to recount the strange circumstances of his call to Ireland, and affirmed that the gods that inspired Moore's return to Ireland were not Asiatic; and talking of local gods and of the Druids, A. E. heard his friend proposing that they should go forth together and preach the Danaan divinities —A. E. as Paul, and himself as Luke to take down Paul's words. 'It would be your own thoughts, my dear Moore, that you would be reporting, not mine,' was the acute reply. But there is no unkindness in Moore's long, lingering regard of A. E.; indeed the cunning elaboration that forms the portrait of his friend presents the subject much as a 'figure in a carpet.' More truly yet might it be said that in Moore's eyes A. E. is like the prized carpet, as real as the Aubusson, as finely proportioned, as subtly hued, and almost as fondly gazed upon by the eyes of ownership. There is something wonderful in the art that can charge a portrait with such opposites—with invention and verisimilitude, romance and literality, making it at once an image of the subject and a reflection of the artist. It is A. E. who listens, or is presumed to listen, to Moore's speculation upon the Druids and the Renaissance, A. E. who answers concerning everything, saying at one moment, Admire the bridge without troubling yourself as to what its fate will be when you are gone ; and at another, Men knew great truths thousands of years ago, and it seems to me that these truths are returning. . . . Moore does not invent out of nothing ; he develops, and brings his oaks from acorns, his A. E. from what his eye has seen, his ear heard, and his unresting imagination rained its seasons upon. In his memories of A. E., he says, there must be so much of himself, that he hesitates to attribute some of these reminiscent phrases to his friend ; such as, for example, ' The folk-tales of Connaught have ever lain nearer to the hearts of the people than those of Galilee.' A. E., it is recorded, floating as easily above lowlier minds as did Coleridge when Hazlitt heard him (he, too, entranced), finished a wonderful evening by drawing a portrait of Moore—' clearly the work of one who has been with the Gods, for in it my hair is hyacinthine, and my eyes are full of holy light.'

It may be, he admits, that he is caricaturing A. E., as he proceeds to sharpen the outline and deepen the shadows : but A. E. remains the one of all his friends whose spirit burns with the purest and most constant energy, giving the simplest of all light amid the confusions which un-happily make up—I had almost said compose—national aspirations in Ireland. Moore does not laugh at A. E., he does not measure or question him, but accepts and admires. Scruples of conscience are his speciality, he admits with an epicurean smile ; but he does not look for them in that clear and unhaunted nature. He finds them in Gill, who seems to have been flashed into visibility in order to give substance to the mistrust which so soon supplanted the first enthusiasm for Cathleen ni Houlihan. Should Gill accept office under the English Government ? ' Gill should have consulted me, for he would have gotten from me the advice that would have been agreeable to him ;' but men do not consult their friends when their deter-mination is to walk the thorny path. I need not remind the reader that Gill is the target for those swift and sharp arrows which Moore shoots with faultless accuracy, if not always with perfect coolness. He delights in displaying in Gill the follies and vanities of human nature—follies and vanities so numerous, so unmercifully displayed, that you wonder that a single head can contain them all, yet never wonder long enough to question the consistency of the imaginary portrait. What was it, do you ask, that provoked this subtle constructive surgery? I cannot tell —a physical antipathy, perhaps, the first sight of the beard which brushes so many pages of *Hail and Farewell*. I will not plunge into the history of the Irish Renaissance, and only ask myself whether it is not obscurely necessary that a Renaissance bring with it offences of one kind and another; in one country offences against morals, in another offences against manners. My concern is the simple one of tracing the character, not of A. E. or Gill, but of the artist who has composed their effigies, and of the influence upon him of long acquaintance with the particular stars of that now darkened firmament. *Hail and Farewell* is remarkable in its devotion to an antipathy. It was not published until some time after Moore's sojourn in Ireland was over, and to few men is it given to nurse either their admiration or their contempt with such perfect success as he achieves. Admiration cools, gods are dethroned or diminished in glory, and the contempt which we feel one year fades to indifference the next; but Moore's admiration of A. E. and his manifest affection for Edward Martyn do not perceptibly dwindle, nor does time rob him of his contempt for others. Men are sometimes ashamed of an overweighted dislike; but Moore has avowed his desire not to conceal or be ashamed of anything, no, not even of the touch of inhumanity which gives a final salience to his amazing inventions.

This portrait of Gill, to take the chief instance, is a portrait of one Irishman by another, and the artist has genius to speed him. Gill, too, gives him opportunities, which had to be found somewhere, of reflections upon the personalities which made the Celtic Renaissance conspicuous and pathetic; the opportunity, for instance, of saying that the Celt is so ineffectual because his dreams go one way and his actions go another. Every race produces more Gills than Davitts; and when, he proceeds, in 1901 he went to live in Ireland, he found Gill the centre of the Irish Literary and Agricultural Party, and looked on as the one man who could weather the political peril. ' A cheerful, superficial nature!' Some men, he says, in speaking of Gill, spend their lives watching bees or ants, noting down the habits of these insects; his own pleasure is to watch the human mind, noting how unselfish instincts rise to the surface and sink back again; and so he watches this kindly-tempered man who had floated down the tide of casual ideas into the harbour of thirteen hundred a year. Moore sees himself as sacrificed for Cathleen ni Houlihan, again and again playing with that attractive theme; and Gill had the satisfaction, perhaps more permanent and also more perplexing, of seeing himself as a sacrifice to Moore's art. But it was an involuntary sacrifice, since few who are not men of genius can bear to look ridiculous.

Gentle enough, however, is the earlier treatment of Gill in comparison with that chapter of *Vale* in which Gill and Plunkett are joined in martyrdom for the purposes of this matchless entomologist. Moore complains that others have complained that instead of creating such characters as Esther Waters and Dick Lennox, he has wasted himself in mere portrait-painting of his friends; and he answers that we all use models, and that he used models for Esther Waters and Dick Lennox. The models are presented for intelligent study, and the artist must use them; and has not Flaubert presented models for Moore's use? When he wrote *Bouvard and Pecuchet* he thought he was creating, but he was really giving new names to Nature's own creations, Plunkett and Gill.

Our novelist, it seems, was interested in a Co-operative Egg Society, which his brother had prompted Plunkett to establish, and he wanted to discuss the co-operative egg when he met Plunkett; finding, however, that nothing bored him so much as detail and that, like every other Irishman, he loved dreaming. But the dreams of Plunkett and Gill were influential, for a substantial Government grant was obtained, in order to found a Department of Agriculture and Art in Ireland; and it is at this point that the dreamers are invested with the mask of Flaubert's types.—It is thirty years, says Moore, since he read *Bouvard and Pecuchet*, but his unscrupling study of his friends revives his memory of that masterpiece, and he proceeds with the tenderness of Fabre towards a spider, or a spider towards two flies, in the task of re-identifying or re-incarnating the French writer's conception. . . . Flaubert, says our novelist, had he seen what I see, would have murmured regretfully, I have been anticipated; Plunkett and Gill have transferred dreams into real life. The adventure of the calf that died, the adventure of the Ballina shoe factory, the Galway oyster-beds, the piers, the eggs, the cheese, and—consummation of inestimable folly!—the adventure of Asses in Ireland, all these are briefly recited amid such comments as, ' They found consolation in the thought that experimentation is the source of all knowledge '; and ' Pecuchet hesitated, with his usual instinct for compromise.' I dare not attempt to select the most exquisite of all the exquisite touches of ungentle mockery which make *Vale* unforgettable—it is not for me to say unforgivable also; even to a generation that has won a great war and discovered the cost afterwards, these incidents are astonishing. The justice of the satire may be most properly questioned by those concerned in the development of the Co-operative Society with which

Sir Horace Plunkett has been so honourably associated. But whether it is questioned or not, this chapter illustrates more than any other the perfect detachment which our author succeeded in cultivating until he had become all eyes for others' humours and weaknesses, all ears to every echo, and all ice to every little naked imp of pity. This disillusionment, disharmonization, disintegration—call it what you will—was a gradual process, hastened by certain antipathies, retarded by obstinate affections, but slowly going on until he found himself simply out of humour with Ireland. The process embraced most of the men he was in the habit of meeting and thinking about, and the forbearance of the injured would surely have been impossible had *Hail and Farewell* been a less perfectly wrought piece of imaginative art. Generosity and a love of English literature may even have persuaded Dr. Hyde to pardon such a sentence as this that tells of the anticipated disappearance of the Gaelic League, if not the earlier sentences which it would be too cruel to repeat here.

'It drifted back whence it came. Worn and broken and water-logged, it drifted back to the original Connemara bog-hole, to sink under the brown water out of sight of the quiet evening sky, unwatched, unmourned save by dear Edward, who will weep a few tears, I am sure, when the last bubbles arise and break.'

It was one day while he was walking with John Eglinton that Moore mentioned his fancy for writing a volume of short stories about Irish life, and he adds for our information that his search for subjects was immediately rewarded by the theme of "The Wedding Gown," budded from *A Mummer's Wife*; the new story proving so pleasant in the eyes of a priest that it was translated into Irish, and thought by the late Kuno Meyer to exhale in the Irish version a folk-flavour wanting in the English original. Other stories followed and, like the first, were printed in *The New Ireland Review*; but after a while the priestly censorship of subjects for that Review created difficulties, and those difficulties became a grief to the Irish Turgenev. Father Tom and himself, he reflects, had lain side by side in harbour for a while; but he began to feel that these stories were drawing him away from Catholic Ireland.

So liberated, other stories came, incident following upon incident, he recollects, with bewildering prodigality. Thus the best of the stories in *The Untilled Field* was founded upon an episode of the country, and received the title 'The Wild Goose'; but at the moment I do not wish to think of this short story as literature only, but as indicating that deepening dissent from Catholicism which was to hasten our author's separation from the leaders of the Celtic Renaissance. He saw, through the magic casement of this short story, how impossible it was to enjoy independence of body and soul in Ireland. 'They bring their Catholicism with them wherever they go. . . . Every race gets the religion it deserves.' In his half-bantering, half-serious way he launches his perplexity at dear Edward, fearing lest it cool before it has pierced the triple brass of his friend's consistency. The decline of art was coincident with the Union of the Irish Church with Rome, and it is impossible to deny that Irish Catholics had written very little. Father Tom had admitted that. Excited, and standing as he thought on the verge of a great discovery, he cries, Which is at fault—the race or Catholicism? A long discussion ensues, reverting to the dawn of recorded time and ending with the nineteenth century and the remark, How strange that nobody should have seen before that Catholicism is an intellectual desert!—How often, let me add, has it happened that one has waked in early morning, with a remnant of a dream in one's head or eyes, a half-formed vision; and in that delicious ferment of the brain it has seemed that the greatest conceptions of the imaginative world are about to be captured and confined to verse or prose. The dream fades, the vision clouds, excitement wanes, and the aspect of the world is common again. With such extravagant, deluding swiftness of mind does Moore awake with his new opinion, excited by it as the dreamer with his dreams. ' In Mayo, almost in my own parish, was fought the most famous battle in Irish legend; from Mayo came Davitt, the Land League, and a new discovery which will recreate Ireland. The shepherds will fight hard, but the sword I found in my garden will prevail against the crozier, and by degrees the parish priest will pass away, like his ancestor the Druid! '

In default of this salvation from faith it is not merely an intellectual desert that he foresees, but a depopulated Ireland as well, Ned Carmody's lament in 'The Wild Goose' being Moore's own lament. The impulse which had borne him to Ireland had begun to shake when he noticed that the nuns upon whose garden his own garden in Ely Place looked were gradually absorbing the neighbourhood; and when, one day, in the course of an afternoon walk, he counted eight monastic houses in a single small district of South Dublin, he dreamed of the time when all Dublin would be a convent. With eyes so washed of their sometime blindness, he stared at the thronging priests and seminarists, the great cathedrals and comfortable presbyteries, and the newspapers with their tales of a kind of blackmail levied by the Church upon the landed and landless alike. There was no heresy in Ireland, and the Modernist movement won no adherence; Ireland, it seemed, was as incapable of independent thought as Thibet; and paradoxically he calls it an essentially unreligious country, himself being one of the few Irishmen interested in religious questions. The reality of his exasperation may be judged from this confusion of religion with religious discussion. . . . I have always felt like a stranger in my own country, he muses, in a phrase of sore lucidity.

I have remarked that it was art that took him to France and art (assisted by a hatred of the English oppression of a pious South African people) that sent him back to Ireland. And it was clearly not in the interest of Protestantism, then, that he hastened first to A. E. (who accepted the discovery as commonplace) and next to Gill, with whom he discussed all the possible reasons for secession from Rome, adding his new reason— literature. And with this postulate before them, Moore and Gill walked the streets of the Celtic Florence, darting swallow-like for Catholic gnats up and down the stream of time. . . . The two whetstones of the mind are sex and religious discussion, and we must keep passing our intelligence up one and down the other:—and so pondering he decided for good and all that he owed the preservation of his intelligence to his theological interests. Sex, it seemed, no longer counted as an interest in the urgency of this great discovery and impending divorce from the mind of his native country.

Of the sincerity of this obstinate questioning there need be little doubt. He could not keep his discovery to himself. From Gill he hurried to Eglinton with— ' My belief is that Catholic countries haven't produced a book.' Somewhere in *Ave* he had written, ' Let us be content with the theory, and refrain from collecting facts to support it, for in doing so we shall come upon excep- tions, and these will have to be explained away ' ; but that attitude would not suit him now, and he discussed the facts and exceptions untiringly and with such a concession to reason as to put it precisely that ninety-five per cent. of the world's literature had been produced by Pro- testants and Agnostics. By literature, of course, he meant literature excluding theology and mainly consisting of imaginative work; and, confirmed by all that he had said to Eglinton, he proceeded to Martyn, who answered the Columbus of ideas with a smile—'What, another! I thought you had come to the end of them. Your first was the naturalistic novel, your second impressionistic painting'—and the third, retorted Moore, was Martyn's plays and the Irish Renaissance, which was but a bubble. Of what use is it to change the language of Ireland, since Catholics cannot write? But when his friend asked, 'What, then, about your mission?' Moore was overwhelmed; it seemed that his life had been sacrificed for a bubble.

After Martyn, Meyer. Plant an acorn in a vase and the oak must burst the vase or become dwarfed, and from Meyer he obtained the support of German literature; and concluded pathetically that his life was at an end. He had been led to Ireland in the hope of reviving the language, for a new language was required to enwomb a new literature; but Ireland would not forego her superstitions for the sake of literature, and dogma and literature were incompatible.

Justice, however—that wilful, sardonic deity—demanded that a Catholic should be heard in the defence of Catholicism; and who better than his brother might defend it? 'You don't mean to tell me that you have brought me all the way from Mayo to argue with you about religion?' Whereupon our author explained that he had come to Ireland (obedient to a heavenly visitant) to help literature, and if he found that dogma and literature were incompatible, he must say so. Catholics may not speculate, and the greatest literature had come out of speculation on the value of life. 'What I'm saying to you to-day,' he cried, 'will be written to-morrow or after—I'm using you as an audience.' It is an exercise that he loves; even in the most simple and familiar conversations of Ebury Street the charmed visitor may suspect that he is being used as an audience.

We often criticize our friend, he says, truly enough, and he sitting opposite to us, little thinking how he is being torn to pieces; but I suppose that no one has carried that practice to such perfection as George Moore. 'There are people of to-day, to-morrow, and yesterday; and the Colonel is much more of yesterday than of to-day.' He finds his brother a subject for that somewhat icy painter Velasquez, who painted the true Catholic in all his portraits of Philip, never failing to catch the faded, empty Catholic look. It has been Moore's fortune, and ours, that, sitting opposite his friends, he has not simply torn them to pieces but also put them together again— making them different, perhaps, but making them certainly whole; no mere incredible collection of the fortuitous, but characters of coherence and animation, if not of literal likeness. It has been our ill-luck, however, that none of his friends has done this for Moore; but in this pursuit of an idea we may catch something of his superficial and more of his profounder personality, and we are helped by that wonderful dramatic candour which tells us so much of his mind as well as his art.

'The lamp burned brightly on the table, and rising from the arm-chair to light a cigar, I caught sight of my face and wondered at my anger against my brother, a sort of incoherent, interior rumbling, expressing itself in single words and fragments of sentences. An evil self seemed to be stirring within me; or was it that part of our nature which lurks in a distant corner of our being and sometimes breaks its chain and overpowers the normal self which we are pleased to regard as our true self? Everyone has experienced the sensation of spiritual forces at war within himself, but does he ever suspect that the abnormal self which has come up to the surface and is influencing him may be influencing him for his good; at all events, for some purpose other than the generally received one—the desire to lead poor human nature into temptation?'

With that keen, unrelenting gaze he watches the Colonel, outward and inward man together, while he develops his discovery and launches the fatal question, ' Why have your sons educated by priests? Protestantism is harmless, for it leaves the mind free.' . . . Such words followed, according to Moore, that further discussion was impossible ; there was but the one phrase—' It will be a great grief to me if you declare yourself a Protestant.'

But the grief of one must not cause another to stumble. Moore confides to A. E., or to the pages of *Salve*, the quarrel with his brother, saying that the Colonel had mentioned accidentally that his grandfather was not a Catholic, and the news that there was only one generation of Catholicism behind him came sweetly as the south wind. He would declare himself a Protestant. But since that declaration would grieve his brother, he must leave Ireland as soon as the lease of his house expired. Meanwhile he was kept out of St. Patrick's every Sunday by his promise to the Colonel, and his fretting at this restriction was only eased by receiving an invitation to stay with friends in England ; this in turn leading to his being asked to read the lessons in the parish church. For several weeks he read the lessons, and when he returned to Ireland he had acquired a superficial but real admiration of the language of the Bible, and resolved to read it through from beginning to end. His discovery of the Bible he kept as little to himself as his discovery of paragraph and punctuation : his wonder is as instinctive and communicative as a child's. Pondering upon things in the Old Testament that repelled him, for his squeamishness was very considerable, it suddenly occurred to him to read the Gospels ; and straightway he became indignant with the teachers of the Gospels who had so utterly neglected the great literary art of the Founder of Christianity. I cannot at this stage enter into a discussion of Moore's appreciation of the Bible, and I pass at once

to his letter to the Archbishop in which he announced
that since he came to live in Ireland his thoughts had
been directed towards religion, and now it appeared that
the purest form of Christianity was to be found in the
Anglican rather than in the Roman Church; how could
he become a member of the Anglican Church? Obviously
some special direction would be necessary for the leader
of the Celtic Renaissance who had just been devastated
with a sense of incompatibles, and obviously, too, he must
demand a purer and æsthetically more satisfying mode of
conversion than that by which others had been constrained into the ranks of orthodoxy. The common man,
he reminded himself, makes the same mess of pottage out
of religion as he does out of art. Moore's tastes in art
have never been common, and as for religion, have we
not the witness of *Evelyn Innes* and *Sister Teresa*?

Perhaps because of mere circumstance, perhaps out of
wisdom, perhaps out of simple perplexity, the Archbishop
referred our novelist to his parish priest. An icy sentence
was dropped by the parish priest at the first interview—
'It is quite possible that there is more intelligence in
Protestantism than in Catholicism, but we are concerned
with spiritual rather than with æsthetic truths.' Wrangling
about texts followed; until Moore cried, *I take my stand
upon Paul!* but a prayer said with the parish priest
melted all difficulties, he grew happy, and for a moment
did not care whether the world thought him a Protestant
or Catholic.

Only for a moment. A review of *The Untilled Field*
upset him by speaking of the author as himself a Catholic;
And is this shame eternal? he cried. Merely because his
father was a Papist must he remain one? Enraged, he
composed a letter to the press, declaring his formal
passage from the Church of Rome to the Church of
Ireland, and consulted A. E., not to get his opinion but
only to get his approval. The publication of such a letter,

conceived in pique and brought forth in anger, was unnecessary to convince us of the depth of Moore's divorce from Catholicism and the Irish Renaissance; it is used, however, to mark the end of *Salve* and the essential completion also of Moore's romantic autobiography; for *Vale* adds little to the inward story of the ten years spent in Ireland. But *Vale* repeats and extends what we have heard already, and by mere insistence helps us to see that Moore's concern with Ireland and Catholicism was not idle.

> ' Ever since the day that I strayed into my garden and it had been revealed to me as I walked therein that Catholics had not written a book worth reading since the Reformation, my belief had never faltered that I was an instrument in the hands of the Gods, and that their mighty purpose was the liberation of my country from priestcraft.'

But how achieve it? The instrument of the Gods was no preacher, and the artist in him could not be suborned to fashion the new gospel into play or novel, until one day the form was revealed to him—it must be autobiography! Truly an unusual form for a sacred book, but a remembrance of St. Paul sufficed to overcome his hesitation; *Ave* was begun in the full sense of his mission; then *Salve*, following his memory of a long search for divinity; and after *Salve* the conviction came that the autobiography would bring his long sojourn in Ireland to a close. For would it not be in bad taste (surprisingly he asks) to remain in Dublin and meet continually his models in the streets—friends and lost friends, acquaintances and men never more to be acquaintances? And far more persuasively—Would not exile (even self-ordained exile, as we see it) give the autobiography a final distinction? Never was such self-consciousness since Rousseau's, nor was it ever so well justified of its children. The great design was to begin in the Temple and end at Moore

M

Hall; but why revisit Moore Hall? Yet, since one is never sure of what may be seen, and since the book wanted that particular conclusion and not another, and since, again, the last eighty pages of *Vale* had to be wrought into something finer than the first hundred, the visit was paid and the needed effect assured. Another advantage—not, I think, an uncalculated one—is that the visit enables Moore to end on a pleasanter note, and so diminish the sense of acerbity which might else have been too plain.

But even in this visit the religious question lies sword-like between the affections of the brothers. The novelist recites a proposal which he made in the course of this visit—that his eldest nephew should be brought up a Protestant, and that recompense should be secured to him in this world as well as in the next. Argument ensued, and was prolonged for the rest of the visit, as it is recalled in *Vale;* a visit of which the chief satisfaction was the moment of farewell; for he felt glad to escape from a wrangle that had become unendurable.

'He had said the night before last that we had better not see each other, and though the words seemed hard I could not resist their truth. It was a relief to get away from him. "Catholics and Protestants don't mix; we are never comfortable in their society. We tell them by a foolish ecstasy, a foolishness in their faces difficult to define, but——" At that moment the guard blew his whistle, the train moved up the platform, and the Colonel passed out of my sight. "So this is the end of it all, and there is no help for it. We never knew it before, and might never have known it if I hadn't come down to Mayo. It was while revisiting the scenes of our youth that we discovered how hopeless is our estrangement! He thinks, no doubt, that I have changed: we have both changed, and the fault is neither with him nor with me."'

Yes, the thought seemed unendurable—but no thought lasts. His mission in Ireland was over, and the time for leaving was come. And whither now—Paris or London? No, it could not be Paris, for *Hail and Farewell* must be finished, cried once more that mysterious voice out of the circumambient profundity. It was precisely between Mullingar and Dublin that he realized more acutely than ever that this task was the cause of his being; he had been led by the hand like a little child to write it, but he knew not by whom he had been led. And now it was borne in upon him (again at whose bidding he knew not) that a sacrifice was asked of him, and that he must leave friends and native land, and even forego the briefly held vision of obedient wife and extraordinary son, for the sake of his book—a book of liberation. He knew the book to be the turning-point in Ireland's destiny, yet prayed that he might be spared the pain of writing. But no man escapes his fate. Something was propelling him out of Ireland.

The sublimation of common causes and effects has seldom reached a greater rarity, and perhaps a less than supernatural impulse would justify the renunciation so loftily conceived; indeed we have already glanced at a humbler reason, without being struck with its inadequacy. He had seen himself as the prophet of the Celtic Renaissance, but the fire had died away, and as it died the new Florence collapsed into ashes.

Yet since the faults of *Hail and Farewell* rankle, and spring from the author's mind into which we are looking, they must not be ignored. Speaking of *The Faithful Shepherdess*, Lamb remarks that if Chloe was meant to set off Clorin by contrast, Fletcher should have known that such weeds by juxtaposition do not set off, but kill sweet flowers. As ill-conceived a juxtaposition is that which Moore has arranged for certain amorous passages in the third volume of his trilogy; for between conversations with Edward Martyn and the journey to Moore Hall, a dozen wanton pages occur in the style of: ' You don't mind, darling, if I don't see you to-night? I prefer to tell you, —— has asked me if he might come to my room; I can't well refuse. You don't mind?' It is not a stain that spreads, but it is one that does not fade, and although the author of *Vale* earns a quick pardon, the necessity for pardoning something so puerile is resented; why, you ask, why cannot he respect his own art and spare this schoolboy smutching? If it be urged that you must take an author as he is, and not as you would have him, the answer is simple :—Moore as he essentially is does not raise this offence; he yields too readily to the tricksy spirit that lives in whispers and furtive smiles and senile chuckles, a spirit which is not of himself, but which he oddly fancies to be a spirit of moral and intellectual liberty. Temperamental differences, however, will determine a reader's attitude in the end, and the only objection to be urged here is the serious objection that such episodes as this, in such a book as *Hail and Farewell*, signify a brief, maddening failure of the artist.

The other fault is also temperamental in origin and has already been noted—a fondness for the cruellest caricature. There can be no question of George Moore's devouring zeal for art, when it involves this general sacrifice of friends and acquaintances. His eye is acute, his tongue merciless, his judgment cynical, and having discovered his power (for it was not always apparent to himself) he proceeds to a malicious employment; yet not because of deliberate malice, but because he cannot abstain from the sharpest exercise of this newly-found gift. He can admire his victims, but they are his victims none the less, and he admires nothing so much as his own ingenuity when he looks again and again at the palpitating shapes that once were theirs. When

he wrote *Confessions of a Young Man* it was himself
that he

> 'Carved with figures strange and sweet
> All made out of the carver's brain;'

not content to show himself as he was (a task inadequately
fascinating), but rather as he wished to appear; but when
his descendant practised with a defter hand upon others,
he forgot that the same freedom with his material might
hardly be granted, and repeated the inventive process
with undisguised ardour. Once again he carved strange
figures, figures without sweetness, but figures made out of
the carver's brain, as freakish in his craft as Puck, as
perverse as Caliban. Never have the privileges of friendship and the accidents of acquaintance been more richly
misused; the fretful porcupine has no more painful quill
than that of the author of *Hail and Farewell*. Small
consolation is it to the fantastically twitching corpses that
Moore has displayed his own character with at least equal
clearness, and breathed a morose or amused *Non dolet*.
His intemperate candour is, I think, another expression
of that unscrupulous licence of speech of which we are so
often reminded in the present study. He will say things
in his own name, as of himself, and he will say things of
others, which most men would shrink from saying out
of mere prudence or generosity; and it is the same
impersonal wantonness that impels him, the same fear of
being ashamed or seeming ashamed of any thought or
imagination which comes into his head. *Hail and Farewell*
is romantic biography as well as romantic autobiography,
and when all is said, in praise and in excuse, it remains
equally admirable and inexcusable. But time will
diminish the offence without dulling the beauty, and the
trilogy will assuredly remain a delight long after most of
the victims of it are forgotten.

What was his model? A remembrance of Sterne, of

Heine's *Florentine Nights,* of the wonderful third book of
Montaigne's *Essays,* of his admired Landor? Perhaps
some or all of these, moving beneath the rippling
surface of his mind, suggested the form; but in truth it is
original—a wandering narrative, now clouded, now clear,
and anon enbowed by such strange light as rejoices the
mind in looking seaward or landward from Howth Head.

In a preface to the revised text of *The Lake,* Moore has
explained the origin of the book and also the origin of
The Untilled Field; but as we have already glanced at
these, I need only say that the two books should be read
as one, being separated for the mysterious purposes of the
publisher. The author's own words upon this matter may
be cited: '*The Lake,* too, in being published in a separate
volume, lost a great deal in range and power, and criticism
was baffled by the division of stories written at the same
time and coming out of the same happy inspiration . . .
the return of a man to his native land, to its people, to
memories hidden for years, forgotten, but which rose
suddenly out of the darkness, like water out of the earth
when a spring is tapped.'
These Irish stories, a village Odyssey, which he finds
very near to his heart, are a witness to that fondness for
story-telling which has become a chief characteristic of
our author. It is easy to understand why that fondness
should especially enfold "So On He Fares," for that is a
story born of a mood, a story naturally flowing from the
memory of a face, voice, river or shade; and indeed all
these stories clearly have the same effortless origin which
it scarcely needed Moore's own preface to suggest. He has
little to complain of when he laments the attitude of the
clerical mind confronted by "In the Clay" and "The Wild
Goose," for has he not employed the powers of art against
the powers of the Irish priesthood? If his stories had been
treated as Rodney's clay was treated, he might have been

angry, but he could not have been surprised ; but there is something ingenuous in his complaint, and the instinct of defence is a perpetual astonishment to him. But I need not pursue the religious question :—pleasanter is it to turn to *The Lake* and to remark that it is the finest of the Irish stories, and hitherto the only one which the author has found it necessary to revise. No longer is a controversial note dominant; like Turgenev, he has allowed the landscape to dominate him, and in this book the beauty, the desire, the sorrow, the constraint, are expressed not simply in character and incident, but also in the lake itself, the reeds and shallows, the trees, the clouds resting upon the trees, and the dark, slow-heaving mountains that form the sullen limits of this remote western world.

It was by the superabundant kindness of Providence that Moore was permitted to write, for justification of his ten delusive years in Ireland, *The Lake* as well as *Hail and Farewell*. The autobiography may seem the work of one who came to pray and remained to scoff, but *The Lake* is the work of another who came to scoff and remained to pray. The friction with Catholicism is sunken in the stream of beauty that flows tide-like over the narrative, washing the few lonely characters and the lonely landscape with equal power and sureness. The book sums up, not an attitude to Church and priest, but an attitude to man and nature. That the man in whom it is presented should be himself a priest is immaterial, for Moore's vision does not centre upon priest and the world, but upon flesh and spirit, desire and matter. Superficially it is the story of Father Gogarty, who denounces the village schoolmistress because she, a young unmarried girl, is about to become a mother. The girl is driven from the parish, but the priest finds that his responsibility does not end with his parish ; his own act, and her possible fate, haunt him, and not until he learns that she is safe in London and earning a living for herself and her baby, not until a frank correspondence takes place, does he know why he is haunted. It is because he loves her; but he can never see her again, and his life stretches out before him in an endless chain of crawling, empty years. He does not know clearly whether the girl has become the mistress of her employer or not, but as she travels about the world and sends letter after letter to the priest, he realizes that she is living and he is dead :—

> ' She seemed a thing that could not feel
>   The touch of earthly years.'

But within the superficial story there is another, and the lake itself is but a symbol. Something of the eternal was the girl's animation, and something of the infinite was his desire ; and thus the book discloses the gradual enfranchisement of the spirit by the primary means of a sensual attraction. The flesh, he writes in another book, the flesh had redeemed the spirit, a thing which does not often happen, for it is usually the spirit that redeems the flesh. That at any rate is the theme, stated abstractly ; more vividly, it is the story of the liberation of Oliver Gogarty, the righteous, by Nora Glynn, the sinner. ' There is a lake in every man's heart, and he listens to its monotonous whisper year after year, more and more attentive, till at last he ungirds.' It is in flying from Ireland and the past that he says this, having already told Nora in his last letter to her, ' I thank you for the liberation you have brought me of body and mind. I need not have added the words " body and mind," for these are not two things but one thing. And that is the lesson I have learned.'

Moore's reason for liking *The Lake* is related to the very great difficulty of the telling, for, as he points out in the preface to the revised text, the one vital event in the priest's life befell him before the story opens ; but he adds that the difficulty overcome is a joy to the artist, for in his conquest over the material he draws nigh to his idea. The idea of the book is the essential rather than the daily life of the priest, and he thinks there will always be a few who will find as much life in *The Lake* as in *Esther Waters;* not so wide a life, perhaps, but what counts in art is not width but depth. . . . For all the difficulty that confronted him, *The Lake* is the simplest book in the world to read, and although a large part of it takes the form of letters, the device of letters is accepted as a natural thing. But he remained conscious of the difficulty, and feared that even if he had overcome it he had not achieved the final conquest of concealing it. Hence the patient revision, extending even to names (as though to hypnotize a reader who would like to revert to the earlier text), and in some degree letters are replaced by reveries.

And here, I think, the significance ot *The Lake* is touched. It is a beautiful creation, of clear outline and sparse colour, a large conception reduced to its simplest and smallest elements ; but it points to something outside itself—to other books of a new prose, expressing more largely the very mood of *The Lake*. It is the mood of imaginative reverie, and the prose expressing it is the discovery of George Moore. *The Lake* bridges the gulf, the deep and mysterious gulf, between *Sister Teresa* and *Memoirs of My Dead Life,* and leads you from a scented, languid, babble-echoing air to the serene clarities of *The Brook Kerith* and *Héloïse and Abélard.* Plain enough is it now that the mood of imaginative reverie is the peculiar kingdom of our novelist, and the communication of it, the expression of its human sweetness and sadness, his peculiar office. *The Lake* is full of instances of thought blended with sense, and sense sunken in thought : ' The beautiful evening did not engage his thoughts and he barely listened to the cuckoo, and altogether forgot to notice the bluebells, campions and cow-parsley ; and it was not until he stood on the hilltop overlooking the lake that he began to recover his self-possession. "The hills are turned hither and thither, not all seen in profile, and that is why they are so beautiful." '

But in this simple and direct phrasing the mood has not yet found its perfect voice. The later books have a new cunning in which the words follow the thought as flaws follow the wind's feet over the water ; and since style is of supreme interest in relation to the personality of an artist, I must dwell for a moment on the dedication of *The Lake* to *Mon cher Dujardin*. It is dedicated in recompense for the larceny committed by Moore in using the title of Dujardin's book, *La Source du Fleuve Chrétien*, for the title of his fictitious Ralph Ellis's work, and also in memory of old kindness between them. It was in August 1905 that this dedication was written, and written in French, and as soon as it was finished Moore hastened to Dujardin to read the dedication to his friend ; but when he read :—

' A Valvins, la Seine coule silencieusement tout le long des berges plates et graciles, avec des peupliers alignés ; comme ils sont tristes au printemps, ces peupliers, surtout avant qu'ils ne deviennent verts, quand ils sont rougeâtres, posés contre un ciel gris, des ombres immobiles et ternes dans les eaux, dix fois tristes quand les hirondelles volent bas ! Pour expliquer la tristesse de ce beau pays parsemé de châteaux vides, hanté par le souvenir des fêtes d'autre-fois, il faudrait tout un orchestre. Je l'entends d'abord sur les violons ; plus tard on ajouterait d'autres instruments, des cors sans doute ; mais pour rendre la tristesse de mon pauvre pays là bas il ne faut drait pas tout cela. Je l'entends très bien sur une seule flute placée dans une île entourée des eaux d'un lac, le joueur assis sur les vagues ruines d'un réduit gallois ou bien Normand——'

Dujardin wondered what might be the effect of such

phrasing in English, unconsciously suggesting to his bilingual friend the possibility of a prose that should renew the swallow's flight. Falling into so favourable a soil the suggestion could not die, but shot green above the ground and grew into the shady and murmurous branches of *Memoirs of My Dead Life*. It may perhaps be doubted if a discovery is ever so sudden and isolated as Moore thinks this discovery to have been ; clearly *The Lake* had prepared his mind for the seed, and had it not been Dujardin it would have been another. *The Lake* is nearer to *Hail and Farewell* than to *Evelyn Innes;* the new mood itself begot the new prose. The equal significance of mood and prose is not diminished by remembering that (with the luckless exception of the disinterred *Modern Lover*) *The Lake* is the last of Moore's novels; he was to become an imaginative writer of another kind, and the novel was to thrive and languish where we find it now.

Three years after *The Untilled Field* came *Memoirs of My Dead Life*, of which a new English edition was issued in 1921 with such additions as testify again to George Moore's peculiar passion for grafting fresh shoots upon old wood. The new mood is expressed in the first words, in the whole of the first scene entitled ' Spring in London '— a spring that invades poor streets like a flood, and makes the wretched rejoice ; and as serenely beautiful is the chapter that follows, ' Flowering Normandy,' marred only by such a prettification as the river 'looping up the verdant landscape as if it were a gown, running through it like a white silk ribbon, and over there the green gown disappearing in fine muslin vapours.' Already in this chapter he is essaying that favourite dual journey, through space to Paris, through time to youth ; as yet a not quite perfect attempt, but certainly forecasting the success of later pages and later books.

Among the *Memoirs* one might expect to find what is in

fact found, some clear echoes of earlier voices; and one of these is the voice of an Irish waitress, who served in a café in the Latin Quarter. Her face as well as her voice spoke of Ireland, a face showing now but a pale, deciduous beauty. It was of her, the pale phthisical Irish girl, that those verses already cited from *Confessions of a Young Man* were written, beginning :—

> ' We are alone ! Listen, a little while,
> And hear the reason why your weary smile
> And lute-toned speaking are so very sweet.'

In a slightly different form the same verses appear in *Pagan Poems* of 1881—'À Une Poitrinaire.' It was after a first and last meeting that he wrote the poem, haunted by the girl's previsioned and near death ; for nothing could save her. 'Twenty years have passed,' he writes, ' and I think of her again. . . . I bow my head and admire the romance of destiny which ordained that I, who only saw her once, should be the last to remember her.' And again, fifteen years later, he will say, ' I can see her, the poor little Irish waitress, sitting where you sit, as plainly as I can see you.' Of impressions so brief, so permanent, is art achieved.

As simply rendered, and only less pathetic, are other incidents of Moore's reminiscence, for he is at times deliberately renewing fading memories, anxious to revive his dead life and in reviving to give it the shape that pleases him now. He cannot look upon Paris without emotion, for he thinks it made him, and now he exists in two countries and is furnished with two sets of thoughts and emotions, especially the pleasure of a literature which is his without being wholly his. He calls himself the youngest of the naturalists, the eldest of the symbolists ; a decayed terminology, truly, in the ears of 1921. He speaks, in the chapter on ' Spent Love,' of women as the legitimate subject of a man's thoughts, saying that women are forgotten when men think about art, though only for a little while; but the writing of these *Memoirs* itself proves, with the support of so much besides, that this is untrue. Again, he remarks that the passing of things is always a moving subject for meditation, but the taking of a pen would destroy the pleasure of meditation. He would give much for another memory, but memory may not be beckoned.

As token, or instead of another memory, you are offered a long episode, 'The Lovers of Orelay.' It is a curiously artificial piece, a garrulous simulation, into which wantonness creeps like a cold, crystal trickling of water. A psycho-analyst has lately decided (in *The Erotic Motive in Literature*) that it is Moore's habit to write of his own adventures; but the credulity of certain psycho-analysts is too perfect to be followed by plain folk. Literature, to take one definition of a thousand, is an art of discriminations, and I cannot refuse such a primary discrimination as that between a violet and an oyster for smell, or Shakespeare and Jonson for sound; nor can I so easily smother that other simple sense which shows so plainly the difference between what happened once in time and what happened once in idea. It is his crystalline coldness that robs our author's offence of offence, and makes the wantonness of this episode a purely intellectual adventure. There still remains the wonder why a writer of George Moore's genius should care to waste himself in these dubious excursions, but I have already touched this recurring problem too freely to raise it anew on this least provocative occasion.

The natural disorder of the *Memoirs* is an advantage when the author, passing from 'The Lovers of Orelay,' needs only a brief transition to the beauty of 'A Remembrance,' in which familiar Sussex country, the neighbourhood of *Esther Waters* and *Spring Days*, reminds you yet again how fondly his thoughts revert to early scenes and eddy round a few clear island figures. He had first met the subject of his reminiscence when he was only eighteen, and was deeply interested in religion and philosophy; he meets her later when disease has touched but not destroyed her beauty:—

' She turned and looked at me with that love in her face which an old woman feels for a young man who is something less and something more to her than a son. As a flush of summer lingers in autumn's face, so does a sensation of sex float in such an affection. There is something strangely tender in the yearning of the young man for the decadent charms of her whom he regards as the mother of his election, and who, at the same time, suggests to him the girl he would have loved if time had not robbed him of her youth. There is a waywardness in such an affection that formal man knows not of.

' I remember that day, for it was the last time I saw her beautiful.'

As exquisite is the closing passage—' I thought of memory as a shrine where we can worship without shame, of friendship, and of the pure escapement it offers us from our natural instincts. . . . I knew how much more intense and strangely personal was my love for her than the love which that day I saw the world offering to its creatures.' Such phrases, following so soon after ' The Lovers of Orelay,' make the task of discrimination easy and certain.

The last chapter is entitled ' Resurgam.' His mother was dying and he had been summoned to Ireland, and he tells the story of the hasty journey with a candour which should be met with equal candour by the reader, less accustomed perhaps to looking into his own mind with an eye of double-vision. The long ride through the spring-enkindled country was but a parable, for at the same time his thoughts were roaming back to his own springtide. 'There are times,' he remarks, 'when the present does not exist at all, when every mist is cleared away, and the past confronts us in naked outline;' and perhaps that was why it was painful for him to return home. All he saw was associated with his childhood— and every association was turned to pain; yet amid the pain the unresting mind flows on and he cries, 'We are so constituted that the true and the false overlap each other, and so subtly that no analysis can determine where one ends and the other begins.' The comment is both true and lustrous. He seemed to have become a sheer mentality, a buzz of thought, and it is out of this inward murmuring that his voice issues, now sighing and now singing. He tells of his prolonged prayers—to what God?—and of his terror not so much that he might not see his mother alive, but that he might arrive in time to see her die. Vain terror! 'My mother died certainly on the most beautiful day I have ever seen, the most winsome, the most white, the most wanton, as full of love as a girl in a lane who stops to gather a spray of hawthorn. How many times, like many another, did I wonder why death should have come to anyone on such a bridal-like day.' Sorrow has an ingenious cunning, but few would utter in such words of beauty and brightness an elegy upon one loved and lost, and enhance the brightness by revision many years after. No one dares to speak his thoughts about such a kind of incongruity as death in the midst of quickening spring; but nevertheless he goes on, saying that the day 'moved slowly from afternoon to evening like a bride hidden within a white veil, her hands filled with white blossom; but a blackbird, tiny like a humming-bird, had perched upon a bunch of blossom, and I seemed to lose sight of the day in the sinister black speck that had intruded itself upon it. No doubt I could think of something better were I to set my mind upon doing so, but that is how I thought, the day I walked on the lawn with my brothers, ashamed and yet compelled to talk of what our lives had been during the years that separated us.'

Dual consciousness in times of distress is common enough, and it is only the expression of it that is rare. *Memoirs of My Dead Life* shows, in this single chapter, the clearest following of the double thread; these sixty pages are elegiac as *Lycidas* is elegiac, but no more than *Lycidas* is this prose memory exclusively elegiac. The tenderest of memories are recalled, the simplest of affections, the most human and general of sorrows; and with these there is heard the accent of the detached mind, amid the funereal foliation a jesting face appears, a mocking smile, the elegist becomes satirist, and you turn the page hastily when you find that, at the moment of the Christian burial of his mother, he smiles at the thought of himself escaping that disgrace and murmurs joyfully, 'O death, where is thy sting?' for he sees, with the far-darting eye of the mind, a Grecian urn and a little pile of white ashes.

For it is not alone the true and the false that overlap and defeat analysis, but the pure and the perverse, the simple and the cunning, the spirit and the flesh; one concealing and anon revealing the other, one trampling and now yielding to the other. Here, in this unique prose elegy, the sincere and the assumed, the face and the mask, the spiritually true and the intellectually true, appear and disappear, one passing into the other half imperceptibly, one suddenly drowned by the other, and still almost imperceptibly. Personality has its different truths, its various planes, its unreconciled opposites, its evanescent distinctions; in George Moore's best work these are so delicately disposed and so cunningly dispersed, that to pick and choose among instances, rejecting here and enhancing there, is both delusive and exciting.

The end of the chapter is the end of the book. At the moment when the priest began to intone the *Pater Noster*, Moore's thoughts turned towards the sea, the only clean and holy receptacle for the vase containing his own ashes. ' If it were dropped where the sea is deepest, it would not reach the bottom, but would hang suspended in dark moveless depths where only a few fishes range, in a cool, deep grave "made without hands, in a world without stain," surrounded by a lovely revel of Bacchanals, youths and maidens, and wild creatures from the woods, man in his primitive animality.' But nothing endures, all passes away and returns, and with this ancient idea of eternal recurrence singing in his head, he dreams of worlds and æons, appearing and vanishing and returning again.

Memoirs of My Dead Life, the first attempt in the author's new style of discursive reminiscence, claims a large part of his fondness as he looks back; although that style was as yet imperfectly free in movement, transitions being abrupt or absent and the tone uneven. He has avowed his faith that if any twentieth-century literature linger on into the twenty-first, this volume would probably be among the last stragglers. The revised text (1921) is presented in the beautiful privately-printed form of *Avowals*, and includes chapters which were not offered to the reader of the earlier humble edition. The title-page of the new issue is itself an amusement, as the bibliography will show, but there is a better wit and humour, well matched and moving easily together, in ' Euphorion in Texas.' It is a story of the kind that we look to France to give us, never to England since Sterne died, and even to France often in vain.

Hail and Farewell has its denominated overture, else the *Memoirs* might well stand as overture to the great trilogy that followed it a few years after. Both books (like *The*

N

Lake and *The Untilled Field*) are the immediate result of
the Irish immersion, but they are not the sole result.
A Story-Teller's Holiday (1918), the first of the famous
privately-printed books and the only one in which the
author has taken advantage of the immunity peculiar to a
private issue, springs out of the same inspiration, and is
characterized by his common virtues and excesses. In a
brief preface, entitled 'A Leave-Taking,' he speaks half
regretfully to his family of readers of the steadfast
persecution of his writings ever since *Flowers of Passion*
was published. *The Brook Kerith* had but lately been
submitted to the indignity of magisterial writs, and yet
more recently the unhappy *Lewis Seymour and Some Women*
had become the subject of a libel action, a certain producer
of revues complaining that his name had been used by our
author. Mr. Justice Darling found even harsher terms
than I have used to describe the book, and although the
action failed, the humiliation of appearing as defendant
was profound. Moore did well, therefore, he thinks, to
retire into an arcanum in which he could practise his art
in dignified privacy, and write for men and women of
letters exclusively. With Landor he might murmur, 'I
would excite the pleasure (it were too much to say the
admiration) of judicious and thoughtful men;' but he
could not quite truthfully proceed, 'I would neither soothe
nor irritate these busybodies. I have neither honey nor
lime for ants.' There is a careless wisdom in such arrogance, but it is only partially reached by George Moore.
. . . The book betrays the story-teller's proneness to
repetition, passages appearing here almost precisely as
they appear elsewhere, and critical *obiter dicta* being
expressed, if not in the same terms, at any rate to the
same purpose as in other books. The repetitive tendency
is sometimes disguised, and memories of his own childhood
and youth are given by another's tongue; hence you find
the story of Appely told once again, and told the less

effectively. But the virtues are more conspicuous than the flaws; Moore may become more garrulous when he speaks of his childhood, and show the common proclivity in telling the same story over and over again; but when he speaks of his revisiting journey, of spring stepping always a little ahead and putting beauty into everything animate and inanimate, he speaks with the freshness of an enchanted child. In these warm and sunny pastorals, these humbler prose complements to *A Sensitive Plant* and *Endymion*, there is a breath of that wandering beauty whose passage redeems the mortal world. And it must be admitted, too, that the other personality whose shadow falls so freakishly across the reader's path wanders here also, telling stories that are not common in English literature but common enough in the language of Boccaccio. The primitive animality of which Moore speaks in *Memoirs of My Dead Life* suggests the character of the proper audience for certain of these stories, and indeed indicates a quality which he esteems more highly as a vital quality than I can. Once again I am driven to the mere assertion of unreasoned differences and antipathies, the look that glances through the tangle of amorous stories being the look of a younger and wilder Dr. Fell. . . . Strange to me is this intertwisting of the simple and the sensual, but it is a fact that cannot be ignored; he complicates one thing with another, and were he imagining a Don Quixote he would interfuse with that great nobility something of Sancho Panza, or with Pantagruel something of Panurge, his sympathy naturally and unerringly seeking out the grossly human in the most divinely human of characters. Idealistic sentiments find no sanctuary in his mind; he welcomes them, sometimes, only to mate them with a masculine or feminine grossness, and present the twin-minded offspring to the Muse. Sometimes in *A Story-Teller's Holiday* he delights you with a flower of strange beauty and significance

even in the midst of a debateable story : ' Luachet is
beautiful, but it wasn't her beauty altogether that drew
me. Well, this much I can say with truth, that there is
something beyond the lust of the eye, the desire of the
flesh, something that is beyond the mind itself, and maybe
that thing is the soul ; and maybe the soul is love, and
whosoever comes upon his soul is at once robbed of all
thought and reason, and becomes like a flower.' And
another verity is glimpsed by Marban when he adds :
' It may be that yesterday I would have denied the truth
of what I'm now saying to you all. All the same it is the
truth I'm telling you.'

And all the same, the reader may remark, it is the truth
that the author's sense of beauty does not always save
him, for the last story in this curious medley'd volume, a
story which he is still strangely inclined to prize, shows
him exercising an ingenuity which only beauty could put
to a sensible purpose ; but beauty is away, and not a touch
of her kindness or mystery is visible. It is the story of
a waiter in a Dublin hotel, who had for many years passed
as a man but was born a woman, and who encounters
another in the same case ; and although there is no offence
in the episode, the whole story has yet the irrelevance of
a dream and the harshness of a nightmare. Sex, sex, you
cry impatiently, what is sex doing here ? It is the one
thing you are conscious of, as you turn and turn the
pages, and yet it is without significance ; and at length
you come to perceive that the fault of the story is precisely
the fault we have found in certain earlier stories—that it
is written to a theme and not out of an imagination. Let
me write a story, you may fancy the author saying, in
which a girl shall pass as a man until old age is nearing ;
let her come near to marriage—what shall I make of such
a story ?

Worse still, he has failed to observe how completely
this last story is at odds with all that goes before in

another mood. Ibsen in the midst of the *Decameron* would hardly appear odder than this story at the end of the romantic narratives told in a lush spring-time by men enchanted by spring. For once Moore's art has stumbled, or it has slept; the naturalist that decayed in *Celibates* has been resuscitated for a final exercise, and has written as though there had been no interval since *Celibates*. . . . But this is to labour a fault, and the only justification for doing so is the proof that a hankering after the grotesque can enfeeble the author's instinct for beauty. The two strands of his character as an artist (it is convenient to count them as two, rather than any larger number) have strayed apart, and it is the worser strand that alone is traceable here. For the rest, the book is well-named; the old interest in the story for the story's sake is dominant, and if there is a holiday for anyone, it is not for the artist to whom the visible world appears as fresh and as lovely as to Adam when Lilith was with him, and again when it framed the body of Eve. Some slender tradition may be concealed in the stories told by the author's companion, but they are unembarrassed by the tradition—developed, he says, just as the gipsy develops on his fiddle the snatches of song that he hears the reapers singing in the cornfields.

With *A Story-Teller's Holiday* we may dismiss the consideration of Ireland as an immediate influence upon the mental life of our author. A touch of pleasant melancholy and grieving fondness is seen here and there, when he casts his eyes back to the familiarities of child-hood and murmurs: 'It is our former selves that have vanished; we are always winning and losing something; nothing is permanent within or without.' Yet even while he charges himself with this inconstancy, he shows that the charge is not wholly true, for his memory is un-changed and undying. But his fidelity is wholly personal; scarce another soul in Ireland or of Irish birth can please him; little that is general or national touches his heart for long or deeply; he is as solitary as a hermit, and with the arrogance of isolation can say, 'The falsetto scream that comes out of Ireland and a certain untrustworthiness in the national character may be traced back to the relinquishment of the right of private judgment.' For him the Catholicism of Ireland is never to be forgiven.

Since *The Story-Teller's Holiday* was published Moore has said little of his native country, and that little not as an artist. At whiles he has shown a consciousness of human affairs, writing letters to *The Times* and suggesting what practical steps might be taken to end the Irish chaos. Alas, little as the world heeds the artist when he speaks in his own tongue and of his own heaven, it heeds him not at all when he speaks of politics and the follies of the wise.

CHAPTER V

THE TERMLESS JOURNEY

I do not number my borrowings, I weigh them. . . . Knowledge and truth may be in us without judgment, and judgment also without them ; but the confession of ignorance is one of the finest and surest testimonies of judgment that I know. —*Montaigne*.

I HAVE referred in an earlier chapter to Moore's regret that when he avowed himself a Protestant at heart, his father did not give him a Bible in order that he might be confirmed in his religious conviction. Nevertheless it was, it seems, to his father that he owed his first interest in St. Paul, the memory of a phrase overheard when he was but a small boy being lodged in his mind and only springing into life many years after. The phrase referred to the pre-eminent part of the Apostle in the establishment of Christianity—without St. Paul there would have been no Christian religion; a theme with which our author has now become perfectly possessed, and which has imposed upon him a wondering admiration of the supreme genius among all the Apostles.

The dedication of *The Brook Kerith* shows that it was not until 1898 that a friend gave him a Bible, and although we are not called upon to believe that he lived for more than forty years without a knowledge of the Scriptures, we have his repeated word that this gift became, from 1898 to the publication of *The Brook Kerith* in 1916, his constant companion and chief literary interest. But *The Brook Kerith* was not the first sign of that interest; did not Mike Fletcher, in 1889, talk of a trilogy on the life of Christ? and long after, *The Apostle* of 1911 and *Salve* of 1912 witness to his vivid delight in the literature of the Bible, and his sense of its spiritual value. Thus he surveys the Old Testament in *The Apostle* and repeats his review in *Salve*, finding in Genesis a collection of beautiful folk-tales, in the Book of Job and the Psalms a rhetorical note and an absence of *piano* passages, in Ecclesiastes a beautiful agnostic work, and in the greater and lesser prophets a series of tractates upon morals with but a slight

185

tincture of literature. The prophets, indeed, disgusted the author of *Lewis Seymour* and *Evelyn Innes*—'The filthiest God that ever came out of Asia!' he cried, feeling that he could not stand a moment longer the reek of sacrifice and the howls of dervishes.

The mere force of his own disgust threw him from the Old Testament to the New, and he continued to read until ravishment overcame him; how was it that he had so long been persuaded that Christianity had brought nothing into the world but chastity and melancholia? The question falls not quite without surprise upon our patient ears, for has it not seemed that Christianity is confounded with Catholicism, and substance with shadow, in the curse which George Moore has so frequently invoked in the name of art, from the day of *Confessions of a Young Man* to the day of these confessions of an older man? That note of presumption which the former essay in autobiography sounded in its reference to religion may seem gross and unpardonable as a lapse in civilized manners, until it is remembered that ignorance, pure ignorance, can be pleaded for it; for ignorant youth is both presumptuous and pardonable. And as the *Confessions* show Moore at his worst, a merely imitative writer who would be thought French and audacious, so *Hail and Farewell* and *The Brook Kerith* show him at his best, no longer an imitative writer, looking with other eyes upon things which had never before troubled his ignorance with questions.

It is as a man of letters—again and again must we remind ourselves that Moore is wholly and exclusively a man of letters—that he approaches the New Testament and the character of Christ; and when he seeks to discover the clear image of Jesus in the four Gospels his distinctions are purely æsthetic. Thus he is able to decide that St. Luke is an earlier sleek Maeterlinck, and even those who share this enlightened appreciation of Maeterlinck may fail to agree that the Gospel according

to St. Luke is like *The Treasure of the Lowly*. He passes
on to St. Matthew, and again his professional eye is strict,
finding the first Gospel a canvas that has passed through
the hands of a restorer. St. John, as the work of a later
ecclesiastical writer, is yet more briefly dismissed, and it
is not until St. Mark's Gospel is reached that Moore
catches a glimpse of 'the magnificent heretic.' His admiration is reserved for St. Mark's narrative, in which he
discovers the qualities that we admire in Maupassant; a
concise, explicit, objective narrative, the truth of which,
in fact, we shall never know, though the imaginative
truth is plain. But it is when he leaves the Gospels for
the Acts of the Apostles that he is conscious of passing
from legend to history, and it is still the æsthetic test that
he applies in distinguishing a new voice—the voice of St.
Paul. How could St. Luke have written the story of
St. Paul's farewell to the Ephesians? The blind and the
deaf know nothing of the art of writing.

It is St. Paul that fascinates him—and how could he
not, and whose is the imaginative mind which has not
been subdued by the great Apostle? The very figure of
St. Paul rises up before him as clearly as Don Quixote—
a man of middle height, with round head covered with
dark curly hair, a short neck, square shoulders, long body
and thick legs. The Epistles of St. Paul seem to him the
most natural literature in the world, and their author
the most human of writers. Inevitably he welcomes the
Apostle's discussion of sex, for St. Paul knew how to come
to terms with life and thus lived as intensely in the flesh
as in his theology. 'But deeper even than the sex
mystery is the mystery of Being; we all ask sometimes if
there is divinity and if we are related to the divine, no
matter how remotely.' It is in touching, lightly enough, on
this mystery that our author finds himself approaching the
heart of another—How is it that the Apostle never speaks
of the sayings of Christ and seems to have known nothing

of the life of Christ but three things—the Last Supper
and Betrayal, the Crucifixion and the Resurrection? At
once he turns to John Eglinton for enlightenment, and his
questions are partly answered and partly forgotten in the
mention of a book which contained the views of a certain
doctor on the Resurrection. The doctor was inclined to
think that Christ had suffered from a cataleptic swoon
which had been mistaken for death, and thus His subsequent appearances were not supernatural at all.

Moore was already aware of an old legend that after
His crucifixion Jesus preached in India, and had read too
that He was supposed by some to have been an Essene
monk. Why, then, should not He have returned to the
monastery, after His wounds had been healed by Joseph
of Arimathea? And why should not St. Paul, many years
later, have knocked at the door of that monastery after a
day's labouring among the people of the hills? A wonderful meeting it was, as he swiftly pictured it, the climax of
a story which possessed him completely and compelled
him to dictate the scenario of *The Apostle*. But why
publish it, do you ask? Because he could not refrain from
telling his imagination over and over again, until others
wanted to collaborate with him in producing a play or a
story upon the great theme; and since he feared that the
story might drift into the common mind, and somebody or
other write it in a way that would be painful to the
only begetter, Moore decided to anticipate the imaginary
offender with *The Apostle*. *The Apostle* is but a rough
sketch for a more deeply considered work. The story of
The Apostle is an invented story, but the story of *The
Brook Kerith* is imaginative; and it is unnecessary to show
in detail the profound difference between the two. You
may read the former, but only with difficulty; you will
read the latter not without difficulty perhaps (since it is a
work of art), but with abundant delight. Moore, in fact,
as we have seen again and again, needs to brood upon his

first thought ; or, to change the metaphor, the roots of his conception need to strike deep before they reach the nourishing soil ; and only when the roots have struck the rich darkness of his mind does his conception lift its head beautifully in the light.   Hence the hasty *Apostle* has certain invented scenes and fancies which were found too crude, too violent, for the uses of imagination ; but the purer romantic biography which is given in *The Brook Kerith* is purged of these and has a harmony of its own—a harmony between the character of Jesus Christ as Moore discovers it, and the incidents upon which that character plays or by which it is moved.

The Brook Kerith is a simple imagination, and it is the least of its praise that it achieves easily what Renan failed to achieve.   From his own allusions you may gather that Moore was in ignorance of Renan's work, and even of the intention of that work, when *The Brook Kerith* was conceived, and when the book was reviewed he wrote eagerly to explain to his critics the genesis of his imaginary biography ; but now, at any rate, he is familiar enough with Renan's *Vie de Jésus* to detest it for the prettification of its subject. . . . Nowhere in St. Matthew, St. Mark or St. Luke did he find that Jesus claimed divinity ; but his main difficulty in reading the synoptic gospels was to form a distinct conception of the character of Jesus ; for at one time He is meek as an Essene, and at another rages like the Baptist.   He found a clue to the answer in remembering that there was an Essene settlement on the eastern bank of the Jordan ;—what was more natural than that a young shepherd should fall under the influence of the Baptist, who was preaching in the neighbourhood ?   It seemed that there was reason for holding that Jesus was the disciple of John, and not John the disciple of Jesus ; and what was more natural, again, than that Jesus, preaching the doctrine of the Essenes, should become obsessed by the idea of the time, namely, the approach of the end of the world? Our author believes this to be his own exegesis, and says that it helped him to catch a glimpse of a man amid the gospel mists. But this was not all, for the story-teller quickening in him again, he imagined a man coming out of a swoon to find all his beliefs false. In such a theme, it appeared, there was a grand opportunity for the psychological narrative that always tempted him. How would life reconstruct itself for Jesus? Would He not take refuge in His trade, returning to His rams and ewes, and keeping all thoughts of the past out of His mind?

He complains that criticism reproached him with the silence of the Essenian Jesus regarding His crucifixion, but that is part of the psychology of Moore's narrative, for he has been careful to represent Jesus as not only unable to speak of the Crucifixion and the ideas that led to it, but unable even to think about them. Immersed in His old shepherd's duties, twelve years pass before He begins to look back; and after that long silence He would find some difficulty in telling His story. Hence it is not until He is too old for the lonely life of the hills and makes over His flock to another shepherd, that He is able to tell the story to Hazael.

Much of all this is familiar to those who have read Renan, and less popular authors than Renan. The French writer, for example, sedulously discredits the divinity of Jesus; he too suggests the possibility of Jesus being an Essene, at least in spirit; he too mentions the influence of anchorites such as Banu, who in the *The Brook Kerith* directs Joseph of Arimathea to the Baptist; and he too emphasizes the transition from the exalted tenderness of Jesus at one time, to His exaggerated harshness at another. But Renan's is only one of the many inventions. The idea of the removal of the body of Jesus by Joseph of Arimathea is to be found in earlier fictional lives, with such an epilogue as that He afterwards appeared to Mary, lived with the Essenes, met the disciples at the Mount of Olives and, taking leave of them, walked up the mountain until a cloud concealed Him; returning then to the Essenes, and only at rare intervals reappearing in human affairs; the occasion chiefly to be noted just now being an encounter with St. Paul on his way to Damascus. Other inventions relate that Joseph of Arimathea, himself an Essene, used Jesus as his tool, and bribed the Romans to permit his rescue of the still animated body from the cross, so that he could remove it to his own tomb and resuscitate it; and hence it is alleged that the Christian Church had its origin in the Essene order. Yet another alleges that as the Baptist came forth from the Essenes and thought himself Elias, so Jesus, thinking Himself the Messiah, preached a spiritual kingdom, being encouraged by the Essenes and helped by Joseph. The Essene origin of the life of Jesus, and the revival of His body after crucifixion, are features common to many of the earlier imaginary biographies which we owe to Germany.

That other minds had for long been moving in the same direction as George Moore's is, however, of little significance; the question of historical primacy is not an important question in a matter of art. The letter killeth, it is the spirit that giveth life; and Moore's apprehension of his theme is vividly imaginative. He approaches it as an artist, and what I notice infallibly is the ease with which the imaginative tendency is harmonized with the rationalizing tendency. He sees Jesus as a shepherd overswayed by His passion for righteousness, and thinking at length that only His sacrifice can save the world—a painful extravagance of the mind, in Moore's eyes; and all that he says of Jesus is said from that point of view. And then he sees the shepherd resuming His common life after that lofty and woeful aberration, when the belief for which He suffered—the belief that the Kingdom of Heaven was at hand—had been found false. But when time and loneliness have enabled Him to look back upon that aberration, St. Paul, the great apostle of the tragic mistake, comes journeying to Rome and testifying to the risen Christ. . . . Everything in the divine story is rationalized—rather say, everything is humanized; and it is a tribute to the eternal freshness of the life of Jesus Christ that this re-statement in mere human terms of the divine elements of that life should hold so much of beauty and so much of truth. The author's nature has been subdued to what it works in; and in the midst of our inquisition into his nature, does it not seem remarkable that the subdual should have been so complete? Again and again are you made aware of his homage to the figure of Jesus Christ as his imagination perceives it; and more than this, or more than such a recognition, cannot be asked of any man. His attitude has been resented, but can it be resented that he should attempt what painters have attempted? To suggest such a comparison seems unfair, but I ask myself which represents the finer tribute: the orthodox, unimaginative life of Jesus by Dean Farrar, or the unorthodox, imaginative life by George Moore? Insincerity would have made *The Brook Kerith* detestable, but I do not find insincerity. Some will detest the humanizing of a figure which for two thousand years has borne divine attributes, but it is not a relevant objection. Moore is careful to call his book 'A Syrian Story,' and not the life of the Messiah; and my own surprise is not that he should have treated his subject in a spirit of rational imagination (the term, I hope, will be allowed), but that he should be almost alone among English writers to treat it thus.

He approaches his subject as an artist, I said; and from the humble technical position his manner of approach seems to me of singular beauty. He looks through the eye of a child, and Joseph of Arimathea is all but the first child among Moore's characters. With what a melodious phrase does the book open—'It was at the end of a summer evening, long after his usual bedtime, that Joseph, sitting on his grandmother's knee, heard her tell that Kish, having lost his asses, sent Saul, his son, to seek them in the land of the Benjamites and the land of Shalisha, whither they might have strayed. But they were not in these lands, Son, she continued, nor in Zulp, whither Saul went afterwards.' Happily the method of our study does not enjoin upon me the summarizing of the story, but it permits my pointing out anew Moore's characteristic virtues. He is said to indulge in an incredible prolixity, and that is only partly true; indeed, at times his narrative moves with only too much swiftness, and you are compelled to read narrowly in order to note important transitions, such as that from the gentle to the terrible Jesus. Generally, however, the favourite manner of reflective recapitulation is indulged in freely, and if it results in making a long book, it is because incidents are many and thoughts are legion, and only life is short. He indulges, too, in another favourite method in his third chapter, when he resorts to a picturesque recital of the visit of vagabonds to Tiberias, a chapter in which mediæval Europe is thrust back to the first century and a full foretaste of the romance of *Héloïse and Abélard* is offered.

Imagination, again, transcending the necessities of invention, is evident in his presentation of the central figure at first through the loyal and affectionate eyes of Joseph of Arimathea, and then directly, without the intervention of another, when Joseph is dead and Jesus returns to His old pastures. That vast and significant transition (at which we have already glanced) is managed quite simply by means of an incident occurring when Joseph is about to lead Jesus back to the old settlement. A wandering breeze carries the smell of the

o

camel-driver's sheepskin straight into Jesus' nostrils, and like one in a dream He questions the camel-driver regarding the quality of the flocks. Who was thy master? asks the camel-driver; and Jesus replies that His acquaintance with sheep came from His association with the Jordan Essenes. His thoughts are at once immersed in His old task, and when the two travellers reach the monastery it is with a simple phrase that Hazael greets Him—'So thou hast come back to us!' forbearing to ask questions concerning the three years of separation, since the shepherd's face forbids inquiry. If things are said or done that remind Jesus of His late experiences, He covers His face for sorrow, since His memory is clear enough to make the reminder easy and bitter. A day may come, says Joseph privately to Hazael, when Jesus will tell His story; and with hardly another word for our ears Joseph himself passes out of the narrative, being slain by the Zealots in Jerusalem as one of the Nazarene's friends. News of Joseph's death on His account reaches Jesus and He grieves with more than mortal grief. A shepherd's preoccupation was necessary, it has been said, to save Jesus from complete despair by saving Him from thought; and it is in the recital of this that Moore's imagination is most happily alive; the finest instance being his relation of the search of Jesus for a ram to renew the flock of the Essenes and His return (the symbol or the parable is left for the reader's perception) with the ram in His bosom. But it is not until the conclusion of the book draws near that the lyric becomes dramatic, with the advent of St. Paul preaching the risen Christ on his way to Rome. I repeat that the historical truth of the episode is irrelevant when an imaginative story is being considered.

And here I might note again the change that takes place between *The Apostle* and *The Brook Kerith;* for in the former the hero is St. Paul and the story develops

around the Apostle, the more impressive figure; but in
The Brook Kerith he is a secondary figure, and the reader
looks at him with the eyes of Jesus, and not at Jesus
through the eyes of the Apostle. . . . Is any imaginative
synthesis more quick with passion than this of St. Paul's
encounter with Jesus—St. Paul on his way to preach the
risen Christ and the salvation of the world by faith, and
Jesus vainly striving to dissuade him from preaching an
illusion? At first the vehement Apostle denies that Jesus
is the crucified Jesus risen from the tomb, and a great
pity for him takes possession of Jesus as they walk side
by side across the hills; but when at length St. Paul
can no longer dispute His identity he answers, 'Thou'rt
Jesus of Nazareth, I deny it not, but the Jesus of
Nazareth that I preach is of the spirit and not of the
flesh, and it was the spirit and not the flesh that was
raised from the dead.' Painful and profound is the
moment when Jesus shows His hands and feet for
testimony that it was indeed He that was crucified and
removed from the tomb; and again the Apostle answers
inflexibly that his Christ is not of this world. And painful
too is that other moment when Jesus tells him that it is
in His mind to go once more to Jerusalem, so that the
priests may know that He whom they believe to be raised
from the dead still lives in the flesh; and so the world be
saved from a delusion.

The English language has been brought to a new
exercise in the prose of Moore's story, and that is honour
enough for an author and joy for a reader. I have already
referred to the lovely pastoral episode of Jesus' journey
for a young ram, but I have not recorded an illustration of
one manner in which an imaginative writer works. It
was while his mind was full of the story that Moore,
walking in Ireland, was troubled by the incessant bleating
of a lamb which the shepherd said was without a mother;

the ewe (the yoe, as our author prefers to call it) having been killed by a stray ball. It would be dead by the next morning, said the shepherd, for another ewe would not feed it. How could it be saved? Imagine Jesus receiving a forlorn lamb, how could He save it? Another shepherd was asked, and he had saved many lambs by cutting a stem of elder, extracting the pith, and tying a rag at one end for the lamb to suck while the ewe's milk was poured in at the other. So the episode was complete in his mind, and Jesus, saving the young ram by this device, was Himself saved by His care for it from the despair caused by the news of Joseph's death.—The incident is trifling, but the mental processes of an artist are never insignificant, and it is not superfluous to remember that the mind does not create out of nothing. The pastoral note, sounding so lightly in this reference, is heard throughout the narrative, and is dominant in those many passages in which music and colour are employed in the reading of landscape. It is not the traditional Palestine but the soft, green, remembered Ireland that is presented again and again;— *Christ in Ireland* might well be used as a sub-title, if regard be given chiefly to Moore's water-colour. Nor is it simply that the prose is beautiful; it is radiant with a beauty which Moore did not discover by his single visit to the Holy Land, but by the idleness of earlier days in his native country. Compare a brief passage such as :—

'Every breath of air brought a new and exquisite scent to him, and through the myrtle bushes he could hear the streams singing their way down to the lake; and when he came to the lake's edge he heard the warble that came to his ear when he was a little child, which it retained always. . . . But suddenly from among the myrtle bushes a song arose. It began with a little phrase of three notes, which the bird repeated, as if to impress the listener and prepare him for the runs and trills and joyous little cadenzas that were to follow. A sudden shower of jewels it seemed like, and when the last drops had fallen the bird began another song, a continuation of the first, but more voluptuous and intense ; and then, as if he felt that he had set the theme sufficiently, he started away into new trills and shakes and runs, piling cadenza upon cadenza till the theme seemed lost, but the bird held it in memory while all his musical extravagances were flowing, and when the inevitable moment came he repeated the first three notes——'

with a passage by Mr. G. K. Chesterton :—

'One can only say that the whole landscape was like a leper. It was of a wasting white and silver and grey, with mere spots of decadent vegetation like the green spots of a plague. In shape it not only rose into horns and crests like waves or clouds, but I believe it actually alters like waves or clouds, visibly, but with a loathsome slowness. The swamp is alive. And I found again a certain advantage in forgetfulness ; for I saw all this incredible country before I even remembered its name, or the ancient tradition about its nature. Then even the green plague-spots failed, and everything seemed to fall away into a universal blank under the staring sun, as I came, in the great spaces of the circle of a lifeless sea, into the silence of Sodom and Gomorrah.'

It is plain that in this picture of the unholy spot of the Holy Land, Mr. Chesterton has worked more directly and presented more sharply a vision that is not simply external. George Moore's rendering is translated into memories of childhood and Mayo, and Mr. Chesterton's into memories of moral quake and triumph ; but each is characteristic prose—the one transpicuous and fluent as sliding water, the other vigorous, clamant, startling.

Memory is short, and the discussion—not quite un-deliberately provoked, perhaps — which followed *The Brook Kerith,* may have been quickly forgotten ; and I might remind the forgetful reader that the story was assailed by orthodox writers who were unwilling to admit any other criterion than that of conformity to an accepted type. The violence of objectors became vicious, and the voices of those who welcomed the book were still very small. Moore, in fact, was made to suffer for having written such a story as *Evelyn Innes*. I regret it, because *The Brook Kerith* thus achieved notoriety, and notoriety obscured for a time its simplicity. Unluckily, too, the author made the profound mistake of following his narrative with *Lewis Seymour*, an example of levity which was bound to distress the faithful and rejoice the malicious. And had he not, years before, offended the libraries with the severe morality of *A Mummer's Wife*? So *The Brook Kerith* was banned, and criticism gave way to intolerance. Nor could his admirers derive much comfort from reflecting that he had courted the attack, for it is deplorable that a work of imagination should be regarded as an obscene scrawl. If æsthetic considerations be ignored (and his æstheticism, as we have noted, is the writer's all), there is yet another consideration to be weighed, namely, his own justification for treating Jesus Christ as human and not as the Son of God. Had he printed a single one of the many meditated prefaces, or a single one of the retorts which quivered on his eager tongue, he would have reminded us that the humanity of Jesus Christ is no new assertion, and that Christianity, in its recurrent renewal, may even now be striving towards a new apprehension of the man, rather than maintaining its assertion of the God. . . . But theological argument is apart from my power and purpose, and I am only concerned to remember that an heretical book is not necessarily bad literature.

In an essay by James Elroy Flecker, whose early death robbed our time of a true poet, the unending, needless

quarrel between art and the world is re-phrased in a
dialogue intended for the rebuke of the world that ignores
the living artist and discovers the dead :—

> 'Come out and love, Pentheus . . . leave your
> ridiculous concerns, your childish politics, your
> amusingly ugly towns. There are lands where sun-
> light and harmony are not yet dead; there are
> the absurdest poets leading lobsters on strings and
> charming all the sylvan beasts by their pleasant
> ways. . . .
> 'Then that man answers: My dear sir, I am
> entirely with you. You must not imagine that in
> the midst of more serious pursuits I have neglected,
> or even desired to neglect, the interests of Art. . . .
> I need only refer to my art galleries, to the Royal
> Academies, and to the great efforts I have made to
> provide all who come to the County Council schools
> with a sound grounding in English literature, starting
> with Beowulf, and tracing the gradual development
> of Idealism down to the death of Tennyson.'

The quarrel is unending because it is based upon a
fallacy or confusion of the kind to which human nature
is prone; and it is the artist himself who yields to it,
for, oppressed by failure and discouraged by unworthy
success, he is apt to cry out upon those who pass his
work unheeding. He is apt to complain that the world
does not welcome or even endure art, and he sometimes
fosters a suspicion of hostility when at worst there is but
ignorance and indifference. Driven back upon himself,
he becomes querulous or arrogant—moods that are acid
to his work; and that is far more lamentable than the
injustice of his attitude towards the world. The letters
of George Meredith teem with unhappy evidence of this
confusion, presenting the tragic comedy of a bright genius
in the midst of a world which it disdained to please, yet
could not quietly forgive for not being pleased.

But art does not exist to conciliate the world, nor the world to recognize art. Art exists for itself, an eternal expression of the zest of creation, knowing no joy but in the consciousness of existence, and content if it find space and time for its movement. By its mere existence it atones for the coarseness of the world, whose veins it animates with a finer essence; but the artist has no complaint if the world is ignorant of his aim and indifferent to his emotion, for he is paid and overpaid by that mere consciousness of creation. Enemies he has, but the world is not one of them. His chief enemy hides slily in his own heart, and another is Marvell's enemy :—

> ' At my back I always hear
> Time's wingèd chariot hurrying near,
> And yonder all before us lie
> Deserts of vast eternity.'

Creative art is a world in itself, obedient to other laws, bound by other obligations of honour, than the laws and obligations of the social world. Some men may be called to serve and shape the world, and if the artist is deaf to that call, pursuing an Idea, an imagination of his mind, he is not to lament that the world is deaf to him. The more original his creation, the more vexing it will be to the unimaginative mind, and he need not attempt to make the best of both worlds; for having chosen the immaterial, the material world will probably forget to choose him.

And in this attitude of independence there will be no more than a healthy, natural pride, a pride so near to humbleness that the artist will have no room for rancour. 'The large, dull, indocile world,' he will murmur, 'has no great occasion to delight in what I have done; the delight is mine, and no material recognition, however brave and sumptuous, can reward immaterial creation; I am content.' . . . Sometimes, by the very wildest felicity, material recognition does fall upon the creator—absurd and welcome luck! but it is as incalculable as spring in winter.

George Moore has seldom endured injuries in silence, and I have already alluded to his resentment—perfectly just and perfectly vain—of the attitude of the libraries towards certain of his books. In those books he challenged the world, and the world replied in its old dull-eared way that makes recrimination useless. But there is something finer than resentment in his regard for his calling: there is pride, and a jealousy for the honour of English letters; and although it does not persuade him into muting his tongue to shy whispers and becoming as other men (and therefore less himself), it secures him against worse than casual lapses. His pride extends to the outward form of a book, demanding the same conscience in the type-founding, type-setting and paper-making as he has himself come to observe in the diligent art of an author. *The Brook Kerith* showed the first and admirable sign of this rare concern, but *A Story-Teller's Holiday* is a better as well as a more costly example. The suggestion having been made that in issuing expensive and fine books he is actuated only by a spirit of gain, he answers: A strange charge to bring against a man who has worked for thirty years, week in, week out, at a craft in which he is considered a master-craftsman by common consent without ever making two thousand a year, very rarely one thousand, more often merely a few hundreds! He adds, Let none read in this statement a complaint of injustice done to me. My recompense is the full enjoyment of my craft, and in circumstances so favourable that it is often a wonder to me that I did not do better than I have done. To escape from useless regret I fall to thinking of the difficulties that beset every man who goes forth with an ideal in his mind.

He is bound by those strict, intangible bonds which are at once a trouble and delight, and especially a trouble because the queer wantonness that lurked within the earlier writer has never been quite suppressed in the later. The desultory war between sense and spirit seems to have been revived at times almost with deliberation, as though for his own disengaged pleasure; and the sound of that conflict, even partly hushed, is never wholly pleasant and yields only a speculative interest. ‘Unhappy,’ he once wrote, ‘is he who forgets the morals, the manners, the customs, the material and spiritual life of his country.’ Sometimes his own vision is forgotten or defied, but the more secure he becomes in the art of writing—I mean by that something beyond grammatical or stylistic craft—the less easy is his surrender to the satyr-like mood against which my constant protest is directed. His temptation has not been to court the world but to shock it, a subservience as ill-seeming as any compliance; but the temptation has become weaker, or his strength greater, and he has steadily grown in loyalty to the invisible world of his choice.

His attitude towards his art and his attitude towards the world are discovered, implicit or explicit, in every book, for it is peculiarly true of Moore that his art is a personal one; and he himself has said, in speaking of his admired Turgenev, that the impersonality of the artist is the vainest of delusions. Personality informs not merely his novels, the books (that is) which commonly and alone are called creative art; nor merely his imaginative memoirs, which no definition as yet has covered; but also his criticism, which, as we have already seen, is straightforward and vigorous in *Modern Painting* and *Impressions and Opinions*, but far more intimate and ponderable in *Avowals* and sundry prefaces. *Avowals*, above all, expresses Moore's attitude towards the art through which he looks out upon life. In the perfection of prose fiction he seeks for a lucidity and profundity of apprehension, whereby life shall be manifested as order as well as tumult, deep as well as broad; and *Avowals* is his Odyssey, an Odyssey with disappointment on every day's horizon, but bloomed over with amber clouds and winnowed continually by fresh hopes. He is, he acknowledges, without erudition, as many of the ancients were, but he thinks the eyes of the ancients are his.

His thesis is that only the subaltern mind has attempted prose narrative in England, the English genius having accomplished little or nothing outside poetry. Perhaps there is the merest touch of a grudge in this view, for the author of *Hail and Farewell* is not satisfied that a poet should write nothing but poetry, which he sees as a lyrical flower, sudden and unpredictable, and not the main engagement of a serious mind. On points like these discussion with him is in courtesy impossible. . . . I do not know what degree of complicity in these conversations Mr. Edmund Gosse might admit, but certainly they are so contrived as to present a serious argument with an ease, a vivacity, a brilliance and a simplicity which make *Avowals* the worthiest book to set beside the *Imaginary Conversations* of Landor, of whom Moore gives you the frankest and most assured of reminders. There are felinities of touch which Mr. Gosse might resent, if he did not remember that they are the felinities of friendship and therefore, perhaps, not unpardonable. Waiving the smaller Elizabethan romances, the discussion starts with *Robinson Crusoe*, although our author would rather have started with Fielding; but the reference to Defoe gives him the opportunity of obscuring his thesis with the remark that inferior writers seized upon English prose narrative as a means of getting money. Luckily he does not proceed to assert that writing for money annihilates the creative purpose, but he metaphorizes his objection

by saying that English fiction never finishes gallantly—
it is a hackney, while French and Russian narrative shows
breeding. Nobody, he adds, was more *terre à terre* than
Crusoe, and England expressed herself uncommonly well
in her first narrative. Audacious still, he throws out
hints for the better completion of *Robinson Crusoe*, for he
would fain make it finish gallantly, instead of finishing
dead ; and why, he asks, should we not re-arrange literary
masterpieces ? Because, it may be answered, some George
Moore of the future, surveying a mutilated George Moore
of the past and regarding the offence as rank, might be
pricked to murder ; and, more seriously, a book that lives
long enough to provoke such questions means one thing
to one age, and something else to another. And the
value of a book, as Moore knows as well as any author,
consists in the individuality and not in the commonalty
of its authorship. *Esthev Waters* amended by an aspiring
youth of 1950—no! . . . Already, he would have us
believe, it saddens him to think that the next generation
may be more concerned with his writings than with
Landor's or Pater's, and merely because his own are
inferior. But it is worth while to note this plea of our
author's, for he has illustrated a like discontent and
restlessness in regard to many of his own books, giving
them, if not new ends, new bodies, more athletic and
shapely outlines, and brooding upon his own successes
like a peacock within his tent of splendid plumes.

There is much to argue about in these serenely nimble
conversations, for almost every page has its provocation ;
but in the midst of questionings it is delicious to hear
Moore's tribute to Cervantes, who used an eternal gesture
and whose genius dwarfed even Turgenev's ; for it is
easier for a rich man to enter into the Kingdom of
Heaven than for a popular writer to step within the
brilliant disc of Moore's praise. But when he returns
to the English novel it is to find it silly, illiterate,

sentimental, erudite and so forth by turns, but never
serious; and by his rigid if indefinable standards to declare
that George Eliot was trivial and Sterne serious. Let it be
remembered here that our author does not easily indulge
in paradox, and certainly not when he goes on to say that
A Sentimental Journey recalls antiquity. The chief interest
of the conversations, however, does not lie immediately in
the critical opinions so freshly presented, but in their
illumination of Moore's mind, the candid survey of which
is his own dispassioned concern. The time will come, he
says to Mr. Gosse, when memories will seem like hips
and haws hardly worth the gathering; and he adds that
the feminine trouble will be the first to disappear. If
you are a little weary of yourself, is the reply, it is
because you have lost the habit of reading; and he admits
having invested too much in art. . . . It was in 1885,
when he went to Moore Hall to write *Muslin*, that he
first read *Marius the Epicurean*, and was so overwhelmed
by it that he wanted to return to London in order to
find how such a book was appreciated there. His
mother, he says, asked what matter it was how the book
was received in London since he liked it :—'You're
always asking people for their opinions, but I don't think
you ever take them.' But his idea was not to listen but
to speak and say, with apostolic accent, that Pater had
added a prose work to English literature; and his account
of the guarded personality of his subject has a special
interest. Moore claims a genius for intimacy, and shows
Pater as possessing a genius for disguise and detachment;
and you may imagine something amusing and something
pathetic in the contact or conflict of the two writers.
For intimacy proved impossible, though Moore speaks of
his relation with Pater as having been almost affectionate;
and hence he sums up in a too-neat and narrow phrase—
'A shy, sentimental man, all-powerful in written word,
impotent in life.' Affection seems to have died as

suddenly as it grew; it is a judgment which falls strangely from our author, whose powers have been so faithfully concentrated on the written word, and displayed so negligently in 'life.' Nevertheless the intellectual recognition is constant, for he still regards Pater as the writer of the most beautiful of modern English prose, although without pointing precisely to his supreme achievement—the cold, crystalline, faint-flushed picture of *Sebastian van Storck* and a few other unfading water-colours. Had Moore followed his disparagement with some warmer praise, his portrait of Pater would have been unquestionable.

His appreciation of Pater's prose is almost the only exception to his generally unsympathetic view of contemporary writers. It is fortunately unnecessary to recite instances of depreciation, or to account for it beyond mentioning the commonly noted failure of the imaginative artist, in whatever medium he may work, to apprehend the significance of another's creation. Concentration involves sacrifice, even if it be but an involuntary and unconscious sacrifice; and perfect responsiveness to the imaginations of others is hardly to be expected of an artist who is intensely preoccupied with his own. Henry James, restless analyst as he avows himself, lacked something of the amenity of perfect apprehension, growing into himself, his manner sinking slowly and deeply within, until his later writing appeared to some the ultimate refinement and to some the ultimate perversion of his earlier; and how then could he retain that freshness and immediacy of response which was once to be found in his references to others? But Moore's attitude was already far more inflexible than Henry James's, and his natural readiness less marked, even when his own characteristics were unformed or unrecognizable. James, it seems, thought *A Mummer's Wife* too long, and said (the author concurring) that it seemed to have been thought in

French and inadequately translated; and it is in contrasting *A Mummer's Wife* with *The Portrait of a Lady* that Moore complains that James is mistaking trivial comments about men and women for psychology. That which is firmly and clearly imagined, he adds, needs no psychology; Hamlet and Don Quixote *are* psychologies, and so is Dick Lennox, though a long way off. He found that Henry James was too analytic for creation, an opinion that is not offered as more than an opinion. He is impatient of those etherealized reveries, those infinitely refined discriminations, those wing-like and unabiding shadowings, which distinguish the later novels of Henry James from the earlier as plainly as from all other novels save those of sedulous disciples. Such complexities of narrative tease and bewilder Moore, for his own narrative has steadily become a simpler, single strand, clear as a stream drawing its delicious coolness over a shining bed, beneath green weeds and their shadows. That *The Ambassadors* and *The Golden Bowl* should have flowed inevitably down from the spring that once gave us *The Portrait of a Lady* and *The Passionate Pilgrim* seems not to have occurred to Moore's speculations; yet is it less surprising than that *A Modern Lover* should have trickled on to *Evelyn Innes,* and all the first turgidity been lost in the clear waters of *The Brook Kerith* ?

However Moore may have failed in comprehension of others, he has offered the wise and true doctrine for their acceptance—' If we would appreciate a writer, we must take into account his attitude towards life, we must discover if his vision is mean or noble, spiritual or material.' The sentence comes astonishingly in the middle of an essay in which the merits of Mr. Rudyard Kipling are applauded ; astonishment being thoughtlessly based upon the fact that Moore, who deplored the development of Henry James, should have praised the development of so alien an artist as Mr. Kipling. But astonishment is stupid, for he has so carefully trained himself in candid expression that what he says, whether of Henry James or Kipling, of Dostoeffsky or Turgenev, may be listened to as a kind of acute and innocent thinking aloud; and this remains the grand virtue of *Avowals*. Moore does not attempt the kind of wisdom that the late Remy de Gourmont had attained when he reminded us that, 'If there were an art in writing, it would be nothing more or less than the art of feeling, the art of seeing, the art of hearing, the art of using all the senses, whether directly or through the imagination; and the new, serious method of a theory of style would be an attempt to show how these two separate worlds—the world of sensations and the world of words—penetrate each other.' But the French critic describes precisely Moore's own practice, which achieves in *Avowals* a perfect harmony of his thoughts—flowing on, now bright, now deep, sometimes slowly, sometimes swiftly, and sometimes bearing an echo of the masculine and curt phrase of Walter Savage Landor.

The story in *Celibates* called 'John Norton' has the interest of a reference to the subject of one of the chief works of Moore's later maturity, *Héloïse and Abélard*. Norton, it may be remembered, is the essential celibate who, shrinking from the abyss of marriage, is thankful for the tragedy that saves him from marriage. 'He knew now that he could not have fulfilled the life of marriage. . . . They could not have lived together. They would have had to part. His life and hers would have been irretrievably ruined, and then? John remembered the story of Abélard and Héloïse. A new Abélard—a new Héloïse!' The reference is sufficiently early to suggest that the subject of Moore's romance of Héloïse and the great clerk and great lover was for many years among those teasing and obstinate themes which float in the mind, now on the surface, and now submerged and forgotten. Moore had forgotten Pater's few pages in *The Renaissance* when he composed his own book, and is glad he had forgotten them and was not disturbed by those other harmonies of Pater's early prose. 'True child of light, the humanist, with reason and heart and senses quick,' is Pater's phrase for the great mediæval philosopher who overthrew his rivals until he himself was overthrown by his passion for Héloïse, married her, was separated and mutilated, and stole a flame-like immortality from the few letters attributed to Héloïse and himself. Pater is not concerned with Héloïse, and it marks Moore's distinction from him that the title of his romance should be *Héloïse and Abélard* and not *Abélard and Héloïse*. Pater presents Abélard, in his all too few pages, as an influence rather than as a man and lover—'he prefigures the character of the Renaissance, the movement in which, in various ways, the human mind wins for itself a new kingdom of feeling, sensations and thought;' but Moore in his two volumes presents him chiefly as lover, as gleeman, and far less fully as theologian or philosopher. He quite simply justifies himself by insisting that he is writing *Héloïse and Abélard* and not another book, using the painful story of their love, separation and last meeting, and forbearing to touch that after period with which the letters are concerned. The unhappy monk who cried so solemnly against the beloved sins of the past is an unforgettably sad and great figure; and those sins, that thwarted passion, that pride, that madness of mind and body—they are the features of Moore's portrait of the heretical humanist, broken once upon the wheel of personal revenge, and again upon the wheel of an incensed Church. Thus, while it would be untrue to say that Moore has given you the Abélard of the letters, it is true that he has given you something at least of the faint-traditioned Abélard whose passions were abjured and lamented by the Abélard of the letters. Scholars, of whom I am not even the least, have objected against the

P

unveracity of Moore's history. It is said, to use a small instance, that Héloïse could not, if she would, turn down the leaves of Fulbert's Virgil and Ovid and the rest; that the beautiful and curious missal sent from Argenteuil to the Bishop of Lichfield could not have been in existence when Héloïse stood admiring it after her parting from Abélard; and even that the friars, in whose guise Abélard led Héloïse from her home, had not then made their appearance in European history. Moore promptly answered contentions such as these when suggested by his reviewers; his answer being not that he knew that there were anachronisms and that they were immaterial—a quite simple and admissible answer—but that there were no substantial anachronisms; an answer (he still adds to it by repetition) which scholars, I believe, have gently declined to admit. The point remains a slight one, save in so far as Moore's denial illuminates the tenacity with which he will cling to any position in which he happens to have been opposed.

And after the scholar, the less positive literary critic may object to certain passages, saying that such a phrase as, 'The world within us has been enlarged, horizons have been put back,' comes oddly from a twelfth-century conversation, even when the speaker is the great philosopher himself; and saying, again, that the repetition of 'the grey idealistic eyes' of Héloïse sounds no less oddly in scrupulous ears. He will say that if there is any tediousness in this long narrative, it comes with the introduction of the Courts of Love and the elaboration of scenes which seem but tiresome anticipations of the eighteenth century—a twelfth-century Fête Galante.

But when scholar and critic have said what they would upon such points, there are far more vital things to remember. For our present purpose it is useful to observe the author revealing himself, in his preferences and mental habits, almost as clearly in this historical

romance as in *Esther Waters* and *The Lake*. It is himself
that he portrays when he says, 'It seems to me that
afterwards I talked to everybody who would listen to me,
Abelard answered; taking pleasure in the argument for
the sake of it, caring very little which side I took, my
pleasure being to quicken dead minds, to awaken thought;
for the world, it seems to me, is sloughing its skin of
centuries very slowly.' And again, 'I think thou art
sorry, Héloïse, that I am so immodest a man. And if
that thought come into thy mind I cannot blame thee for
it, for it's often come into mine. Time and again I have
tried to check myself, to conform. . . . It may be, too,
that the time has come for me to make my peace with
the world, for one of our oldest proverbs is, that an old
monkey pleases nobody. But can we change ourselves?'
The very voice is heard, the hand seen waving, and you
understand how hard it is even for the imaginative mind
to be wholly lost in its creation. As clear is the hint of
the author in the infrequent coarseness, in the wantonness that echoes earlier offences—'Thou wilt not chide
me if I spend part of to-morrow with a certain knight?
she said to me. . . . It has fallen out that Malberge has
wept naked in my arms, telling me that I must help her
to obtain some man who has caught her fancy, reminding
me of our long love, her tears flowing on her cheeks.'
Who shall say that such a thing has never happened in
the twelfth or the twentieth century? But who shall
deny that such a thing has a lamentable attraction for our
artist? An early proclivity has looked in yet again and
smirched *Héloïse and Abélard* as evilly as it smirched
Hail and Farewell. More welcomely characteristic is our
author's free indulgence of his fondness for the picaresque,
nowhere developed more beautifully than in the long
flight of Héloïse, Abélard and Madelon from Paris to
Tours. The story of that flight draws river-like through
eighty pages of this prolonged pastoral, and the note is

repeated in other wanderings and other stories, to recur last of all with a new solemnity in the final journey and final parting of the lovers in a world where happiness and unhappiness are but the accidents of unresting travel.

And another habit, the inveterate habit of portraying contemporaries, is surely disclosed in such an outline as that of Sister Angela, with ' round almost foolish eyes, dragging mouth and drooping chin. In her face was the simplicity of the deer, and not even the nun's habit could hide the gracefulness of her long arms and slender hands. Héloïse expected a stupid woman to reveal herself, but an intelligence began to appear—a fitful, disconnected intelligence that broke into the conversation and then left it as abruptly, putting thoughts into Héloïse's mind of animals she had seen at one moment eager to claim human companionship and then, wearying suddenly of it, returning into themselves without apparent reason.' The type is common, but the instance veraciously chosen. It occurs in the scene of the return of Héloïse to her old convent, and that, too, is an example of the simple fondness of Moore's mind for a return to old acquaintance ; for the convent of Argenteuil is the convent of Sister Teresa, the inhabitants are almost the same inhabitants, the musical preoccupation is the same. One feature that mars *Sister Teresa* is happily lacking in the story of Argenteuil—the vulgarity which Evelyn Innes so potently distilled into Sister Teresa. It is nowhere to be found in the later story.

Moore's old preferences are betrayed again in the general, or generalized, picture of the Middle Ages, which *Héloïse and Abélard* slowly unfolds. What he sees in that obscure, passionate period is priestly intrigue and a universal sensualism expressed in the traditions of trouvères and the Courts of Love ; and the least profound of readers will be sure that such simple generalizations are not exhaustive. Candour, however, demands an exception being remarked, namely, the descent of a religious madness upon the world, described in the apparition of a spurious Jesus to Héloïse's child, and the demoralizing frenzy that swept the convent at the same time and preluded its destruction. An enemy hath done this, might well be the cry of a pious churchman of the twelfth or the twentieth century; for horror, quiet, simple, unbearable, swells the tide of the story and culminates in the disappearance of Héloïse's child, Astrolabe. Of Astrolabe it is a joy to speak. His name is historical, but all else in him is pure and high imagination and memory. The absence of children in most of Moore's work will have been noticed by his readers, but Astrolabe is a lovely child in whom the genius of life is radiant. . . . Part of imagination, I repeat, and part of memory has Astrolabe been created. 'I have to tell the reader that he was of an amiable and happy disposition, a docile child, yet a wilful one. . . . Why Nature should have given him such witty eyes——' That is not a description of Héloïse's son, tragically swallowed up in the children's crusade, but of the small George Moore himself; but it describes Astrolabe perfectly. Strange is it that when so many writers of our time have proved how easy it is to write affectedly or absurdly of children, the writer who has so often been dismissed as affected should almost alone have created the natural and beloved child.

Héloïse and Abélard has been called monotonous, and if that term be meant merely as an equivalent to monotoned, it can be admitted. Save for the troubadour element, of which there is an excess, there is no tediousness, and though the narrative flows, as I have said, like a river wandering slowly through willow-hemmed meads, it flows in an atmosphere of light and space and sun and shadow. Sometimes it darkens, and tragic sadness tosses the waves of the river, as in the meeting of wife and husband after many years' separation and silence. With the suddenness and sadness of an apparition Abélard comes, and Héloïse, prepared only by her perpetual thoughts and ache, scarce sees him :—

> 'They brought back some small coins every day, and these Héloïse was counting when the door of the kitchen opened and a monk crossed the threshold and stood, his eyes fixed upon her. On seeing that she did not recognize him, for he stood against the light, he raised his hood, and the surprise was so great that for a moment she felt like dying, and leaned against the wall gasping, to fall into Abélard's arms at last. Neither could speak, nor were words needed ; it was enough for each to know that each was with the other. So thou hast come at last, broke from her sighing lips.'

It is painful to read what follows, for the sadness that purifies or destroys great passion is here.

Moore's aim in writing *Héloïse and Abélard*, so far as, after writing it, he is able to define his aim, was to make a beautiful book. He admits having attempted this before, and curiously instances *Evelyn Innes ;* but he freely adds that he failed there, and smiles if you cordially agree that he failed. The success now is as plain as was the failure then. His own conception of a beautiful book (the phrase is a poor one) may be judged by his constant preference of *Marius the Epicurean* as the imaginative masterpiece of our time; and if I do not share this preference quite without hesitation, it is because *Héloïse and Abélard* rivals Pater's success. An imaginative masterpiece cannot be achieved without a mastery of English prose ; and here is Moore's excellence. To recount the various virtues of *Marius* which are not to be found in Moore's book, would be as foolish as to note the fine qualities of *Héloïse* which are wanting in Pater's philosophical romance. I shall not attempt it, but will only compare what is comparable, and say that Moore's

romance has as surely as Pater's—no, a little more surely
—the note of the purest English prose. The striking
phrase, the eloquent cry, the prepared effect, are not
Moore's; but his are a thousand passages, or rather his is
one prolonged lovely passage breathing the music and
reflecting the motion of : ' Grief hushes like a wind and
breaks forth again in the mind like a wind;' and :—

> ' I am afraid of the forest, Héloïse said, and Abélard
> sought to calm her fears, saying : The forest is wonder-
> ful. Listen to the silence, for silence in the forest
> is different from any other. But the forest is never
> silent, Héloïse interposed; it is always mumbling to
> itself. I am afraid. Shall we go back to Madelon,
> he asked, or sit here among the ferns? And in
> answer to her question if he were afraid, he answered
> that he was not, which was barely the truth, for with
> the decline of the light the forest seemed to have
> put off its casual associations with man and to have
> returned to itself, a strange, remote self, nearer to
> beasts than to man. We are all aliens to the forest,
> he said, all save charcoal-burners and wolf-hunters.'

Pleasant is it to be able to record such a satisfaction as
Héloïse and Abélard yields. The book is the work of a
man of mature, unageing mind. Sometimes, as he will
acknowledge, he is touched by the fear that his powers
as an imaginative artist are declining, for that decline
must come, and time brings it nearer. One day age,
that has approached as yet with such friendly gentleness, will step more swiftly, chilling the activity of his
mind and greying every bright hue ; and, worst of all,
he may not know it except by the report of others,
which he will be both ready and reluctant to believe.
I am glad that such a report is not mine. That it has
been sounded by certain reviewers is due, I am willing
to suppose, to the alleged necessity of prompt notice
being given to a book which can only be valued truly
if it is valued reflectively, and pondered over with the

familiarity that deepens the satisfaction of an exquisite water-colour at which we look so often for what we know we shall find. *Héloïse and Abélard* is a picture hung in the mind;—time may establish or diminish its beauty, and as yet it would be stupid to prophesy; but the immediate quickening of the spirit which it provokes is like the quickening that can be remembered in those first apprehensions of things which have grown into permanent delights.

CHAPTER VI

A WANDERING MIND

Were I to live againe it should be as I have already
lived. I neither deplore what is past, nor dread
what is to come : and if I be not deceived, the inward parts have neerly resembled the outward. . . .
Each thing hath beene carried in season. I have
seen the leaves, the blossomes, and the fruit.—
Montaigne.

The years have added a little fulness to the face, but the face is still that of the small boy who looks at you from the new edition of *Memoirs of My Dead Life* and upon whom his thoughts fall so fondly now. Across the deeps and shallows of six decades he bends towards the early slim figure with the long nose and witty eyes, pleased that a resemblance to his present looks should appear, and teasing himself with speculations upon the equal constancy of intellectual and spiritual characters. It is no more wonderful that the visible and invisible characters should persist than that they should vanish, but the persistence gives room for a complacency which is wholly amiable.

But there is change in likeness. The pleasant mildness of the child's face may be found in the man's, just as the fall of the child's hair is followed sixty years after in the fall of the white hair; but the eye changes, the mouth moves, the face in a moment becomes other than it was. Often the look is broad, mild, contented; the cheeks droop in their fulness, the mouth hangs a little open, the harshness of the voice is dulled, the hand weaves a flowing pattern, and there is a general air of softness and ease. Swiftly falls the change at the challenge of a word, a memory; the eye gleams bright, though the brows be but faintly gathered; the lines in the face deepen, the lower lip hangs heavy beneath the white upper lip, the voice at once is strident—the mildness of the sheep is lost in the sharpness of the hound, alert to defend and attack. The note of expostulation is frequent as the voice rises and flows, belying the assertion of indifference that he will make, for instance, if his thought wanders to such injuries as the banning of his novels by the foolish

219

libraries; but if he returns to his story or speaks, as he will do for an eloquent hour, of his own work achieved or planned, or of Shelley or Pater, his face grows serene again and the whole man sits at ease.

The small-boned, fleshly body, sunken into perfect immobility, fills completely the low chair, but the head and eyes are never still. He loves to talk of poetry, of *Poems and Ballads* and Morris's early work, to which he returns in a renewing ecstasy; but save in a French exercise, he is no longer tempted to write verse. He has no *subject* for poetry, and to please him poetry must be objective; the introspection of modern lyrical poets gives him no delight—it is for subject and story that he cries. Milton, for all his epical narration, does not greatly attract him, although the superbness of style is beyond dispute; indeed, he hates such vast and isolated types as Beelzebub, and cannot endure the mediæval conception of a boiling hell, which Milton so simply admitted. But the beautiful pastoral of Adam and Eve in the Garden has a persistent charm. That charm is wanting when he reads Keats, transpiring only through the Miltonic verse of *Hyperion* :—Shelley, in fact, seems to have spoiled him for Keats. Beautiful to him, like a spring bubbling from a cool and sunny hill, is Shelley's *Hymn to Pan.* Even in translation the poet's gift is magical, and the whole of Shelley remains readable, save *A Vision of the Sea ;* and his fondness does not seem to Moore inconsistent with his demand that poetry should be objective, *Epipsychidion* itself, and the *Stanzas Written in Dejection,* for all their lyrical isolation, being 'about' something other than the personal experience of the poet. Scarce anything later than Morris or Meredith can touch his affections, and even Morris fails in a critical test, for he tried too many things. For Rossetti he can find no fondness hidden anywhere, not even in the memories of youth, his poetry seeming too artificial and wanting the sweetness of Christina's. The early English lyric pleases him by its innocence and religious gaiety, and happy absence of introspection. Innocence always touches an innocence within him.

His indifference to recent poets, to the most honoured among them, is complete and undisguised. Nor is his admiration of contemporary prose writers very much more liberal. Of none is his love so warm and prompt as for a few earlier authors: none competes with Landor for his affection, no other approaches Pater. Moore is not a great reader but he remembers what he reads, and is loyal to his early intellectual loves in spite of scores of years flowing by. He is no less loyal to his prejudices, and the reader of *Avowals* will scarcely want an assurance that the opinions so exquisitely enlarged there, the suggestions so adroitly insinuated, the judgments so weightily announced, are not transient shadows of a shifting mind, but the last expression of an æsthetic and moral attitude which has deepened within him through seventy years of change. Speak of Landor, and he rises from his chair, opens a volume of the *Imaginary Conversations* and, at the invitation of a word or look, reads *The Maid of Orleans and Agnes Sorel* or *Bossuet and the Duchess de Fontanges* :—slowly, clearly, and with something of a child's manner of reading straightforwardly to a listener. He has reflected a little sharply upon Stevenson—the preface to *Lewis Seymour* modifies the earlier derogation—but he will no longer deplore—nay, will rather defend—Stevenson's English, reserving his dislike for the stories. He thinks himself perhaps better at stories than Stevenson, but worse at the critical article; forgetting Stevenson's last story on the one hand, and *Avowals* on the other. And he forgets, too, that Stevenson, a year or two his elder, died while as yet *Esther Waters* was the latest and best of his own books; and a comparison between these bright dissociates in 1894 would have led to another conclusion than is inevitable now. . . . Nevertheless our author, although preoccupied with his own work, is very far from being obstinately satisfied with it. There is a curious petty strife in him of the childlike and the masculine. No man depends more entirely upon his instinct, yet no man mistrusts it more. He may seem arrogant when he speaks of another, but when his own art is touched he is strangely pliable and submissive; and hence you become wary and reluctant to make even a minute suggestion, lest he too hastily adopt it.

Sometimes he is guilty of a pleasant excess of praise— as when he says of Stevenson, again, that he possessed the very model of a perfect style of a kind, *Travels with a Donkey* being as absolute an achievement in prose as such a book can be; but a qualification will follow and you perceive him in two minds about the unhappily lost artist. Hard on the heels of the amateur emigrant comes Mr. Max Beerbohm, whose writing seems to Moore as good as Lamb's. That perfection of small prose, which is like the rarest courtesy of language, pleases him by its lightness and brightness. A kind and queer irrelevance is heard when he says that he would not care to leave Max on 'Servants' lying about in his house, for fear that if a servant read in it she might think it superior and inconsiderate. . . . I have a wandering mind, he says, and caprice is often at his elbow, breathing new phrases for old prejudices, as it is present in the conversation of many less exacting readers; but he burns not the faintest pinch of incense to convention, and prefers his own thoughts to the thoughts of others. Perhaps it is more correct to say that when he talks of writers and the art of writing he forgets all but his own thoughts, and is simply unaware of conventional appreciations.

The case is altered when he speaks of men and women, for he will sometimes show an absurdly youthful fondness for thrusting at conventions. Yet even then he shocks not only because he loves to watch the vexed or chill stare, but also as a protest against what is vaguely called the provincial, the philistine, the suburban, the mechanical. He would fain see the world saved (in the spirit of the *Confessions* of 1888) not from its sins but from its narrow virtues, its coldness, its formalism; he would fain see men going on a pilgrimage again, not to Rome but Touraine, or wandering on to no goal but seeking only the joy of wandering. Humour touches his lips with an odd smile, and the instinct for exaggeration seizes at times upon his voice and gestures, as when he is enraged at an ineffably bad cast for a play—perhaps his own. 'You ask me what I think?' he cries. 'My dear friend, if you came to dine with me and I gave you a lemon, you would probably eat it for politeness; you might even eat a second lemon; but if I gave you a third, a fourth, a fifth lemon, and nothing else, you would get up after the fifth lemon and rush out of the house, as I'm rushing out of your theatre.' He will tell this to one and another with the growing relish of a repeated revenge. . . . Seldom is a man isolated equally by reason of his virtues and his faults; but this is Moore's fate, or fond choice. Alone of the present generation he indulges himself in the humour of the scandalous, and presents to the amused but critical eyes of nineteen-twenty-two the spectacle of an utterly devoted artist ridden at times by a disreputable, outmoded hag misnamed wit, misnamed freedom.

> 'At my back I always hear
> Time's wingèd chariot hurrying near——'

And Time will unseat her at length, and leave her withered in the dust; but I lament that the poor victory should be reserved to Time. Moore bears the dignity of his art in his bosom, yet cannot see how oddly it is overborne now and again by the discreditable hag. That serene dignity, happily, survives, and when all is said of these brief, unadvised subordinations, the finer spirit is found unweakened. It is hardly a moral question that is touched here. Moore has assuredly a quick concern with that universal embarrassment and universal stimulus, morality, yet not with morality as part of the social order, but as a personal and restricted problem. The great artist and Don Juan, he declared in an early book, are antagonistic. In his own work there is not the least clinging wisp of the sociological obsession which darkens over vast tracts of modern prose fiction; but there is a very sharp sense of the questions that beset a man and a woman in their relations with one another. To put it loosely, his morality is not philosophical, nor even falsely philosophical, but strictly experimental. It is not so much that he hates abstractions, as that he cannot breathe the air of abstractions, needing a denser air for his vigorous mental constitution.

Apart from the deliberate and the innocent presentation of himself in a long list of books it is proper to ask, What has George Moore given to English literature? Nineteen-fifty will disregard the judgment of nineteen-twenty-two, and a prophecy is apt to prove a jest; and hence I will not presume to anticipate wiser opinions or the stealthy fingering of decay, nor will I attempt a comparison of Moore's work with that of eminent contemporaries. But the question of his own gift is irresistible.

First of all, then, he has given form to the English novel, *Esther Waters* (to name no other of his novels) making a considerable claim to recognition on this score. I do not speak of his method, for that is not new; he follows a traditional way, using a single thread and never attempting the complexities of alien modes. The method of Henry James, for instance, which the common terms of saturation and suffusion so clearly suggest, is not for Moore; neither does he attempt methods so impossible for his genius as those of *The Brothers Karamazov* and *Mort de Quelqu'un*. It is scarcely a virtue that he refrains from the attempt, for the psychology of his novels is so simple and single-visioned as to show that such intricacies of apprehension are for him repellent as well as impossible. His own method gains greatly from the care with which he has developed a native sense of form. His contempt for others' work, considered under this aspect, is expressed in *Avowals* and is too heedless in its scope; and were his mind free to relish another artist's imaginations, he would have found an exception in *The Return of the Native*, to choose but one of several examples. Nevertheless his charge that English fiction is careless in shape remains substantially true, and so far as the contemporary novel has been touched by any beauty of form, it may be said that *Esther Waters* has been the model. It would be too exacting to ask that a novel should be as rigidly ordered as a sonnet, but we may ask that, like the verse of *Paradise Lost*, it should possess without quite concealing a shape of its own creation. The lesson has been learned by some writers, perhaps by all who are capable of learning, that order and form are not a hindrance to the literary artist, any more than straight lines to an architect. And with this lesson a yet simpler one is intertwined—that neither character alone nor incident alone is sufficient for the presentation of human life in an imaginative shape. Moore has discovered these trite notions for himself, for all that he knows of his own task is self-taught; and thus, while the chief influence upon current prose fiction may be that of Henry James or Mr. Hardy, the art of Moore's best books is scarcely less conspicuous as an example, or a reproach.

Next, he has so dexterously modified an old form as to turn it virtually into a new one in his autobiographical writings; making grave things light, using mockery and

Q

malice for those intellectual revenges which the very kindest of us condone, and arming his prejudices with such satire as the seventeenth and eighteenth centuries dearly loved to sharpen. In the decline of brush and pencil, he has redeemed portraiture from gentleness and made butchery a pleasure. The art of caricature is not a Christian exercise, and *Hail and Farewell* may be reckoned by gentle hearts as a breach in the defences of society; but the difficulty of praising it, if that difficulty exists, is merely a contemporary one, and a later generation may very readily pardon offences which it does not feel, and be thankful for the illumination of figures which, but for this maliciously witty light, had been perhaps quite forgotten. The reminiscent narrative has been of service to our subject in another way, for he has always been interested in persons more than in ideas, and in men more than in women; hence his thoughts have been most brightly stimulated by the friction of opposing personalities. This is but to say that he is an emotional artist, whose intellect is the instrument of fondness and animosities; and wanting that friction—to which he will for a while expose himself readily enough—he is lethargic and another man than the author of *Avowals*. . . . The art of writing cannot be taught, least of all an innovating refinement of art such as the musing, acute reminiscence of the autobiography, and I do not refer to Moore's achievement now except to note it as his own and commend it to the haunted eyes of despair.

But to say all this is perhaps to speak superfluously, since it is implied in whatever remains to be said concerning George Moore's prose. I have already referred in so many places in this book to the qualities of that prose, from its first crudities to its slowly unfolding ease, its maturity of flower, fruit and shade; and listening to his prose and remembering that of his contemporaries, a prime distinction is observed—that Moore's is written from and for the ear, while the prose of most others is written from the eye. The thing heard rather than the thing seen is our author's prompter, and hence his rhythm is the most beautiful thing in contemporary English. And without extravagance, surely, one might add that it is not alone the heard melody, but the sweeter unheard melody—voice of a bodiless bird, breath of an immaterial landscape—that steals out of the intricate simplicities and shallows of his style.

Comparison with other writers is a disagreeable thing to attempt, although it would serve to mark George Moore's place a little more sharply. It is a place which scarcely more than one or two contemporaries can dispute with him. Mr. Conrad suffers from the penalty which is laid on a writer who uses another tongue than his own, for his genius, that has led him into a romantic world dominated by an august morality, looming huge and dark as Arabian djinn over a bewildered pilgrim, cannot teach him the simplicities of the English language, or win that heritage which childhood alone receives. Henry James and Mr. Hardy, Mr. Kipling and Mr. Hudson are masters of an instrument how diversely played, following what clamorous or whispered thought! Comparison between them, or between them and George Moore, would yield small pleasure now; and thus I am compelled to look at random and ask whether, for example, this passage which a leading critical journal lately crowned with its praise is worthy of comparison with the style of *Hail and Farewell, The Brook Kerith* and *Avowals*. The three books are named because the prose of one is not the prose of the others—the dreamlike melody of *The Brook Kerith* being unheard in *Avowals*, and the graver phrasing of *Avowals* adding power to the light of the trilogy.

The following is the passage praised by *The Times*:—

‘ Much thought has been expended, during the war and since, on the fittest way of honouring the dead.

They will not come back, and we, who remember them and think of them, like to believe that they will always be remembered. But let us be just to them. They did not ask, when they gave their lives, that their memories should be preserved. There have been nations (there are some to-day) who make divinities of fame and glory. That has never been the habit of the English people. Our dead were content to save England. If they could see Oxford as Oxford is to-day, with the war won, they would be pleased with that living memorial. Even if they had failed to save England they well knew (though no one can explain it) that their sacrifice had an absolute value, and was not made in vain. We grope for some sign or token of them, and here and there, far away from the graves where they lie, we find it. Their virtue, which was a live thing, cannot be engraved on stone or printed in a book, but it still is here, to be sought for among other live things. The words Courage and Duty—or rather, the ideas of courage and duty, for Englishmen use the words very sparingly—are enriched by a great bequest. Fellowship and friendship mean more to-day than they meant before the war. The air that children breathe, even when they are at play, comes to them tonic, from the heights. These things are the touch of live spirits, present or absent.'

The use of certain unwelcome words, the staccato sentences, the absence of rhythm, the faintness of the pulse, are plain faults on a first reading and harassing if another reading is endured. I do not urge that Moore's prose is the sole kind of good prose, and that other subjects than his cannot be presented save in his later, beautiful manner; but to contrast the paragraph just cited with almost any page in those of his books to which I have just referred, is to be aware of such a contrast as that of pump and waterfall.

The price paid by the artist for his art is the concern of

himself alone. I have heard it objected, in a specious antinomy, that it is better to live a full life than to write a fine book; and without pursuing the subtleties of this misconception, which was applied by the misconceiver to George Moore himself, it is worth while to make a plain remark upon it. The objection in the present case was expressed to the effect that the sacrifice of a man's personal life for the sake of his art is to be deplored, and that an artist who prefers, for example, isolation to marriage, so that he may make his calling and election sure, is choosing amiss. ' Choose, rather, a full life !' How much of conscious choice and how much of unconscious tendency is involved in this isolation I have no means or anxiety to discover ; but the fallacy of the suggestion is clear, for is not the imaginative life a full life? And is there a full life which is not imaginative? Pity that Providence forbade the exercise of one joy except by the forfeit of another ! To live ten lives a day, and to live again the intimate personal life and tangled social life of marriage, is a problem set for some men in all ages; the Church has solved it in one way and again in another, and the creative spirit that inhabits a man here and there urges him into a solution or evasion of the same kind. I cannot think it a narrow, waning life that is lived in the mind and expressed in stone, melody, line or word. Born of the imagination and inheriting the ages, the expressive creation fulfils the dream of a prolonged consciousness, the instinct of maintaining in another the life that fades in one's fiery brain. It becomes itself an instrument and a symbol—an instrument of the mind's desire, a symbol of the whole range of human possibility.

And more simply, the justification—if the term be not an impertinence—is found in that for which the imagined sacrifice is made. Of this it is permissible for the speculative critic to speak, but of the artist's private satisfaction the artist alone can speak. Instead, however, of asking

George Moore to plead for himself, it is more decent to listen to his contemporary, Samuel Butler:—

> 'The world resolves itself into two great classes—those who hold that honour after death is better worth having than any honour a man can get and know anything about, and those who doubt this; to my mind, those who hold it, and hold it firmly, are the only people worth thinking about. . . .
>
> 'As for my own position, if I say the things I want to say without troubling myself about the public, why should I grumble at the public for not troubling about me?'

Contradictions flourish in the bosom of George Moore, and his indifference has not always been perfect; but beneath the superficial querulity there is a steadier disdain, and beneath the disdain a serene pride, and beneath all a humble human thankfulness that he has been called to make something which may endure for a moment in a fleeting and sensitive world.

GEORGE MOORE

A BIBLIOGRAPHY

[1878–1921]

BY

HENRY DANIELSON

PREFATORY NOTE

THE present bibliography of the first editions of the writings of Mr. George Moore has been compiled with the object of satisfying the needs of the collector. At the same time it presents a chronological survey of Mr. George Moore's literary activities in volume form from 1878 to 1921.

Those interested in the values of the works herein mentioned will find, at the end of the bibliography, this aspect touched upon.

I must express my indebtedness to Sir Lucas King for his generosity in lending me his copy of *Martin Luther;* and my thanks are also due to Mr. T. Werner Laurie for his kindness in allowing me to inspect many volumes in his collection.

H. D.

March 11th, 1922.

Flowers of Passion : 1878

Flowers of Passion. | [*French rule*] | By | George Moore.| [*French rule*] | London : | Provost & Co., 36, Henrietta Street, | Covent Garden. | [*A line*] | 1878.

Pott 4to ; pp. iv + 116, consisting of Title-page, as above (verso blank), pp. [i, ii] ; Table of *Contents.*, pp. [iii, iv (incorrectly paged ii)] ; *Dedication* (verso blank), pp. [1, 2] ; Text, pp. [3]–114. Pp. [115, 116] are occupied by advertisements of *Provost & Co.'s* | *Recent Poetical Works*. There is an *Errata* slip (4 lines with heading) pasted between the Title-page and Table of *Contents*. There is no printer's imprint.

Issued in black cloth, lettered up the back in gilt as follows : *Flowers of Passion* In centre of front cover, in gilt, skull and cross-bones with leaves and lyre with broken strings and leaves. Back cover blank. Gilt edges. Cream end-papers. (Some copies were issued with plain edges.)

(2)

Martin Luther : 1879

Martin Luther : | A Tragedy, | In Five Acts. | By | George Moore, | Author of " Flowers of Passion," | and | Bernard Lopez, | Collaborateur de | Scribe, Méry, Auguste | Lefranc, Théophile Gautier, | Alexandre Dumas père, Victor | Séjour, Alboize, Charles Desnoyer, | Gérard de Nerval, Dupenty, Laurencin, | Grangé, Hippolyte Cogniard, Lelarge, | Delacour, Varin, | Charles Narrey, Rochefort | père, Dumanoir,

Clairville et Saint-Georges. | [*A line*] | London:
Remington and Co., | 5, Arundel Street, Strand, W.C. |
[*A line*] | 1879. | [All Rights Reserved.]

Crown octavo; pp. xii + 180, consisting of a Leaf (not
reckoned in pagination) with blank recto, and the
following note, printed within a thin one-line border,
in centre of verso: [a fist] *Managers desirous of
securing the Acting | Rights of this Play should apply to
Messrs. | Remington & Co., who have full powers to |
represent the Authors in relation thereto.*; Title-page, as
above (verso blank), pp. [i, ii]; Quotation: "*Si autem
de veritate scandalum sumitur, utilius permittitur | nasei
scandalum, quam veritas relinquatur.*" | *Saint Gregory the
Great.* | (*Taken from the 17th Century Edition of the* |
"*Bibliothéque* [sic] *Nationale,*" *p. 1225, Vol. I.*) (verso
blank), pp. [iii, iv]; *Dramatis Personæ.*, p. [v]; *Authors'
Note.*, p. [vi], *Sonnet Dédicace | a | Algernon Charles
Swinburne.* | [Sonnet] | *Paris, Janvier, 1879.* George
Moore., p. [vii]; *Ode Dédicace | a | Algernon Charles
Swinburne.* [at end of Ode: *Paris, Janvier,* 1879.
Bernard Lopez.], pp. [viii]–x; *Preface.* (consisting of
Eighteen Letters, ten of which are from *George
Moore to Bernard Lopez*, and the other eight from
Bernard Lopez to George Moore, written between
May 1876 and December 1878), pp. [1]–38; Text,
pp. [39]–179; p. [180] blank. At foot of p. 179 is
the following printers' imprint: [a line] | *Printed by
Remington & Co., 5, Arundel Street, Strand, W.C.*
Signatures: [*a*] (2 leaves); [*b*] (4 leaves); B—M
in eights; N (2 leaves). The sheets are wire stitched.
Issued in red bevelled cloth, lettered across the back
in gilt as follows: *Martin | Luther | A Tragedy | [a
line] | George | Moore | and | Bernardo* [sic] *| Lopez |
Remington,* with conventional gilt decoration and two
lines in black at top and bottom; and across front
cover in gilt, within black borders, as follows: *Martin
Luther | A Tragedy,* with conventional designs in
black at top and bottom. On back cover, same
designs and borders as on front cover, in black. All

edges cut and painted red. Greenish-blue end-papers. There is a paper binders' label pasted on inside back cover, lettered as follows : *Bound by* | *Burn* | *& Co*

(3)

PAGAN POEMS : 1881

Pagan Poems. | By | George Moore. | London : | Newman and Co., | 43, Hart Street, Bloomsbury, W.C. | [*A line*] | MDCCCLXXXI. | (followed by initials of the author in ink " *G. M.*" with very small flourish.)

Crown octavo ; pp. iv + 164, consisting of Title-page, as above (verso blank), pp. [i, ii] ; Table of *Contents*, pp. [iii], iv ; Text, pp. [1]–164. There is no printer's imprint.

Issued in blue cloth, lettered across the back in gilt. The book usually occurs with the title-page torn out.

(4)

A MODERN LOVER : 1883

A Modern Lover. | By | George Moore. | In Three Volumes. | Vol. I. [*Vol. II.*] [*Vol. III.*] | London : Tinsley Brothers, 8, Catherine Street, Strand. | 1883.

3 Vols., Crown 8vo

Vol. I, pp. iv + 256, consisting of Title-page, as above (with printers' imprint in centre of verso as follows : *Printed by* | *Kelly & Co., Printers ,* [sic] *Gate Street, Lincoln's Inn Field ;* [sic] | *and Kingston-on-Thames.*), pp. [i, ii] ; Table of *Contents* (verso blank), pp. [iii, iv] ; Text, pp. [1]–252 ; pp. [253–256] blank.

Vol. II, pp. iv + 240, consisting of Title-page, as above (with printers' imprint in centre of verso as follows : *Printed by* | *Kelly and Co., Printers, Gate Street, Lincoln's Inn Fields ;* | *and Kingston-on-Thames.*), pp. [i, ii] ; Table of *Contents* (verso blank), pp. [iii, iv] ; Text, pp. [1]–239 ; p. [240] blank.

Vol. III, pp. iv + 212, consisting of Title-page, as above (with printers' imprint in centre of verso as follows: *Printed by | Kelly and Co., Printers, Gate Street, Lincoln's Inn Fields ; | and Kingston-on-Thames.*), pp. [i, ii] ; Table of *Contents* (verso blank), pp. [iii, iv] ; Text, pp. [1]–210 ; pp. [211, 212] blank. Inserted between pp. 210 and [211] is a 32-page numbered list (undated) of *Tinsley Brothers' | Catalogue of Publications.* (p. [32] blank).

Issued in light blue cloth, lettered across the back in gilt as follows: *A | Modern | Lover | [a line] Vol. I.* [Vol. II.] [Vol. III.] | *George Moore | Tinsley Bros. ;* and lettered (diagonally) across the front in black as follows: *1883 | A Modern Lover | George Moore* Back cover blank. Top edges unopened, fore and lower edges trimmed. Cream end-papers.

(5)

A MUMMER'S WIFE : 1885

Vizetelly's One-Volume Novels. | [*A line*] | III. | A Mummer's Wife. | By George Moore, | Author of " A Modern Lover," | [*Publishers' device*] | London : | Vizetelly & Co., 42, Catherine Street, Strand. | 1885.

Crown 8vo ; pp. 440, consisting of Blank page, p. [1] ; List of *Vizetelly's One-Volume Novels.* printed within a thin one-line border, p. [2] ; Half-title, *Vizetelly's One - Volume Novels. | [a line] | III. | A Mummer's Wife. | By George Moore.* (verso blank), pp. [3, 4] ; Title-page, as above (with printers' imprint in centre of verso as follows: *London : | Printed by J. S. Virtue and Co., Limited, | City Road.*), pp. [5, 6] ; Dedication : *To my friend, | James Davis, | I dedicate this book, in acknowledgment of a | literary debt.* (verso blank), pp. [7, 8] ; Quotation : " *Change the surroundings in which man lives, and, in two or three | generations, you will have changed his physical constitution, his habits | of life, and a goodly number of his ideas."—Victor Duruy, L'Introduction | Générale à l'Histoire de France.* (verso blank), pp.

[9, 10]; Text, pp. [11]–438; p. [439] is occupied by
a list of *Vizetelly's Popular French Novels.*; p. [440] is
occupied by a list of *Gaboriau's Sensational Novels.*
Printers' imprint at foot of p. 438 as follows: [a line] |
*Printed by J. S. Virtue and Co., Limited, City Road,
London.* At end of volume there is a 20-page
numbered illustrated catalogue of *Vizetelly's & Co.'s
New Books,* | *and New Editions.* dated *September, 1884.*
The title-page is a cancel-leaf.

Issued in light brown cloth, lettered across the back in
gilt as follows: *A* | *Mummer's* | *Wife* | [a line] |
George | *Moore* | *Vizetelly & Co* with decoration in
cherry at top and bottom; and on front cover in
cherry as follows: [ornament in gilt] | *A Mummer's
Wife* | [ornamental line in gilt] | *George Moore.*
[ornament in gilt], with decoration in cherry at top
and bottom. In centre of back cover, publishers'
device in cherry. All edges cut. Light grey end-
papers.

In some copies a small printed oblong slip was inserted
between pp. [2] and [3], bearing the following note:
Notice. | *This book has been placed in the Index Expurga-
torius* | *of the "Select" Circulating Libraries of Messrs.
Mudie and* | *W. H. Smith & Son.* This slip was inserted
after the book had been put into circulation.

(6)

LITERATURE AT NURSE: 1885

Price Threepence | [*A line*] | Literature | at Nurse |
or | Circulating Morals | By George Moore | Author
of "A Mummer's Wife," "A Modern Lover," etc. |
"They stand there, Respectable; and—what more?
Dumb idols; with a skin | of delusively-painted wax-
work, inwardly empty, or full of rags and bran. . . . |
Such bounties, in this as in infinitely deeper matters,
does Respectability shower | down on us. Sad are thy
doings, O Gig; sadder than those of Juggernaut's

Car : | that, with hugh wheel, suddenly crushes asunder
the bodies of men ; thou in thy | light-bobbing Long-
acre springs, gradually winnowest away their souls ! " |
[*A row of seven fullpoints*] | " One day the *Mudie*
mountain, which seemed to stand strong like the other
rock | mountains, gave suddenly, as the icebergs do, a
loud-sounding crack ; suddenly, | with hugh clanguor,
shivered itself into ice dust ; and sank, carrying much
along | with it."—Carlyle's Essays. | London | Vizetelly
& Co., 42 Catherine Street, Strand | 1885

Demy 8vo ; pp. 24, consisting of Title-page, as above
(with an advertisement of a *New and Cheaper Edition,
price 3s. 6d.* of *A Modern Lover. By George Moore.*
in centre of verso), pp. [1, 2] ; Text (beginning with
drop heading as follows : *Literature at Nurse,* | *or* |
Circulating Morals. | [French rule]), pp. [3]–22, with
name of the author at end. Pp. [23, 24] are occupied
by an announcement of *A Mummer's Wife.* | *A
Realistic Novel, in One Volume.* with thirteen Press
Notices, and publishers' imprint at end. The running head-line on the left-hand page is the title
of the work (*Literature at Nurse,*) and on the right-
hand page the sub-title (*or Circulating Morals.*), both
printed in small capitals, with folio outside. There
are no signatures.

Issued as a 24-page pamphlet without wrappers, sewn
with one stitch of thread. All edges cut. The leaves
measure 8⅜ by 5½ ins.

(7)

A Drama in Muslin : 1886

Vizetelly's One-Volume Novels. | [*A line*] | XV. | A
Drama in Muslin | A Realistic Novel. | By George
Moore, | Author of " A Mummer's Wife," " A Modern
Lover," etc. | With a Frontispiece from a Drawing
by J. E. Blanche. | [*Publishers' device*] | London : |

Vizetelly & Co., 42, Catherine Street, Strand. | 1886. | [The Right of Translation is Reserved.]

Crown 8vo ; pp. vi + 330, consisting of Half-title, *Vize-telly's One-Volume Novels.* | [a line] | *XV.* | *A Drama in Muslin.* | *By George Moore.* (with list of *Vizetelly's One-Volume Novels.* | *By English and Foreign Authors of Repute.* on verso), pp. [i, ii]; [Frontispiece : *In the Convent Garden*]; Title-page, as above (verso blank), pp. [iii, iv]; [Prefatory Note] (verso blank), pp. [v, vi]; Text, pp. 1–329; p. [330 blank. Printers' imprint at foot of p. 329 as follows : [a line] | *Chas. Straker and Sons, Bishopsgate Avenue, London, E.C. ; and Redhill.* At end of volume there is a 24-page numbered Illustrated Catalogue of *Vizetelly's & Co.'s* | *New Books,* | *and New Editions.* dated *April, 1886.* In the second edition the catalogue is also dated *April, 1886,* but in the third edition it is dated *November, 1885.* The frontispiece is printed in blue ; in the second and third editions the frontispiece is printed in black.

Issued in light blue cloth, lettered across the back in gilt as follows : [two lines] | *A* | *Drama* | *in* | *Muslin* | [ornament] | *George Moore* | [ornament] | *Vizetelly & Co.* | [two lines], and across the front in navy blue, within a thick one-line border in blind, as follows : *Vizetelly's One-Volume Novels.* | *A Drama* | *in Muslin.* | *By George Moore.* | *Author of " A Mummer's Wife."* In centre of back cover, publishers' monogram in blind with thick one-line outer border in blind. Top edges unopened, fore and lower edges trimmed.

(8)

A MERE ACCIDENT : 1887

Vizetelly's One-Volume Novels. | [*A line*] | XXVI. | A Mere Accident. | By | George Moore, | Author of " A Mummer's Wife," " A Modern Lover," " A Drama in Muslin," etc. | [*Publishers' device*] | London : | Vizetelly

R

& Co., 42 Catherine St., Strand. | Brentanos: New York, Washington, and Chicago. | 1887. | [*A line*] | (The Right of Translation is reserved.)

Crown 8vo ; pp. viii + 5–284, consisting of advertisement of *Vizetelly's Half-Crown Series.*, p. [i] ; advertisement of *The Mermaid Series.*, p. [ii] ; Half-title, *Vizetelly's One-Volume Novels.* | [a line] | *XXVI.* | *A Mere Accident.* | *George Moore.* (with advertisement and quotations from reviews of three of *Mr George Moore's Realistic Novels.* on verso), pp. [iii, iv] ; Title-page, as above (verso blank), pp. [v, vi] ; Dedicatory Letter *To* | *My Friends at Buckingham.* (verso blank), pp. [vii, viii] ; Text, incorrectly beginning p. [5] instead of p. [1]–282 ; p. [283] is occupied by advertisements of *Vizetelly & Co.'s Latest Publications.*; p. [284] is occupied by advertisements of *New One-Volume Novels.* Printers' imprint at foot of p. 282 as follows : *Turnbull and Spears, Printers, Edinburgh.* At end of volume there is a 32-page numbered Illustrated Catalogue of *Vizetelly & Co.'s* | *New Books,* | *and New Editions.* dated *March, 1887.*

Issued in light brown cloth, lettered across the back in gilt as follows : *A* | *Mere* | *Accident* | [ornament in brown] | *George* | *Moore* | [ornament in brown] | *Vizetelly & Co* with two lines in gilt at top and bottom, and across the front in brown, within a thick one-line border in blind, as follows : *Vizetelly's One-Volume Novels.* | *A Mere* | *Accident.* | *By George Moore,* | *Author of* " *A Mummer's Wife.*" In centre of back cover, publishers' monogram in blind with thick one-line outer border in blind. Top edges unopened, fore and lower edges cut. Green end-papers.

(9)

PARNELL AND HIS ISLAND : 1887

Parnell | and his | Island | By | George Moore | Author of | ['] A Mummer's Wife ' ' Drama in Muslin '

etc. | London | Swan Sonnenschein, Lowrey, & Co. |
Paternoster Square | 1887

Small crown 8vo; pp. iv + 256, consisting of Title-
page, as above (with printers' imprint in centre of
verso as follows: *Printed by | Spottiswoode and Co.,
New-Street Square | London*), pp. [i, ii]; Table of
Contents (verso blank), pp. [iii, iv]; Text, pp. [1]–254.
Pp. [255, 256] are occupied by advertisements of
New Six-Shilling Novels. Printers' imprint at foot of
p. 254 as follows: *Printed by | Spottiswoode and Co.,
New-Street Square | London*

Issued in pale yellow printed paper boards, lettered up
the back in black as follows: *Parnell and his Island*
The front cover is lettered across in black as follows:
*Parnell | and his | Island | By | George Moore | [a
line] | Half-a-Crown: Cloth, Three-and-Six | [a line] |
London | Swan Sonnenschein, Lowrey & Co. | Paternoster
Square | 1887* (enclosed within a double-line border).
The back cover is occupied by advertisements of
books, with heading as follows: *Swan Sonnenschein &
Co.'s New Political List*. All edges cut. White end-
papers. Also issued simultaneously in cloth.

(10)

CONFESSIONS OF A YOUNG MAN: 1888

Confessions of a | Young Man. | By | George Moore, |
Author of " A Mummer's Wife," " Parnell and His
Island," etc., etc. | [*Publishers' device*] | London: |
Swan Sonnenschein, Lowrey & Co., | Paternoster
Square. | 1888.

Crown 8vo; pp. iv + 360, consisting of Half-title,
Confessions of a Young Man. | George Moore. (verso
blank), pp. [i, ii]; [*Etched Portrait of George Moore
by William Strang*]; Title-page, as above (verso blank),
pp. [iii, iv]; Text, pp. [1]–357; pp. [358–360] blank.
There is no printer's imprint.

Issued in grey cloth, lettered across the back in gilt as

follows: *Confessions | of a | Young Man | By | George Moore | Sonnenschein* On front cover, design of a woman with right knee on a chair, holding up her right hand to a gas bracket, and lettered in blue *Confessions of a | Young Man* and in gilt *George Moore* Back cover blank. Top edges unopened, fore and lower edges trimmed. Dark end-papers.

(11)

SPRING DAYS : 1888

Vizetelly s One-Volume Novels. | [*A line*] | XXIX. | Spring Days. | A Realistic Novel. | A Prelude to "Don Juan." | By | George Moore, | Author of "A Mummer's Wife," "A Modern Lover," "A Drama in Muslin," | "A Mere Accident," etc. | [*Publishers' device*] | London : | Vizetelly & Co., 16 Henrietta Street, | Covent Garden. | 1888.

Crown 8vo ; pp. iv + 372, consisting of Half-title, *Vizetelly's One-Volume Novels. | [a line] | XXIX. | Spring Days. | George Moore.* (with a list of *Mr George Moore's Realistic Novels.*, enclosed within a thin one-line border, on verso), pp. [i, ii] ; Title-page, as above (verso blank), pp. [iii, iv] ; Dedication, *To | My Friend, | Frank Harris.* (verso blank), pp. [1, 2] ; Preface, pp. [3, 4 (numbered iv)] ; Text, pp. [5]–371 ; p. [372] blank. Printers' imprint at foot of p. 371 as follows : *Turnbull and Spears, Printers, Edinburgh.* At end of volume there is a 32-page numbered Illustrated Catalogue of *Vizetelly & Co.'s | New Books, | And New Editions.* dated *April, 1888.*

Issued in dull strawberry cloth, lettered across the back in gilt as follows : *Spring | Days | A Realistic | Novel | George Moore. | Vizetelly & Co.* with two lines in black at top and bottom, and across the front in black as follows : *Spring Days | A Realistic Novel | George Moore.* In centre of back cover, publishers' monogram in blind. Top and fore-edges unopened.

Green end-papers. Some copies were issued in blue cloth. There are many reissues of the first edition, bound in various cheap cloth bindings.

(12)

MIKE FLETCHER : 1889

Mike Fletcher. | A Novel. | By | George Moore, | Author of | " A Mummer's Wife," " Confessions of a Young Man," etc. | London : | Ward and Downey, | 12, York Street, Covent Garden. | 1889. | [All rights reserved.]

Crown 8vo ; pp. vi + 304, consisting of Half-title, *Mike Fletcher* (verso blank), pp. [i, ii]; Title-page, as above (verso blank), pp. [iii, iv]; Dedication, *To | my Brother Augustus, | in memory of | many years of mutual aspiration and labour.* (verso blank), pp. [v, vi]; Text, pp. [1]–304. There is no printer's imprint.

Issued in peacock blue cloth. The front cover is decorated with conventional designs in compartments in light brown and peacock blue, and lettered across in gilt as follows : *Mike Fletcher* | [a line] | *George Moore*, in an oblong compartment on plain background. The back is lettered across in gilt, on peacock background, as follows : *Mike | Fletcher* | [a line] | *George | Moore | Ward & Downey*, with designs to match the front. In centre of back cover, publishers' monogram in blind. Top and fore-edges unopened, lower edges trimmed. Light grey flowered end-papers. Some copies have an advertisement leaf pasted between the half-title and title-page.

(13)

IMPRESSIONS AND OPINIONS : 1891

Impressions | and Opinions | By | George Moore | Author of ' A Mummer's Wife ; ' | ' A Modern Lover ; ' ' Confessions | of a Young Man,' etc. | [*Ornament*] |

London | Published by David Nutt | in the Strand |
1891

Small crown 8vo; pp. viii + 346, consisting of Half-
title, *Impressions and Opinions* (verso blank), pp.
[i, ii]; Title-page, as above (verso blank), pp. [iii,
iv]; [Note] (verso blank), pp. [v, vi]; Table of *Contents* (verso blank), pp. [vii, viii]; Text, pp. [1]–346.
Printers' imprint at foot of p. 346 as follows : [a line] |
Printed by T. and A. Constable, Printers to Her Majesty, |
at the Edinburgh University Press. At end of volume
there is a 12-page numbered list (undated) of *A
Selection | from | David Nutt's | List of Publications.*
printed on smaller paper than the text.

Issued in green cloth, lettered across the back in
gilt as follows : [gilt decoration] | *Impressions | and |
Opinions | George | Moore* | [gilt decoration with *David
Nutt* in centre]; gilt decoration at top and bottom of
front cover; back cover blank. Top and fore-edges
unopened, lower edges trimmed. White end-papers.

(14)

VAIN FORTUNE : [1892]

Vain Fortune. | By | George Moore, | Author of " A
Mummer's Life [*sic*]," " Impressions and Opinions,"
" Confessions of a | Young Man," " A Modern Lover,"
etc. | With Eleven Illustrations by Maurice Greiffen-
hagen. | London : | Henry and Co., | Bouverie Street,
E.C.

Crown 8vo; pp. Frontispiece + iv + 304, consisting
of Frontispiece, *The Great Critics had each a separate
Audience.*, followed by a leaf of tissue ; Title-page, as
above (with printers' imprint at foot of verso as follows :
[a line] | *Printed by Hazell, Watson, & Viney, Ld.,
London and Aylesbury.*), pp. [i, ii]; p. [iii] is occupied
by the following note : *The Author has to express his
thanks to the Editor | of the " Lady's Pictorial " for his*

kind permission to | reproduce in this volume Mr. Greiffen-hagens illus- | trations.; p. [iv] blank; Text, pp. [1]–296. The printers' imprint, which appears on the verso of Title-page, is repeated at foot of p. 296. Pp. [297–304] are occupied by advertisements of books published by Henry & Co. The misprint on Title-page, viz. *"A Mummer's Life,"* is again repeated on p. [303].

Issued in dark red cloth, lettered across the back in gilt as follows: *Vain | Fortune | George | Moore | Henry & C⁰* On front cover there is a thick line border, with thin inner border, in gilt. The same border is repeated on back cover in blind. All edges cut. Dark navy end-papers.

The illustrations comprise Frontispiece and four other full-page plates, which face pp. 35, 101, 180, and 293, each protected by a leaf of tissue; and six vignette illustrations in the text at pp. 84, 106, 174, 202, 264, and 273. There is no list of illustrations.

(15)

Vain Fortune : [1892]

Large Paper Edition

There was also an edition of 150 copies printed on Large Paper. The collation is the same as the small paper issue, with the addition of a Half-title preceding the frontispiece: *Vain Fortune.* (with certificate of issue in centre of verso as follows: *Only One Hundred and Fifty Copies of this Large Paper Edition | have been Printed, of which this is | No. . . .* This large paper edition was advertised as being numbered and signed by the author, but very few copies were so issued.

Crown 4to; issued in white bevelled cloth, lettered across the back in gilt as follows: *Vain | Fortune | George | Moore | Henry & Co.*, and across the front in gilt as follows : *Vain | Fortune | George Moore* Back cover blank. Top edges unopened, fore-edges uncut and unopened, lower edges uncut. Flowered end-papers. A large number of copies were re-issued in red buckram and published by Messrs. Walter Scott, Ltd.

(16)

Modern Painting : 1893

Modern | Painting | By George Moore | London | Walter Scott, Limited | 24 Warwick Lane | 1893

Crown 8vo; pp. vi + 256, consisting of Half-title, *Modern | Painting* (with list of books *By the same Author* in centre of verso), pp. [i, ii] ; Title-page, as above (with Note in centre of verso), pp. [iii, iv] ; Table of *Contents* (verso blank), pp. [v, vi] ; Text, pp. [1]–248 ; pp. [249–256] are occupied by advertisements of books published by Messrs. Walter Scott, Ltd. At foot of p. 248 is the following printers' imprint: *The Walter Scott Press, Newcastle-on-Tyne.* At end of volume there is a 16-page unnumbered and undated Catalogue of Books published by Messrs. Walter Scott, Ltd., printed on different paper to that of the text.

Issued in dark red cloth, lettered across the back in gilt as follows : *Modern | Painting | George Moore | Walter Scott, Ltd.* Both sides blank. Top edges gilt, fore and lower edges cut. Sage-green end-papers.

(17)

The Strike at Arlingford : 1893

The Strike at | Arlingford | Play in Three Acts | By George Moore | London | Walter Scott, Limited | 24 Warwick Lane | 1893

Crown 8vo ; pp. 178, consisting of Half-title, *The Strike at | Arlingford.* (verso blank), pp. [1, 2] ; Title-page, as above (verso blank), pp. [3, 4]; *Note* (verso blank), pp. [5, 6]; List of *Characters* (verso blank), pp. [7, 8]; Text, pp. [9]–175. Printers' imprint at foot of p. 175 as follows: *The Walter Scott Press, Newcastle-on-Tyne.* P. [176] blank. Pp. [177, 178] are occupied by advertisements of books by George Moore, published by Walter Scott, Ltd.

Issued in dark red cloth, lettered across the back in gilt as follows: *The | Strike at | Arlingford | Play in | Three Acts | [a line] | George Moore* (enclosed within a thin border with scallop-shaped design at top and bottom in gilt) | *Walter Scott* On front cover a large elongated panelled design enclosed within a two-line border in gilt. Back cover blank. Top edges gilt, fore and lower edges cut. Sage-green end-papers.

(18)

Esther Waters: 1894

Esther Waters | A Novel | By | George Moore | London | Walter Scott, Ltd. | 24 Warwick Lane, Paternoster Row | 1894

Crown 8vo; pp. vi + 380, consisting of Blank page, p. [i]; p. [ii] is occupied by a list of six books *By the same Author;* Title-page, as above (verso blank), pp. [iii, iv]; Dedication, *To my Brother, | Major Maurice Moore, | I Affectionately Dedicate | this Book.* (verso blank), pp. [v, vi]; Text, pp. [1]–377; p. [378] blank; p. [379] is occupied by a list of advertisements of *Works by George Moore.;* p. [380] is occupied by an advertisement of the Second Edition of 'Modern Painting.' Printers' imprint at foot of p. 377 as follows: *The Walter Scott Press, Newcastle-on-Tyne.* [The preliminaries consist of 1 leaf (pp. [i, ii]) pasted on to a quarter-sheet (Title-page and Dedication).] At end of volume there is a 16-page unnumbered catalogue of books published by Walter Scott, Ltd., with heading as follows: *Walter Scott's | New Books.*

In some copies this catalogue is printed on thin
paper.

Issued in dark green cloth, lettered across the back in
gilt as follows: *Esther* | *Waters* | *A Novel* | *George
Moore* | *Walter Scott ;* and on upper portion of front
cover in gilt as follows: *Esther Waters* | *A Novel* |
George Moore with an ornamental flower-design in
gilt in lower left-hand corner. Back cover blank.
Top edges gilt, fore and lower edges cut. Navy end-
papers (some copies were issued with light navy
end-papers).

(19)

CELIBATES : 1895

Celibates | By | George Moore | London : Walter
Scott, Ltd. | Paternoster Square | 1895

Crown 8vo; pp. viii + 560, consisting of Half-title,
Celibates (with a list of eight books *By the same Author*,
enclosed within a one-line border, on verso), pp. [i,
ii]; Title-page, as above (verso blank), pp. [iii, iv];
Table of *Contents* (verso blank), pp. [v, vi]; Fly-title
to first story, *Mildred Lawson* (verso blank), pp. [vii,
viii]; Text, pp. [1]–559; p. [560] blank. Printers'
imprint, *Printed by T. and A. Constable, Printers to
Her Majesty* | *at the Edinburgh University Press*, at
foot of p. 559. At end of volume there are 8 un-
numbered pages of advertisements of books published
by Messrs. Walter Scott, Ltd. There are fly-titles
before the different Tales, viz. *Mildred Lawson*, p.
[vii]; *John Norton*, p. [313]; and *Agnes Lahens*,
p. [453].

Issued in dark red cloth, lettered across the back in
gilt as follows: [two double rules] | *Celibates* | *By* |
George Moore | [double rule] | *Walter Scott* | [three
rules]; and across the front in gilt: *Celibates* | *By* |
George Moore Back cover blank. Top edges gilt,
fore and lower edges cut. Dark bluish-green end-
papers.

(20)

The Royal Academy 1895 : 1895

" New Budget" Extras.   No. 1 | The Royal Academy | 1895 | [*A wavy line*] | Criticisms | [*A line*] | By George Moore | Caricatures | [*A line*] | By Harry Furniss | Some of which appeared in The New Budget | Price Sixpence | Published at the Office of "The New Budget" | 69 Fleet Street, E.C. | 1895 | All rights reserved

Pott 4to; pp. 64, consisting of Title-page, as above (with an advertisement of *Graham & Banks,* | . . . | *Decorators and Upholsterers.* on verso), pp. [1, 2]; *Index.* pp. [3], 4 ; Advertisement of *Queen's Hall,* | *Langham Place, W.* p. [5]; Advertisement of *Pleyel Pianos,* p. [6] ; Text (signed at end: *George Moore*), with heading as follows: *The Royal Academy Exhibition.* [a line] | *Criticisms* | *by* | *George Moore.* pp. [7]– 24 ; *Caricatures* | *by* | *Harry Furniss.*, pp. 25–62 ; p. [63] is occupied by an advertisement, with heading: *Mr. N. Vert,*; p. [64] is occupied by an advertisement of the *Blue Posts Tavern*

Issued as a 64-page pamphlet, sewn with stitches of thread.   All edges cut.

(21)

Evelyn Innes : 1898

Evelyn Innes | By | George Moore | London | T. Fisher Unwin | 1898

Tall crown 8vo; pp. viii + 484, consisting of a Leaf, with signature *a* on recto, and list of *Novels at Six Shillings Each.,* enclosed within a thin one-line border, on verso, pp. [i. ii] ; Half-title, *Evelyn Innes* (with publisher's monogram on verso), pp. [iii, iv] ; Title-page, as above (with list of books *By the Same Author* and [*All Rights Reserved.*] on verso), pp. [v, vi] ; Dedication, *To | Arthur Symons and W. B. Yeats | Two Contemporary Writers | with whom | I am in sympathy* (verso blank), pp. [vii, viii] ; Text, pp. [1]–482. Printers' imprint in centre of p. [483] as follows : *Colston & Coy., Limited, Printers, Edinburgh.* P. [484] blank. The title of the work and publisher's name on title-page are printed in red, the other lines are in black. At end of volume there are 8 unnumbered pages of advertisements of miscellaneous books published by T. Fisher Unwin. (In some copies these advertisements leaves are missing.)

Issued in dark green cloth, lettered across the back in gilt as follows : *Evelyn | Innes | George | Moore* (enclosed within a thin one-line border in gilt, and *T. Fisher Unwin* at foot, also enclosed within a thin one-line border in gilt). Both sides blank. Top edges gilt, fore and lower edges trimmed. White end-papers.

(22)

THE BENDING OF THE BOUGH : 1900

The Bending of the Bough. | A Comedy in Five Acts. | By George Moore. [*Double ornament*] | London | T. Fisher Unwin | Paternoster Square | 1900

Crown 8vo ; pp. xx + 156, consisting of Half-title, *The Bending of the Bough* (with an advertisement of 'Evelyn Innes,' headed *By the same Author*, enclosed within a thin one-line border, on verso), pp. [i, ii] ; Title-page, as above (with [*All rights reserved.*] at foot of verso), pp. [iii, iv] ; List of Characters, p. [v] ; p. [vi] blank ; Preface, pp. vii–xx ; Text, pp. [1]–153 ; pp. [154–156] blank. Printers' imprint at foot of p. 153 as follows : *Unwin Brothers, The Gresham Press, Woking and London*

Issued in light blue cloth, lettered across the back in gilt as follows : *The | Bending | of the | Bough | George*

Moore | *T. Fisher Unwin*, and across the front in gilt as follows: *The Bending of the Bough* | *George Moore* Back cover blank. Top and fore-edges unopened. White end-papers.

(23)

SISTER TERESA : 1901

Sister Teresa | By | George Moore | [*Publisher's device*] | London | T. Fisher Unwin | Paternoster Square | 1901

Crown 8vo; pp. viii + 248, consisting of a Leaf, with signature *a* on recto (verso blank), pp. [i, ii]; Half-title, *Sister Teresa* (with an advertisement of two books by the same author, divided into three compartments and enclosed within a thin one-line border, on verso), pp. [iii, iv]; [Portrait of George Moore, with facsimile signature: *Always yours* | *George Moore*, printed on imitation Japanese vellum, followed by a leaf of tissue]; Title-page, as above (with *All Rights reserved* at foot of verso), pp. [v, vi]; *Preface*, pp. vii, viii; Text, pp. [1]–236. Printers' imprint at foot of p. 236 as follows: *Colston & Coy. Limited, Printers, Edinburgh* Pp. [237–248] are occupied by advertisements of *Books for* | *Recreation* | *and Study*, published by T. Fisher Unwin.

Issued in dark green cloth, lettered across the back in gilt as follows: *Sister* | *Teresa* | *By* | *George* | *Moore* (enclosed within a thin one-line border in gilt), and *T. Fisher Unwin* at foot (also enclosed within a thin one-line border in gilt). Both sides blank. Top edges gilt, fore-edges unopened, lower edges trimmed. White end-papers.

The Frontispiece-Portrait of George Moore is by Henry Tonks, Slade Professor.

(24)

ᴀɴ ᴄ- úʀ-ʒoʀᴄ : [1902]

ᴀɴ ᴄ-úʀ-ʒoʀᴄ. | [*Rule*] | sʒéᴀlᴄᴀ | ʟe seóʀsᴀ
ó móʀóᴀ ; | ᴀiʀᴄpiʒᴄe ó'ɴ sᴀcʀbéᴀpʟᴀ | ᴀʒ |
pᴀ́óʀᴀiʒ ó suiʟʟeᴀbᴀiɴ, ᴅ.ᴀ. | [*Rule*] | Dublin |
Sealy, Bryers & Walker.

> Royal 8vo; pp. xii + 116, consisting of Half-title, ᴀɴ
> ᴄ-úʀ-ʒoʀᴄ. (verso blank), pp. [i, ii]; Title-page, as
> above (with [a line] | *All Rights Reserved.* [a line] in
> centre of verso), pp. [iii, iv] ; *Dedication.* (verso blank),
> pp. [v, vi] ; Table of Contents, ᴀɴ cʟᴀʀ. (verso blank),
> pp. [vii, viii] ; Preface, pp. [ix–xii (incorrectly paged
> [i]–iv)] ; Text, pp. [1]–115 ; p. [116] blank.   At foot
> of p. 115 is the following printers' imprint : [a line] |
> *Printed by Sealy, Bryers and Walker, Dublin.*

> Issued in grey printed paper wrappers, with the
> lettering on title-page repeated on front cover, with
> ᴀoɴ sʒiʟʟiɴʒ in upper right-hand corner.   Back cover
> blank.   Cut edges.

(25)

The Untilled Field : 1903

The Untilled Field | By | George Moore. | London |
T. Fisher Unwin | Paternoster Square. | ᴍ·ᴅ·cccc·ɪɪɪ.

> Crown 8vo; pp. viii + 424, consisting of Half-title, *The
> Untilled Field.* (verso blank), pp. [i, ii]; List of *New
> Six Shilling Novels.*, enclosed within a thin one-line
> border, p. [iii]; List of Books *By the same Author.*,
> enclosed within a thin one-line border, p. [iv] ; Title-
> page, as above (with (*All Rights Reserved.*) on verso),
> pp. [v, vi] ; Table of *Contents* (verso blank), pp. [vii,
> viii] ; Fly-title, *In the Clay.* (verso blank), pp. [1, 2] ;
> Text, pp. 3–[420] ; pp. [421–424] are occupied by
> advertisements of books published by Mr. T. Fisher
> Unwin.   Printers' imprint at foot of p. [420] as
> follows : *Printed by Sealy, Bryers and Walker, Mid.*

Abbey St., Dublin. There are fly-titles before the different 'Stories' into which the work is divided, at pp. [1], [27], [117], [153], [175], [199], [221], [241], [259], [269], [279], [299], and [395]. Pp. [2], [28], [116], [118], [152], [154], [174], [176], [198], [200], [222], [240], [242], [258], [260], [270], [278], [280], [300], [394], and [396] blank. The title of the work and the author's and publisher's names on title-page are printed in red, the other lines are in black.

Issued in scarlet cloth, lettered across the back in gilt as follows : *The | Untilled | Field | By | George | Moore* (enclosed within a thin one-line border in gilt), and *T. Fisher Unwin* at foot (also enclosed within a thin one-line border in gilt). The front cover is decorated with design of intertwined sprays and publisher's monogram in blind, and lettered on upper portion in gilt as follows : *The Untilled Field | By George Moore* Back cover blank. Top edges gilt, fore-edges cut. White end-papers.

(26)

The Lake : 1905

The Lake | By | George Moore | Author of 'Esther Waters,' 'Evelyn Innes,' etc. | [*Publisher's device, by William Nicholson*] | London | William Heinemann | 1905

Crown 8vo ; pp. vi + 336, consisting of Half-title, *The Lake* (with a list of *New 6s. Novels* on verso), pp. [i, ii] ; Title-page, as above (with *Copyright. New York : D. Appleton & Co. 1905. | Copyright. London : William Heinemann. 1905. | This Edition enjoys copyright in | all countries signatory to the Berne | Treaty, and is not to be imported | into the United States of America.* on verso), pp. [iii, iv] ; *Dedicatory Letter, A Edouard Dujardin,* pp. [v], vi ; Text, pp. [1]–334 ; printers' imprint, *Billing and Sons, Ltd., Printers, Guildford* at foot of p. 334 ; pp. [335, 336] blank. [The preliminaries consist of a quarter-sheet (2 leaves) with the Dedicatory Letter (1 leaf) pasted between Title-page and p. [1] of text.]

Issued in dark red cloth, lettered across the back in gilt as follows: *The | Lake | George | Moore | Heinemann,* and across the front in gilt as follows: *The Lake | George Moore* In centre of back cover, publisher's windmill device (by William Nicholson) in blind. Top edges cut, fore-edges trimmed, lower edges uncut. White end-papers.

A second impression appeared in the same month. It is exactly similar in binding and format, but the two lines of Copyright on verso of Title-page are transposed, and the following note is added in centre of verso: *First printed, November, 1905 | Second Impression, November, 1905*

(27)

REMINISCENCES OF THE IMPRESSIONIST PAINTERS : 1906

The Tower Press Booklets | Number Three [*Two ornaments*] | Reminiscences of the | Impressionist Painters | By George Moore. [*Ornament*] | Dublin : Maunsel & Co., Ltd., | 60 Dawson Street. MCMVI.

Foolscap 8vo ; pp. xvi + 9–48, consisting of Blank leaf, pp. [i, ii] ; Half-title, *Reminiscences of the | Impressionist Painters | By George Moore.* (verso blank), pp. [iii, iv] ; Title-page, as above (with printers' imprint at foot of verso as follows : *Printed at the Tower Press, Thirty-eight Cornmarket, Dublin.*), pp. [v, vi] ; Dedicatory Letter, beginning *My dear Steer,* pp. [vii–xv] ; p. [xvi] blank ; Text, pp. 9–48.

Signatures (A)–c in eights ; D, 4 leaves.

Issued in light grey printed paper wrappers, with large design of a tower, printed in black, on front, lettered below in black as follows : *The Tower Press Booklets | Number Three* [three ornaments] | *Reminiscences of the | Impressionist Painters. | By George Moore.* P. [2] of cover blank. P. [3] is occupied by a list of volumes in the same series, headed *The Tower Press Booklets.*

P. [4] blank. Top edges unopened, fore and lower edges uncut.

(28)

MEMOIRS OF MY DEAD LIFE: 1906

Memoirs of | My Dead Life | By | George Moore | [*Publisher's Windmill device, by William Nicholson*] | London | William Heinemann | 1906

> Crown 8vo; pp. viii + 336, consisting of Blank leaf, pp. [i, ii]; Half-title, *Memoirs of My Dead Life* (with list of *Works by George Moore* on verso), pp. [iii, iv]; Title-page, as above (with *Copyright 1906 by William Heinemann.* in centre of verso), pp. [v, vi]; Table of *Contents* (verso blank), pp. vii, [viii]; Text, pp. [1]– 335; printers' imprint at foot of p. [336] as follows: *Printed by T. and A. Constable, Printers to His Majesty | at the Edinburgh University Press*
>
> Issued in navy blue cloth, lettered across the back in gilt as follows: *Memoirs | of My | Dead Life | George | Moore* (enclosed within a thin border with scallop-shaped design at top and bottom in gilt) | *Heinemann* On front cover, a large elongated panelled design enclosed within a two-line border in blind. On back cover, in lower right-hand corner, publisher's device (the Whistler variety) in blind. Top and fore-edges cut, lower edges uncut. White end-papers.

(29)

AVE: 1911

'Hail and Farewell!' | [*A line*] | Ave | By | George Moore | London | William Heinemann | 1911

> Crown 8vo; pp. vi + 368, consisting of Blank page, p. [i]; p. [ii] is occupied by an advertisement of two books ('Memoirs of My Dead Life' and 'The Lake') *By the same Author;* Half-title, '*Hail and Farewell!'* (with '*Hail and Farewell!'* | *A Trilogy* | *I. Ave* | *II. Salve* [*In preparation* | *III. Vale* [*In preparation* in s

centre of verso), pp. [iii, iv]; Title-page, as above (with *Copyright, London, 1911, by William Heinemann,* | *and Washington, U.S.A., by D. Appleton and Co.* at foot of verso), pp. [v, vi]; *Overture,* pp. [1]–39; Text, pp. 40–367; printers' imprint, *Billing and Sons, Ltd., Printers, Guildford* at foot of p. 367; p. [368] blank. The title of the book, *Ave,* is printed in red, the other lines are printed in black.

Issued in navy blue cloth, lettered across the back in gilt as follows: *Hail and* | *Farewell* | [a line] | *Ave* | *George* | *Moore* (enclosed within a thin border with scallop-shaped design at top and bottom in gilt) | *Heinemann* On front cover a large elongated ornamental design enclosed within a two-line border in blind. On back cover in lower right-hand corner publisher's device (the Whistler variety) in blind. Top and fore-edges cut, lower edges trimmed. White end-papers.

There is a much later issue, of which some copies are printed on thinner paper, with pp. [i, ii] of the preliminaries omitted.

(30)

The Apostle: 1911

The Apostle | A Drama in Three Acts | By George Moore | Dublin: Maunsel and Co. Ltd. | 96 Middle Abbey Street | 1911

Large crown 8vo; pp. viii + 104, consisting of Half-title, *The Apostle* (verso blank), pp. [i, ii]; Title-page, as above (with *All rights reserved.* | *Printed by Maunsel & Co., Ltd., Dublin.* on verso), pp. [iii, iv]; Dedicatory Letter, beginning *My dear Mary Hunter,* (verso blank), pp. [v, vi]; Table of *Contents* (verso blank), pp. [vii, viii]; *A Prefatory Letter* | *on Reading the Bible* | *for the First Time,* pp. 1–35; p. [36] blank; Fly-title to the play, *The Apostle,* p. [37]; *Persons in the Play,* p. [38]; Text, pp. 39–100; p. [101] blank; pp. [102–103] are occupied by advertisements of *The*

Works of J. M. Synge; p. [104] is occupied by advertisement of books by Lady Gregory.

Issued in mauve cloth, lettered across the back in gilt as follows: [a line] | *The* | *Apostle* | *A Drama* | *in Three* | *Acts* | *George* | *Moore* | *Maunsel* | [a line]. The front cover is lettered across in gilt as follows: *The Apostle* | *A Drama in Three Acts* | *By* | *George Moore*, with a one-line border in blind, and a uniform outer border in blind on back cover. Top edges cut, fore-edges unopened, lower edges uncut. White end-papers.

(31)

SALVE: 1912

'Hail and Farewell!' | [*A line*] | Salve | By | George Moore | London | William Heinemann | 1912

Crown 8vo ; pp. iv + 380, consisting of Half-title, '*Hail and Farewell !*' (with '*Hail and Farewell !*' | *A Trilogy* | *I. Ave* | *II. Salve* | *III. Vale* [*In preparation* on verso), pp. [i, ii] ; Title-page, as above (with *Copyright, London, 1912* on verso at foot), pp. [iii, iv] ; Text, pp. [1]–379. Printers' imprint at foot of p. 379 as follows: *Billing and Sons, Ltd., Printers, Guildford ;* p. [380] blank. The title of the book, *Salve*, is printed in red ; the other lines are in black.

Issued in navy blue cloth, lettered across the back in gilt as follows: *Hail and* | *Farewell* | [a line] | *Salve* | *George* | *Moore* (enclosed within a gilt border with scallop-shaped design at top and bottom) | *Heinemann* On front cover, a large elongated ornamental design enclosed within a two-line border in blind. On back cover, in lower right-hand corner, publisher's device (the Whistler variety) in blind. Top and fore-edges cut, lower edges untrimmed. White end-papers. There is an *early issue* with the border-design on back in light green.

(32)

ESTHER WATERS: A PLAY IN FIVE ACTS: 1913

Esther Waters | By George Moore | A Play in Five Acts | London: William Heinemann | 1913

> Demy 8vo; pp. xvi + 156, consisting of Half-title, *Esthers Waters | By George Moore* (with a list of *Works by George Moore* enclosed within a one-line border on verso), pp. [i, ii]; Title-page, as above (with *Copyright 1913* in bottom left-hand corner of verso), pp. [iii, iv]; Table of Acts into which the play is divided (verso blank), pp. [v, vi]; Reprint of the Programme of the Play for the first production at the Apollo Theatre, on December 10, 1911 (verso blank), pp. [vii, viii]; *Preface*, pp. ix–xv; p. [xvi] blank; Text, pp. 1–[153]; at foot of p. [153] is the following printers' imprint: *Printed by | Ballantyne & Company Ltd | at the Ballantyne Press | Tavistock Street Covent Garden | London;* pp. [154–156] blank.
>
> Issued in drab green paper boards, with white paper name and title-label on back lettered across in green as follows: *Esther | Waters | A Play in | Five Acts |* [ornament] *| George | Moore |* [ornament] *| London: Heinemann | 1913* (enclosed within a thin one-line border). Both sides blank. All edges cut. White end-papers.

(33)

ELIZABETH COOPER: 1913

Elizabeth Cooper | A Comedy in Three Acts | By George Moore | Maunsel and Co. Ltd. | Dublin and London | 1913

> Crown 8vo; pp. 80, consisting of Half-title, *Elizabeth Cooper* (verso blank), pp. [1, 2]; Title-page, as above (with *Copyright 1913, George Moore* in centre, and the following printers' imprint at foot, of verso: *Printed by | Ballantyne & Company Ltd | London*), pp. [3, 4];

Note of First Performance and List of *Persons in the Play*, p. [5] ; p. [6] blank ; Text, pp. 7–80.

Issued in drab green cloth, lettered across the back in gilt as follows : *Elizabeth | Cooper | A | Comedy | By | George | Moore | Maunsel* The front cover is lettered across in gilt as follows : *Elizabeth Cooper | A Comedy By | George Moore,* with a one-line outer border in blind, and a uniform outer border in blind on back cover. All edges cut. White end-papers.

(34)

VALE: 1914

'Hail and Farewell!' | [*A line*] | Vale | By | George Moore | London | William Heinemann

Crown 8vo; pp. iv + 364, consisting of Half-title, *' Hail and Farewell ! '* (with

> *' Hail and Farewell ! '*
>
> *A Trilogy*
>
> *III. Ave*
>
> *II. Salve*
>
> *III. Vale*

on verso), pp. [i, ii] ; Title-page, as above (with *Copyright, 1914.* on verso below), pp. [iii, iv] ; Text, pp. [1]–363. Printers' imprint at foot of p. 363 as follows : *Billing and Sons, Ltd., Printers, Guildford ;* p. [364] blank. The title of the book, *Vale,* is printed in red ; the other lines are in black.

Issued in navy blue cloth, lettered across the back in gilt as follows : *Hail and | Farewell | [a line] | Vale | George | Moore |* (enclosed within a thin border with scallop-shaped design at top and bottom in gilt) | *Heinemann* On front cover, a large elongated ornamental design enclosed within a two-line border in blind. On back cover, in lower right-hand corner, publisher's device (the Whistler variety) in blind. Top and fore-edges cut, lower edges trimmed. White end-papers.

The *second issue* was issued with a cancel Half-title, with the above misprint on verso, and the second 'E' in 'Farewell' on recto, corrected.

In the *third issue, Copyright, 1914.* on verso of title-page is altered to *London : William Heinemann. 1914.* | *Copyright.*

(35)

MUSLIN : 1915

Muslin | By | George Moore | [*Publisher's device, by William Nicholson*] | London | William Heinemann

    Crown 8vo ; pp. xx + 344, consisting of Half-title, *Muslin* (with list of *Works by George Moore* on verso), pp. [i, ii] ; Title-page, as above (with the following bibliographical note in centre of verso : *Originally published under the title of* | '*A Drama in Muslin,*' *1886.* | *New Edition, September, 1915.* ; and *London : William Heinemann. 1915.* at foot of verso), pp. [iii, iv] ; *Preface*, pp. v–xx ; Text, pp. [1]–343 ; p. [344] blank. At foot of p. 343 is the following printers' imprint : [a line] | *Billing and Sons, Ltd., Printers, Guildford, England.* At end of volume there is a 16-page numbered catalogue (undated) of *A List of* | *Current Fiction* | *published by* | *William Heinemann* | *at 21 Bedford St., London, W.C.* | [Publisher's device, by William Nicholson.]

    Issued in navy blue cloth, lettered across the back in gilt as follows : *Muslin* | *George* | *Moore* (enclosed within a thin border with scallop-shaped design at top and bottom in gilt) | *Heinemann* On front cover a large elongated panelled design enclosed within a two-line border in blind. On back cover, in lower right-hand corner, publisher's device (by James McNeill Whistler) in blind. Top and fore-edges cut, lower edges uncut. White end-papers.

(36)

THE BROOK KERITH : 1916

The Brook Kerith | A Syrian Story | By George Moore | Printed for T. Werner Laurie Ltd. | By the Riverside Press Ltd., Edinburgh | 1916

Demy 8vo; pp. viii + 472, consisting of Blank page, p. [i] ; p. [ii] is occupied by a list of three books *By George Moore*, printed within a thin one-line border ; Half-title, *The Brook Kerith* (verso blank), pp. [iii, iv] ; Title-page, as above (verso blank), pp. [v, vi] ; *A Dedication* (verso blank), pp. [vii, viii] ; Text, pp. 1–471 ; Printers' imprint, *The Riverside Press Limited, Edinburgh*, in centre of p. [472].

Issued half bound, with tan imitation leather back and corners, and conventional marbled paper sides. On the back are five raised bands and three medallions in blind, and printed paper name and title-label, lettered across in black as follows : *The | Brook | Kerith | [ornament] | George | Moore | T. Werner Laurie, Ltd. | London* Top edges cut, fore-edges uncut and unopened, lower edges uncut. White endpapers. Issued without a duplicate paper name and title-label.

Owing to the orders coming in so rapidly, the publishers had to increase the size of the edition, and as the binders had saved only a certain amount of tan imitation leather, they were instructed to use the nearest material they could find to bind the balance ; these remaining copies were bound in half brown pegamoid.

Two hundred copies of the first edition were bound in light grey cloth, lettered across the back in black as follows : *The | Brook | Kerith | [a line] | George | Moore | T. Werner | Laurie Ltd*. Publishers' monogram within a circle in black in centre of back cover ; front cover blank. All edges (the leaves measuring 8½ by 5½ ins.) cut. This issue was put into grey cloth for the exclusive use of the Circulating Libraries.

(37)

THE BROOK KERITH : 1916

Édition de Luxe

The Brook Kerith | A Syrian Story | By George
Moore | Printed for T. Werner Laurie Ltd. | By the
Riverside Press Ltd., Edinburgh | 1916

Demy 8vo ; pp. x + 472, consisting of Blank leaf, pp.
[i, ii] ; Half-title, *The Brook Kerith* (verso blank), pp.
[iii, iv] ; Title-page, as above (verso blank), pp. [v,
vi] ; *A Dedication* (verso blank), pp. [vii, viii] ;
Certificate of Issue, as follows : *The Brook Kerith* |
[a line] | *This edition de luxe consists of* | *250 copies,
numbered and signed.* | *This is No.* .... (followed
by the number of copy written in ink) (followed by
the author's signature in ink : *George Moore*) (verso
blank), pp. [ix, x] ; Text, pp. 1–471 ; printers' imprint,
The Riverside Press Limited, Edinburgh in centre of
p. [472].

Issued in light grey boards, with cream parchment back,
with paper name and title-label on back at top
lettered across in royal blue as follows : *Edition de
Luxe* | *The* | *Brook* | *Kerith* | [ornament] | *George* |
Moore | *T. Werner Laurie, Ltd.* | *London* (printed
within a one-line border). Top and fore-edges unopened, lower edges uncut. Grey end-papers.

(38)

LEWIS SEYMOUR AND SOME WOMEN : 1917

Lewis Seymour | and Some Women | By | George
Moore | [*Publisher's device, by William Nicholson*] |
London | William Heinemann

Crown 8vo; pp. xii + 310, consisting of Half-title,
Lewis Seymour | *and Some Women* (with list of *Works
by George Moore* on verso), pp. [i, ii], Title-page, as
above (with *London : William Heinemann. 1917.* at

foot of verso), pp. [iii, iv] ; *Preface*, pp. v–xi ; p. [x] blank ; Text, pp. [1]–310. Printers' imprint at foot of p. 310 as follows : *Billing and Sons, Ltd., Printers, Guildford, England* At end of some copies there is a blank leaf following p. 310.

Issued in navy blue cloth, lettered across the back in gilt as follows : *Lewis | Seymour | and | Some | Women | George | Moore* (enclosed within a thin border with scallop-shaped design at top and bottom in gilt) | *Heinemann* On front cover a large elongated panelled design enclosed within a two-line border in blind. On back cover, in lower right-hand corner, publisher's device (the Whistler variety) in blind. Top and fore-edges cut, lower edges uncut. White end-papers.

At end of some copies there is a 16-page numbered catalogue (undated) of *A List of | Current Fiction | published by | William Heinemann | at 21 Bedford St., London W.C.*

(39)

A STORY-TELLER'S HOLIDAY : 1918

A Story-Teller's | Holiday | By | George Moore | London | Privately Printed for Subscribers Only by | Cumann Sean eoταιρ nα h Éιρeann | 1918

Demy 8vo ; pp. x + 356, consisting of Blank leaf, pp. [i, ii] ; Half-title, *A Story-Teller's Holiday* (verso blank), pp. [iii, iv] ; Title-page, as above (verso blank), pp. [v, vi] ; *A Leave-Taking*, p. [vii (incorrectly paged v)] ; p. [viii] blank ; Certificate of Issue, as follows : *A Story-Teller's | Holiday | [a line] | This edition consists of 1000 copies, | numbered and signed. | This is No.........* (each copy numbered automatically) | (signed in ink by the author :) *George Moore* (verso blank), pp. [ix, x] ; Text, pp. 1–355 ; printers' imprint, *The Riverside Press Limited, Edinburgh* at foot of p. 355 ; p. [356] blank.

On p. 48 the second and third words in line 14, viz. *Nouvelle Athènes*, are obliterated.

Issued in pale blue boards with cream parchment back,

with white paper name and title-label on back
lettered across in brown as follows : *A | Story-Teller's |
Holiday | [ornament] | George | Moore | Privately |
Printed* Top edges unopened, fore-edges uncut and
unopened, lower edges uncut. Pale blue end-papers
to match the sides.

'A Story-Teller's Holiday' was issued for private
circulation by the Society for Irish Folk-Lore, for sale
to subscribers through the Society's agents, T. Werner
Laurie, Ltd.

(40)

AVOWALS: 1919

Avowals | By | George Moore | London | Privately
Printed for Subscribers Only by | Cumᴀnn Seᴀn eoᴌᴀiꞃ
nᴀ ʜ Éiꞃeᴀnn | 1919

Demy 8vo; pp. x + 312, consisting of 2 blank leaves,
pp. [i–iv] ; Half-title, *Avowals* (with *By George
Moore | (Privately Printed) | The* [sic] *Story-Teller's
Holiday . July 1918 | Avowals . . . . September 1919 |
Abelard and Héloïse . . (In preparation)* on verso), pp.
[v, vi]; Title-page, as above (verso blank), pp. [vii,
viii]; Certificate of Issue, as follows : *Avowals | [a
line] | This edition consists of 1000 copies | numbered
and signed. | This is No.* .... (each copy numbered
automatically) | (signed in ink by the author:) *George
Moore* (verso blank), pp. [ix, x]; Text, pp. 1–310;
printers' imprint, *The Riverside Press Limited,
Edinburgh* in centre of p. [311]; p. [312] blank.

Issued in pale blue boards with cream parchment back,
with white paper name and title-label on back
lettered across in sepia as follows : *Avowals |
[ornament] | George | Moore | Privately Printed* Top
edges unopened, fore-edges uncut and unopened,
lower edges uncut. Pale blue end-papers to match
the sides. Uniform with 'A Story-Teller's Holiday.'

'Avowals' was issued for private circulation by the
Society for Irish Folk-Lore, for sale to subscribers through
the Society's agents, T. Werner Laurie, Ltd.

(41)

ESTHER WATERS: 1920

Esther Waters | By | George Moore | London |
Privately Printed for Subscribers Only by | Cumann
Seᴀn eoᴌᴀıʀ nᴀ h Éıʀeᴀnn | 1920

Demy 8vo; pp. x + 416, consisting of Blank leaf, pp.
[i, ii]; Half-title, *Esther Waters* (with a list of books
By George Moore | (Privately Printed) on verso), pp.
[iii, iv]; Title-page, as above (verso blank), pp. [v, vi];
Certificate of Issue, as follows: *Esther Waters* | [a
line] | *This edition consists of 750 copies | numbered
and signed. | This is No.* .... (each copy numbered
automatically) | (signed in ink by the author :) *George
Moore* (verso blank), pp. [vii, viii]; *Epistle Dedicatory*,
pp. [ix, x (incorrectly numbered v, vi)]. [The preliminaries consist of a half-sheet (4 leaves), with the
Certificate of Issue (1 leaf) pasted between the Title-
page and *Epistle Dedicatory*.] Text, pp. [1]–415;
printers' imprint at foot of p. 415 as follows: *Billing
and Sons, Ltd., Printers, Guildford, England.* ; p. [416]
blank.

Issued in pale blue boards with white parchment back,
with cream paper name and title-label on back lettered
across in brown as follows: *Esther | Waters | [orna-
ment] | George | Moore | Privately Printed* Top edges
cut, fore-edges unopened, lower edges trimmed.
Pale blue end-papers to match the sides.

'Esther Waters' was issued for private circulation by
the Society for Irish Folk-Lore, for sale to subscribers
through the Society's agents, T. Werner Laurie, Ltd.

(42)

THE COMING OF GABRIELLE: 1920

The Coming of | Gabrielle | A Comedy | By | George
Moore | London | Privately Printed for Subscribers
Only by | Cumᴀnn Seᴀn eoᴌᴀıʀ nᴀ h Éıʀeᴀnn | 1920

Demy 8vo; pp. xxxii + Certificate of Issue + 148, consisting of Half-title, *The Coming of Gabrielle* (verso blank), pp. [i, ii]; Title-page, as above (with a list of books *By George Moore | (Privately Printed)* in centre of verso), pp. [iii, iv]; Certificate of Issue, as follows: *The | Coming of Gabrielle | [a line] | This edition consists of 1000 copies | numbered and signed. | This is No.* .... (each copy numbered automatically) | (signed in ink by the author :) *George Moore* (verso blank) [The Certificate of Issue is a separate leaf pasted between the Title-page and first page of *Preface,* and is not reckoned in the preliminaries]; *Preface,* pp. v–xxx; p. [xxxi] blank; *People in the Play,* p. [xxxii]; Text, pp. 1–146; printers' imprint, *The Riverside Press Limited, Edinburgh* in centre of p. [147]. Pp. [50] and [148] blank.

Issued in pale blue boards with cream parchment back, with white paper name and title-label on back lettered across in grey as follows: *The | Coming | of | Gabrielle | [ornament] | George | Moore | Privately | Printed* Top edges unopened, fore-edges uncut and unopened, lower edges uncut. Pale blue end-papers to match the sides.

'The Coming of Gabrielle' was issued for private circulation by the Society for Irish Folk-Lore, for sale to subscribers through the Society's agents, T. Werner Laurie, Ltd.

(43)

HÉLOÏSE AND ABÉLARD: 1921

Héloïse and Abélard | By | George Moore | In Two Volumes | Volume I [*Volume II*] | London | Privately Printed for Subscribers Only by | Cumann Sean eolair na h Éipeann | 1921

2 Vols., Demy 8vo

Vol. I, pp. x + 264, consisting of p. [i] with printers' signature "ı.—*a*" in bottom left-hand corner; pp. [ii–iv] blank; Half-title, *Héloïse and Abélard* (with a list

of books *By George Moore* | (*Limited Editions*) in centre
of verso), pp. [v, vi] ; Title-page, as above (with
Dedication in French *A Madame X* in centre of
verso), pp. [vii, viii] ; Certificate of Issue, as follows :
Héloïse and Abélard] | a line] | *This edition consists
of one thousand | five hundred copies, numbered and |
signed. | This is No.* .... (each copy numbered
automatically) | (signed in ink by the author :) *George
Moore* (verso blank), pp. [ix, x] ; Text, pp. 1–262 ;
printers' imprint, *The Riverside Press Limited,
Edinburgh* in centre of p. [263] ; p. [264] blank.

Vol. II, pp. 256, consisting of Half-title, *Héloïse and
Abélard*, with printers' signature " II.—A " in bottom
left-hand corner (verso blank), pp. [1, 2] ; Title-page,
as above (verso blank), pp. [3, 4] ; Text, pp. 5–252 ;
printers' imprint, *The Riverside Press Limited, Edinburgh*
in centre of p. [253] ; pp. [254–256] blank.

Issued in pale blue boards with cream parchment back,
with white paper name and title-label on back lettered
across in brown as follows : *Héloïse | and | Abélard. |*
[one star (two stars on Volume II)] | *George | Moore |
Privately | Printed*   Top edges unopened, fore-edges
uncut and unopened, lower edges uncut.   Pale blue
end-papers to match the sides.   Uniform with ' A
Story-Teller's Holiday ' and ' Avowals.'

' Héloïse and Abélard ' was issued for private circulation
by the Society for Irish Folk-Lore, for sale to subscribers
through the Society's agents, T. Werner Laurie, Ltd.

(44)

FRAGMENTS FROM HÉLOÏSE & ABÉLARD : 1921

Fragments from | Héloïse & Abélard | By George
Moore | London | Privately Printed for Subscribers
by | Cumann Sean eoláir na h Éipeann | 1921

Demy 8vo ; pp. 24, consisting of Title-page, as above
(verso blank), pp. [1, 2] ; Sonnet in French, with
heading in italic capitals as follows : *La Reponse de*

Georges Moore en | forme de Sonnet a son ami Edouard |
Dujardin (l'Auteur de " La Source | du Fleuve Chretien")
qui l'avait | invite a Fontainebleau | pour manger de |
l'alose, p. 3; p. [4] blank ; *Preface,* pp. 5–7; p. [8]
blank; Text, pp. 9–23; printers' imprint in centre
of p. [24] as follows: *Printed by | The Riverside Press
Limited, Edinburgh*

Issued in pale blue paper wrappers, lettered across the
front at top in dark brown as follows: *Fragments
from | Héloïse & Abélard | By George Moore* Pp.
[2, 3, and 4] of cover blank. Sewn with a double
stick of pale blue imitation embroidery silk. Top
edges unopened, fore-edges uncut and unopened,
lower edges uncut, with the wrappers overlapping.

There is no Certificate of Issue. Two thousand copies
were printed.

' Fragments from Héloïse & Abélard ' was issued for
private circulation by the Society for Irish Folk-Lore,
for sale to subscribers through the Society's agents,
T. Werner Laurie, Ltd.

(45)

Memoirs of My Dead Life : 1921

' Moore Hall ' Edition

Memoirs | of My Dead Life | of | Galanteries , Medi-
tations | and Remembrances | Soliloquies or Advice to
Lovers, | —with many miscellaneous Reflections | on
Virtue & Merit | By | George Moore of Moore Hall
Co Mayo | [*Woodcut Illustration*] | London | Published
by Heinemann.

Demy 8vo; pp. xx + 292, consisting of Half-title,
Memoirs of My Dead Life (with list of *Works by
George Moore* on verso), pp. [i, ii] ; [*Frontispiece :
Daguerreotype Portrait, in colours, of George Moore at
the age of ten*] ; Title-page, as above (with *London :
William Heinemann, 1921.* at foot of verso), pp. [iii,
iv] ; Certificate of Issue, as follows: *Memoirs of My*

Dead Life | [a line] | *This edition, printed from hand-set* | *type on English hand-made paper,* | *is limited to one thousand and thirty* | *copies, of which one thousand are for* | *sale.* | *This is No.*.......... (each copy numbered in ink) | (signed in ink by the author :) *George Moore* (verso blank), pp. [v, vi]; *Epistle Dedicatory,* to *My dear Gosse,* pp. vii–ix ; p. [x] blank; *Prelude,* pp. xi–xviii ; Table of *Contents* (verso blank), pp. [xix, xx]; Text, pp. [1]–290 ; at end of text : *The End of this Volume.* ; printers' imprint at foot of p. 290 as follows : [a line] | *Printed in Great Britain by Richard Clay & Sons, Limited, Bungay, Suffolk.* ; pp. [291, 292] blank.

Issued in pale blue boards with white parchment back, with white paper name and title-label on back lettered across in brown as follows : *Memoirs* | *of My* | *Dead Life* | *George Moore* | *Heinemann* Top edges unopened, fore-edges uncut and unopened, lower edges uncut. Pale blue end-papers to match the sides.

(46)

PIPING HOT!: 1885

Piping Hot! | (Pot-Bouille.) | A Realistic Novel. | By | Émile Zola. | Translated from the 63rd French Edition. | Illustrated with Sixteen Page Engravings, | from Designs by Georges Bellenger. | London : | Vizetelly & Co., 42 Catherine Street, Strand. | 1885.

Thick crown 8vo ; pp. ii + xviii + 9–384, consisting of 2 pages of advertisements, with *Press Notices*, of *New Realistic Novels.* . . . *A Mummer's Wife. By George Moore*, . . . (not reckoned in pagination) ; Half-title, *Piping-Hot !* (with list of *Zola's Realistic Novels.* on verso), pp. [i, ii] ; [Frontispiece : *Valérie in hysterics at the Wedding Ball.* | *p. 160.* (not reckoned in pagination)] ; [Illustrated Title-page : *Piping Hot !* | *(Pot-Bouille.)* | [Illustration] | *Jubilation of the Josserands at Berthe's Engagement. p. 102.* | *By Emile Zola.* (not reckoned in pagination)] ; Title-page, as above (verso blank), pp. [iii, iv] ; *Preface.* (by George Moore), pp. [v]–xviii ; Text, pp. [9]–383 ; p. [384] blank. At end of volume there is a 20-page numbered illustrated catalogue of *Vizetelly & Co.'s New Books,* | *and New Editions.* dated *December, 1884.* There is no printer's imprint.

Signatures : *a* (8 leaves) ; A (6 leaves) ; B—2A in eights. The illustrations, of which there is no list, face pp. [Frontispiece and Illustrated Title-page], 24, 50, 61, 88, 98, 134, 168, 190, 192, 246, 282, 288, 318, and 358.

Issued in brown cloth, lettered across the back as follows: *Piping | Hot ! | Émile Zola | Illustrated | Vizetelly & Co* with lines in blind at top and bottom ; and on front in gilt as follows: *Piping Hot ! | A Realistic Novel |* [Illustration in gilt on brick-red background, surrounded by ornamental border in black] *| By Émile Zola. | Illustrated.* On back cover, three-line border in blind. Top and fore-edges unopened, lower edges cut. Flowered end-papers of daisies on brown background.

(47)

THE RUSH FOR THE SPOIL: 1885

The | Rush for the Spoil | (La Curée). | A Realistic Novel. | By | Emile Zola. | Translated without Abridgment from the 34th French Edition. | Illustrated with Twelve Page Engravings. | London : | Vizetelly & Co., 42 Catherine Street, Strand. | 1885.

Crown 8vo ; pp. vi + viii + 9–290, consisting of Half-title, *The Rush for the Spoil | (La Curée). | A Realistic Novel.* (with a list of *Zola's Powerful Realistic Novels.* on verso), pp. [i, ii]; Illustrated Title-page: *The | Rush for the Spoil | (La Curée).* | [Illustration] | *Maxime discovers his Father at the Maison Dorée. | p. 120. | By Emile Zola.* (verso blank), pp. [iii, iv]; Title-page, as above (verso blank), pp. [v, vi]; *Preface.* (signed at end: *George Moore.*), pp. [i]–viii; Text, pp. [9]–290. There is no printer's imprint.

Issued in royal blue cloth, lettered across the back in rust-red as follows: *The | Rush | for the | Spoil | Émile Zola | Illustrated | Vizetelly & C°* with four lines at top and bottom, and across the front in rust-red as follows: *The Rush for | the Spoil | A Realistic Novel | Émile Zola.* with four lines at top and bottom. Back cover blank. Top edges unopened, fore and lower edges trimmed. Flowered end-papers.

T

(48)

PIPING HOT!: 1886

Large Paper Illustrated Edition

Piping Hot! | (Pot-Bouille.) | A Realistic Novel. | [*Illustration, with lettering below as follows:* The Josserands' Delight at Berthe's Engagement.] | By Émile Zola. | Illustrated with 104 Engravings from Designs by French Artists. | London: | Vizetelly & Co., 42, Catherine Street, Strand. | 1886

Royal 8vo; pp. xvi + 314, consisting of Half-title, *Piping Hot!* | (*Pot-Bouille.*) (verso blank), pp. [i, ii]; Frontispiece, *Valérie in Hysterics at the Wedding Ball.* | P. 129. (recto blank), pp. [iii, iv]; Title-page, as above (verso blank), pp. [v, vi]; *List of* [47] *Page Engravings.* pp. [vii, viii]; *Preface,* signed at end: *George Moore.* pp. [ix]–xvi; Text, pp. [1]–312; p. [313] is occupied by a list of *Zola's Realistic Novels.*; p. [314] blank. There is no printer's imprint.

Issued in light peacock blue cloth, lettered across the back in gilt as follows: *Piping* | *Hot!* | *Émile Zola* | *Illustrated* | *Edition* | *Vizetelly & Cº.* with three lines in dark blue at top and bottom; and lettered on front cover as follows: *Piping Hot!* (in gilt) | *A Realistic Novel* (in brick red) | [Illustration in gilt on dark blue background, surrounded by ornamental border in gilt] | *By Émile Zola.* (in brick-red) | *Profusely Illustrated.* (in gilt), the whole surrounded by an ornamental border in dark blue. On back cover, ornamental border with publishers' device in centre in blind. All edges cut. Conventional figured endpapers printed in brown on white background.

(49)

POOR FOLK: 1894

[*Illustration, by Aubrey Beardsley*] | Poor Folk | translated | from | the Russian | of | F. Dostoievsky | by |

Lena Milman | with an | Introduction | by | George Moore | London | Elkin Mathews | and John Lane | [*A line*] | Roberts Brothers | Boston | 1894

> Crown 8vo ; pp. xx + 192, consisting of Half-title, *Poor Folk* (with *Copyrighted in the United States* | *All rights reserved* in centre of verso), pp. [i, ii] ; Title-page, as above (with printers' imprint at foot of verso as follows : *Edinburgh : T. and A. Constable, Printers to Her Majesty*), pp. [iii, iv] ; p. [v] is occupied by the device of 'The Keynote Series' ; p. [vi] blank ; *Preface* (by George Moore), pp. vii–xx; Text, pp. [1]–191 ; p. [192] blank ; Printers' imprint at foot of p. 191 as follows : [a line] | *Printed by T. and A. Constable, Printers to Her Majesty* | *at the Edinburgh University Press* At end of volume there is a 16-page numbered *List of Books* | *in* | *Belles Lettres,* dated (on p. [3]) *March 1894* The title of the book, *Poor Folk,* is printed in red ; the other lines are in black.
>
> Issued in yellow cloth, lettered across the back in gilt as follows : *Poor* | *Folk* | [ornament] | *Fedor* | *Dostoievsky* | [key in black] | [ornament] | *Elkin* | *Mathews* | *and John* | *Lane* [ornament]. On front cover, design in black by Aubrey Beardsley, and lettered across in black as follows : *Poor Folk* | *A Novel* | *by* | *Fedor Dostoievsky* | *Translated* | *from the Russian* | *by* | *Lena Milman* | *With* | *A Critical Introduction* | *by* | *George Moore* In centre of back cover, key design with date 1894. Top and fore-edges unopened, lower edges uncut. White end-papers.

This is Volume II of 'The Keynote Series.'

(50)

The Heather Field and Maeve : 1899

The Heather Field | and | Maeve | By | Edward Martyn | Author of "Morgante the Lesser" | With an Introduction by | George Moore | [*Publishers' device*] | London | Duckworth & Co. | 3 Henrietta Street, W.C. | MDCCCXCIX

T 2

Pott 4to ; pp. xxviii + 132, consisting of Half-title, *The Heather Field* | *and* | *Maeve* (with *All Rights Reserved.* in centre of verso), pp. [i, ii] ; Title-page, as above (verso blank), pp. [iii, iv] ; Dedication : *I Dedicate these Two Plays to* | *George Moore, W. B. Yeats* | *and* | *Arthur Symons.* | *E. M.* (verso blank), pp. [v, vi] ; *Introduction* (signed at end : *George Moore*), pp. vii–xxviii ; Fly-title to *The Heather Field* | [a line] | *A Play in Three Acts* (with *Dramatis Personæ* in centre of verso), pp. [1, 2] ; Text of 'The Heather Field,' pp. 3–83 ; p. [84] blank ; Fly-title to *Maeve* | [a line] | *A Psychological Drama in Two Acts* (with *Dramatis Personæ* in centre of verso), pp. [85, 86] ; Text of 'Maeve,' pp. 87–129 ; Printers' imprint in centre of p. [130] as follows : *Printed by* | *Turnbull and Spears,* | *Edinburgh* ; pp. [131, 132] are occupied by advertisements of *Messrs Duckworth & Co.'s* | *New Books.* | *Modern Plays.*

Issued in light green cloth, lettered up the back in brown as follows : [two Shamrock designs] *The Heather Field* [two Shamrock designs], and across the front in brown as follows : *The Heather Field* | *and Maeve* [two Shamrock designs] | *By Edward Martyn* | [three Shamrock designs] | *With an Introduction by* | *George Moore* [two ornaments]. Back cover blank. Top edges unopened, fore and lower edges trimmed. White end-papers.

(51)

An Irish Gentleman : [1913]

An Irish Gentleman | George Henry Moore | His Travel | His Racing | His Politics | By | Colonel Maurice George Moore, C.B. | With a Preface | by | George Moore | [*Heraldic arms, with inscription in Irish*] | London | T. Werner Laurie Ltd. | Clifford's Inn

Demy 8vo ; pp. xxviii + 404, consisting of Blank leaf, pp. [i, ii] ; Half-title, *An Irish Gentleman* | [a line] | *George Henry Moore* | [a line] | [Publishers' device]

(with a list of *Books of Travel*, enclosed within a one-line border, on verso), pp. [iii, iv] ; [Portrait of *Col. Maurice Moore, C.B.*] ; Title-page, as above (verso blank), pp. [v, vi] ; *Preface*, pp. vii–xx ; Table of *Contents*, pp. xxi–xxvi ; *List of Illustrations*, p. xxvii ; p. [xxviii] blank ; Text, pp. 1–385 ; p. [386] blank ; *Index*, pp. 387–396. Pp. [397–404] are occupied by advertisements of books. At foot of p. 396 is the following printers' imprint : *The Northumberland Press*[,] *Thornton Street, Newcastle-upon-Tyne* A small slip, bearing the following Note : *What the Prefacer writes regarding the | mode of his father's death must be taken | as expressing his wishes, and not the facts. | The Author.* is inserted between the Title-page and first page of *Preface*.

Issued in dark red cloth, lettered across the back in gilt as follows : *An | Irish | Gentleman | George | Henry | Moore | [Shamrock design] | M. G. Moore | T. Werner Laurie L*$^{td}_{-}$ (enclosed within a one-line border in gilt), and across the front in gilt as follows : *An Irish Gentleman | George Henry Moore | His Travels | His Racing | His Politics | [Shamrock design] | M. G. Moore* (enclosed within a one-line border in gilt). In centre of back cover, publishers' device in blind. All edges cut. White end-papers.

(52)

THE GENIUS OF THE MARNE: 1919

The | Genius of the Marne | A Play in Three Scenes | By | John Lloyd Balderston | With an Introduction | by | George Moore | Nicholas L. Brown | New York - - - - - MCMXIX

Crown 8vo ; pp. ii + xx + 90, consisting of Blank leaf (not reckoned in pagination), pp. [i, ii] ; Half-title, *The Genius of the Marne* (verso blank), pp. [i, ii] ; Title-page (with *Copyright, 1919, by | Nicholas L. Brown* in centre of verso), pp. [iii, iv] ; Dedication *To a Lady* . . . (verso blank), pp. [v, vi] ; Fly-title to

Introduction | by | George Moore (verso blank), pp.
[vii, viii]; *Introduction*, pp. ix–xv; p. [xvi] blank ;
List of *Characters* (verso blank), pp. [xvii, xviii]; Fly-
title to the Play, *The Genius of the Marne* (verso
blank), pp. [xix, xx]; Text, pp. 1–86; pp. [87–90]
blank. There is no printer's imprint.

Issued in dark grey boards with pale blue paper name
and title-label on back lettered across in blue as
follows : [a line] | *The | Genius | of the | Marne |
Balderston | George Allen | & Unwin Ltd.* | [a line], and
pale blue paper name and title-label in centre of
front cover, lettered across in blue as follows : *The |
Genius | of the | Marne | John L. Balderston | Introduc-
tion by | George Moore* Back cover blank. All edges
cut. White end-papers.

There is a printed slip inserted between the half-title
and title-page, lettered in red as follows : *This Book
is now published by | George Allen & Unwin, Ltd. |
Ruskin House, | 40, Museum Street, | London, W.C.*

NOTES ON THE VALUES OF THE FIRST EDITIONS OF THE WRITINGS OF GEORGE MOORE

(1) *Flowers of Passion, 1878.* Excessively rare and seldom occurs for sale. At Sotheby's (April 5, 1921) a copy realized £29 10*s.*, and again in the same rooms (July 18, 1921) £21. Another copy at Sotheby's (December 14, 1921) with a Poem in the handwriting of the author, entitled *The Ballad of Lovers,* and addressed *To Fluffie,* consisting of three 8-line stanzas and Envoy of four lines, signed and dated *Feby.* 11, 1871, realized £50. 'Flowers of Passion,' like all George Moore's first editions, has considerably appreciated in value during the last few years. Gleeson White's copy was catalogued by Lionel Isaacs in 1899 at 7*s.* 6*d.*

(2) *Martin Luther, 1879.* The last record is at Anderson's Auction Co., New York (January 29, 1919), when a copy realized $51.00. The present value of the book is probably about £20.

(3) *Pagan Poems, 1881.* Excessively rare, especially with the title-page. At Anderson's Auction Co., New York (January 29, 1919), a presentation copy inscribed *To Violet Fane from the Author,* with a 3-page Autograph Letter from the author to the recipient, realized $540.00. The last English record is at Puttick & Simpson's (January 20, 1915), when a copy with the title-page realized £15 : the present value, however, is about £60, or probably more. Gleeson White's copy was catalogued by Lionel

Isaacs in 1899 at 12s. 6d. In 1920 Messrs. Henry Sotheran & Co. catalogued a presentation copy *To William Rossetti with many compliments, George Moore, 1881*. On the fly-leaf of this copy was the following inscription by the late W. M. Rossetti : *This book raised some clamour, and I think it was withdrawn from circulation, W. M. R., 1906*.

(4) *A Modern Lover, 3 vols., 1883.* There is no recent record of a copy having occurred for sale in the auction rooms. A shabby copy at Puttick's (April 29, 1919) realized £5 5s. To-day a fine copy would probably realize about £25.

(5) *A Mummer's Wife, 1885.* Very scarce, especially in fine state. A fine copy to-day would probably realize about £10. A copy at Sotheby's (April 5, 1921) realized £7.

(6) *Literature at Nurse, 1885.* An uncommon pamphlet, which seldom occurs for sale. A copy at Hodgson's (May 27, 1921), inscribed by the author *With the writer's compliments*, realized £13.

(7) *A Drama in Muslin, 1886.* A copy at Sotheby's (April 5, 1921) realized £6 5s. The book is very scarce in fine state.

(8) *A Mere Accident, 1887.* Value of a fine copy about £3 3s. to £3 10s. The book usually occurs for sale in shabby condition.

(9) *Parnell and his Island, 1887.* A copy at Anderson's Auction Co., New York (January 29, 1919), realized $17.00. A copy to-day in England would probably realize £4 to £4 10s.

(10) *Confessions of a Young Man, 1888.* At Puttick's (June 15, 1921) a presentation copy, with autograph inscription by the author, realized £18. Another presentation copy (Hodgson's, March 5, 1920) realized £22. Value of an ordinary copy about £10 to £12.

(11) *Spring Days, 1888.* First issues in the correct binding are very rare. Value about £3 3s.

(12) *Mike Fletcher, 1889.* A copy at Hodgson's (June 2, 1921) realized £5 2*s.* 6*d.*

(13) *Impressions and Opinions, 1891.* A copy at Dowell's in Edinburgh (February 22, 1921) realized £3 12*s.* 6*d.* At Hodgson's (November 3, 1921) a presentation copy from the author with autograph inscription realized £12 12*s.*

(14) *Vain Fortune* [*1892*]. Value about £2.

(15) *Vain Fortune, Large Paper Edition* [*1892*]. First issues in white cloth are very scarce : value about £5 5*s.* Value of second issue about £3 3*s.*

(16) *Modern Painting, 1893.* A copy at Sotheby's (April 5, 1921) realized £3 5*s.*

(17) *The Strike at Arlingford, 1893.* Value about £1.

(18) *Esther Waters, 1894.* Copies in fine state are rare. Value of fine copy about £2. Copies in average condition realize from £1 5*s.* to £1 10*s.*

(19) *Celibates, 1895.* This book was 'remaindered' a few years ago and is still quite common. Value 10*s.* to 15*s.*

(20) *The Royal Academy 1895,* 1895. There is no record of a copy having been sold at auction. The copy used for the purposes of collation by the present compiler was kindly lent to him by Mr. C. Millard, who listed the same in his *Spring* 1922 Catalogue at £2 10*s.*

(21) *Evelyn Innes, 1898.* At Hodgson's (March 5, 1920) a presentation copy from the author, with autograph inscription, realized £12 5*s.* Value of an ordinary copy about 15*s.* to £1.

(22) *The Bending of the Bough, 1900.* Value about £1 5*s.* for a fine copy.

(23) *Sister Teresa, 1901.* Value about 15*s.* to £1.

(24) *The Untilled Field* (*in Irish*) [*1902*]. There is no record of a copy having occurred for sale. Probable value about £3.

(25) *The Untilled Field,* 1903. Value about 10*s.* to 15*s.*

(26) *The Lake, 1905.* Value about 10*s.* to 15*s.*

(27) *Reminiscences of the Impressionist Painters, 1906.* Copies at Sotheby's have realized £3 15*s.* (June 29, 1921) and £4 10*s.* (December 13, 1920).

(28) *Memoirs of My Dead Life, 1906.* At Sotheby's (July 26, 1921) a copy realised £7 15*s.*

(29) *Ave, 1911.* Value about £2 10*s.*

(30) *The Apostle, 1911.* A copy at Sotheby's (April 25, 1921) realized £1 12*s.*, but £1 1*s.* to £1 5*s.* is about the average value of the book.

(31) *Salve, 1912.* Value about £1 5*s.* Copies of the first issue, which are extremely rare, are probably worth about £6 6*s.*

(32) *Esther Waters : a Play, 1913.* Value about 10*s.*

(33) *Elizabeth Cooper, 1913.* Value about 15*s.*

(34) *Vale, 1914.* Copies of the *first issue* are excessively rare, and no copy is known to have occurred for sale in the auction rooms. £10 is a probable price for a copy. Value of *second issue* about £3 to £3 10*s.* The *third issue* is common : value about 15*s.*

(35) *Muslin, 1915.* Value about 10*s.* to 15*s.*

(36) *The Brook Kerith, 1916.* Value about £1 10*s.* to £2 2*s.* The Circulating Library issue is very scarce : value £3 3*s.* to £4 4*s.*

(37) *The Brook Kerith, Édition de Luxe, 1916.* Value about £8 8*s.*

(38) *Lewis Seymour and Some Women, 1917.* Value about 12*s.* 6*d.* to 15*s.*

(39) *A Story-Teller's Holiday, 1918.* Value about £5 5*s.*

(40) *Avowals, 1919.* Value £4 4*s.* to £4 12*s.* 6*d.*

(41) *Esther Waters, 1920.* Value about £2 2*s.*

(42) *The Coming of Gabrielle, 1920.* Value about £1 10*s.* to £1 15*s.*

(43) *Héloïse and Abélard,* 2 vols., *1921.* A copy at Sotheby's (July 22, 1921) realized £4 6*s.*

(44) *Fragments from Héloïse and Abélard, 1921.* Value about 5*s.*

(45) *Memoirs of My Dead Life, 1921.* Value about £3 3*s.* to £4 4*s.*

(46) *Piping Hot! 1885.* The book is scarce in fine condition. Value of fine copy £1 1*s.* to £1 10*s.*

(47) *The Rush for the Spoil, 1885.* Value about 15*s.* to £1 1*s.*

(48) *Piping Hot! Large Paper Illustrated Edition, 1886.* Very scarce. Value about £2.

(49) *Poor Folk, 1894.* Value about £1 5*s.* to £1 15*s.*

(50) *The Heather Field and Maeve, 1899.* Value about £1 10*s.*

(51) *An Irish Gentleman* [*1913*]. Value about 7*s.* 6*d.* to 10*s.*

(52) *The Genius of the Marne, 1919.* Value about 5*s.* to 7*s.* 6*d.*

PRINTED IN GREAT BRITAIN BY
RICHARD CLAY & SONS, LIMITED,
BUNGAY, SUFFOLK.